PHILADELPHIA

WILLIAM PENN
Proprietor and Governor
of Pennsylvania · Founder of
the City of Philadelphia · 1682

PHILADELPHIA

BY

HORACE MATHER LIPPINCOTT - *1877*

FOREWORD
· AND ·
ILLUSTRATIONS
BY

THORNTON OAKLEY

Ira J. Friedman Division
KENNIKAT PRESS
Port Washington, N.Y.

PHILADELPHIA

First published in 1926
Reissued in 1970 by Ira J. Friedman Division, Kennikat Press
Library of Congress Catalog Card No: 78-124995
ISBN 0-87198-511-X

Manufactured in the United States of America

KEYSTONE STATE HISTORICAL PUBLICATIONS SERIES NO. 11

Foreword
By the Illustrator

See you in your imagination, O Philadelphians, the coming of your city's founder? Call you before your eyes a day of wind and gulls: a river all advance with wave and light: a ship arriving free from a far, intolerant world, canvas dazzling in a new realm's sun, upon her bow, his eyes upon the virgin shores, an eager figure—Penn—first Governor of Pennsylvania!

William Penn! What would be your thoughts if where once you built the first house of your envisioned colony you today again could stand, behold the towers of your city reaching to the heights of Heaven, could sail beneath the bridge that with its cloud-dimmed span soars conqueror above the once majestic bay?

And Franklin, what of Franklin? Do ye, Philadelphians, and ye strangers too within the city's gates, as ye tread the canyon streets, mingle with the rush and turmoil of the traffic, do ye oft call to mind the picture of this supreme amongst supreme Americans? For in history who beyond the exalted Penn stands more the guiding genius of the city? Here Franklin lived, here Franklin toiled, here upon Penn's rock foundations he carried on the mighty framework of the new-born nation.

Ah, Philadelphia, city invincible, thou that tak'st thy place amongst all-potent cities of the world, forget not that it is not in cloud-capped towers, not in roar of industry, that thy true greatness lies. In the vision of thy founders dwells the reason of thy fame. Hast thou not stood, wilt thou not stand for that for which they built thee?—for Freedom, Tolerance, for Truth; for Love amongst mankind? Revere your shrines, O Philadelphians!—be blinded not by golden marts of a wealth-bedazzled world. Let your hallowed monuments ever keep alive your passion for ideals. See! search but a few short steps amidst your shadowed thoroughfares and you will find the spots where was born imperishable history— the very walls within which the sires of your nation conceived the Constitution of a new era for mankind. Here stood the house of Penn: here Franklin plied his press: here immortal Washington attended divine service: here met the first Continental Congress: here, ah here, a deep-tongued bell acclaimed the Signing of the Declaration. Rich in romance art thou Philadelphia, rich in splendor of thine heritage. May the purpose of thy fathers be increasingly fulfilled as thou stridest forward into the untold future of the world!

Introduction

In this year of the celebration of the one hundred and fiftieth anniversary of American Independence Philadelphia is being presented to its visitors and to its citizens in many different aspects, some of them very similar to those of other American cities.

The city founded by William Penn and his English Quaker friends has, however, some unusual and interesting qualities, largely preserved from its substantial and wise origin, which have retained for it a distinction not shared by its Colonial sisters. It is this flavour as one might call it, of quaintness and originality that this book aims to briefly set before you. You will hear, see and read, just now much about bigness, and greatness, and speed of which we Americans seem obsessed, of commerce and industry and of the more ordinary things of cities, but here in Philadelphia there are other qualities remaining which we like to think are among the refinements of life, that make it a good place to live in. A large part of the Quaker reserve and balance of our forefathers remains in the old town and Philadelphians do not feel a necessity or a propriety in shouting about their importance or usefulness. After all it is enough to just *be it*.

Eastern Pennsylvania possesses a beauty and more agreeable diversity of surface than most sections of our country and we owe to Penn's sagacity not only the selection of such a fortunate location, but the choice and encouragement of men of solid worth and industry as its first settlers.

The wealth of history attached to the city which was the metropolis of the Colonies is often referred to. Some

of it is not so well known. Here the founders of the
Republic were playing their parts and many useful institutions were originated. The Free Library, the Medical and
the Law Schools of the University of Pennsylvania, the
Pennsylvania Hospital, the American Philosophical Society and the Academy of the Fine Arts were successfully
established in Philadelphia before there were any similar
attempts elsewhere. The English Bible and Testament,
Milton, Shakespeare and Blackstone were all produced
for the first time in America in Philadelphia and the earliest book written by Thackeray first appeared here. The
first protest against slavery came from Germantown
Friends' Meeting in 1688 and the earliest Abolition Society in the world was organized in Philadelphia in 1774.
The Declaration of Independence and the Constitution of
the United States were written and adopted here and for
ten years the city was the American Capitol during the
Presidencies of George Washington and John Quincy
Adams. Robert Morris financed the Revolution, Stephen
Girard the War of 1812, and Jay Cooke the Civil War,
and perhaps most important of all, here lived Benjamin
Franklin.

This book portrays old-fashioned things—things which
are typically Philadelphian and for which we who have been
here for 250 years (and what Philadelphian has not!) have
an affectionate regard. We often speak of our family
and of our cousins to the remotest generation, and quote
our grandfathers as oracles, alongside the sages of Plutarch.
Do not smile at such an one, observe him as he enters
a room or speaks to a servant. Do not think our ideas
of old-fashioned courtesy and high-breeding are provincial.
It is the fashion nowadays to proclaim against this aristoc-
racy of culture, refinement and gentleness. Have we
substituted anything better for it or are we ruled more

justly? Philadelphians are frequently laughed at because of their interest in these ancestral matters. Perhaps in an odd moment this generation may find time for the bow, but it is at most an imitation—theirs was the reality. Is not this Philadelphia flavour worth while in American life?

Acknowledgment is made to the many sources of information, both books and individuals, consulted in the preparation of this piecing together of our fragments of colour.

Particular gratitude is due to the J. B. Lippincott Company for permission to use material used in *Early Philadelphia* published by them and by the same author in 1917.

HORACE MATHER LIPPINCOTT

Chestnut Hill
Fourth Month, 1926.

CONTENTS

ILLUSTRATIONS

I : The Founding of the City

THE Province of Pennsylvania differed from the other Colonies in America in that no other had such a mixture of languages, nationalities and religions. It differed also through the wise plan of its founder in the character of its settlers, who were men of varied capacity and industry. They were free from mediæval dogmas and far advanced in the line of the Reformation, particularly the first settlers and earliest purchasers. These were nearly all Quakers who were the most advanced sect, and the effect of their liberalism on the growth of Pennsylvania was marked. The Quakers were well-to-do people at home who had sold their property in England and sought refuge in America to escape severe persecution. They had servants and were well supplied with clothing, and there was no such cry of distress from Penn's colonists as was heard from Plymouth and Jamestown after their first winters. These early settlers were not gathered by the force of material or temporary inducements or the desire for physical betterment, but for religious liberty. They were radicals and revolutionists in thought, but they did not resist authority and were bound by rules of conduct. They were not militant and suffered rather than resist or disturb law and order, believing in the final supremacy of moral and intellectual forces. Peaceful, careful, thrifty and dependable, they and their colony soon grew wealthy.

The Founder of Pennsylvania displayed his wisdom in no greater way than in the encouragement he gave to the settlement of his province by men of sterling worth. In striking contrast to the Colonies of the South there came to Pennsylvania artisans and farmers who were to build a foundation of lasting prosperity There were no Cavaliers in silks and plumes to greet the Proprietor upon his landing at New Castle, but we read that there were welcoming shouts from settlers in woodland garb, the men in leather breeches and jerkins, the women "in skin jackets and linsey petticoats." Penn writes that the land is like "the best vales of England watered by brooks; the air, sweet; the heavens, serene like the south of France; the seasons, mild and temperate; vegetable productions abundant, the chestnut, walnut, plums, muscatel grapes, wheat and other grain; a variety of animals, elk, deer, squirrel, and turkeys weighing forty or fifty pounds, water-birds and fish of divers kinds, no want of horses; and flowers lovely for colour, greatness, figure and variety." What golden opportunities are here presented for the industrious men who settled in this new country!

Philadelphians like to think of their city as "typically American" and indeed it has been so characterized by many distinguished visitors. Certainly no American city has maintained more of its original character, customs and institutions than that founded by William Penn. No city owes its origin more definitely to the genius of one man nor can any city find among its founders one of more capacity or personality. Simplicity, dignity, and reserve are still the characteristics of Philadelphia, and something of the old Quaker directness, the robust candour not easily subdued, are still to be found here. There is still the decorum which prevents the jostling of her sister cities, which stills the cries of triumph amid the hustle for existence. Noise and excitement do not disturb her mental balance nor crowd out an appreciation of names and things still honoured. Her traditions and opinions of yesterday are maintained with a solidity of thought which recalls their lessons and builds slowly but surely with clear perspective and the saving grace of modesty. The beginnings of all this are laid so nearly to the personality of the Founder that it is well to touch briefly upon his fruitful life at the outset of this book. Indeed no account of Philadelphia should omit a grateful tribute to this great man who seized the opportunity of the Crown's debt to his father to carry out the great purpose of George Fox and the early Quakers to establish a refuge for them in the New World. The discussion of their plans reached his ears at College and twenty years afterwards he wrote: "I had an opening of joy as to these parts in the year 1661 at Oxford."

William Penn, scholar and gentleman, politician and statesman, lover and Minister of Christ, was born October 14, 1644, on Tower Hill, London, the son of Admiral Sir William Penn and the gentle Lady Penn, daughter of John Jasper, a merchant of Rotterdam. The Penns seem to have been of Welsh origin, sometime settled in the counties of Bucks and Wilts, England. They were well-to-do country gentry until Giles Penn, the grandfather of William, took to a seafaring life which his son continued and became a Vice-Admiral of England at thirty-one. William Penn was born in troublous times for one who was destined to become a man of peace. He was, however, essentially a man of action, of unbounded energy. His portraits express great determination, a religious face but not that of the hard ecclesiastic or the sour Puritan. A gentle, sympathetic, heroic soul looks out from the eyes. A carving, which seems to be the most authentic likeness, shows him in later years to be of serene and cheerful countenance, an evidence that he was fully sustained in his worst trials and anxieties by a courageous temperament.

The Admiral was at sea when William was born and

soon his mother took him from the little court close to the
Tower of London and went to live in the pretty village of
Wanstead, near Essex, where he passed his boyhood and
went to school. The family were Royalists and Penn's
close relations with King Charles and King James afterward made him more so, but he imbibed principles of free
government and liberty in his early schooling at Wanstead,
among the Puritans, which made him liberal in his views
as well. When he was but eleven years old he had a
religious experience—"He was suddenly surprised with an
inward comfort; and, as he thought, an external glory in
the room, which gave rise to religious emotions, during
which he had the strongest conviction of the being of God,
and that the soul of man was capable of enjoying communication with Him. He believed also that the seal of
divinity had been put upon him at this moment, or that he
had been awakened or called upon to a holy life." This
was of course before he had heard of George Fox or the
Quaker message.

In 1660 Penn was sent to Christ Church College, Oxford, as a part of his father's design toward preferment
and a career. Oxford at this time of the Restoration was
still under some Puritan influences, and Penn seems to have
sympathized with these, to have engaged heartily in
athletics and led a life of freedom in body and mind. To
such a healthy, unbound soul the Quaker message was sure
to appeal when he met it in the preaching of Thomas Loe,
to whom he one day accidentally listened. We may pass
over his troubles with his father and his college on this
account, his sojourn in France and his first experience of
persecution in the whipping he received at home. The
journey to France, and to Italy, too, broadened and polished him so that in after life he was a much more effective
instrument in what he had to do. A considerable portion

of his two years abroad had been spent under the guidance of Moses Amyrault, a professor of the Reformed French Church, in perfecting his theological studies. So we can see how he could correspond in Latin with Sewell the Quaker historian, read and speak Greek, French, German and Dutch, and add to his essays or pamphlets quotations from all the ancient and modern authors that he could find in support of his Theses. In his "Treatise on Oaths" there are over fifty opinions of some Greek or Roman philosopher, statement or father of the Church. In "No Cross No, Crown" there are over 130 of these instances from remote antiquity to men of his own day, so that we can judge of his intellectual equipment, diligence and patience. A large part of his enthusiasm came from his reading. He had a passion for the biographies of all who had achieved, learned from their experiences, and was inspired by the most progressive and philanthropic ideas that had been suggested in the whole course of written human history. He was intimate with the most distinguished as well as the lowliest men of his time. His liberality was developed at the expense of many practical qualities and he was not a shrewd judge of the characters by whom he was surrounded in after life. Thus he often failed in carrying into practice the great ideas that came to him. He managed his colony well while living in it only, and was a careless business man. He was so far ahead of his time in everything and so vigorous and enthusiastic that he suffered many temporary defeats. He was a voluminous writer, much of his work being done in prison. "No Cross, No Crown," written in the Tower of London, was his greatest work and passed through several editions during his lifetime. We may pass his many trials for conscience sake which are well known. He suffered imprisonment many times, though often confounding the Jurists when brought to trial and standing up manfully and ably for an Englishman's rights upon all occasions. His was no meek submission to wrong but a vigorous leadership against all injustice. The whole of his life indicates the power of his personality. He showed his force when he went to jail for a matter of conscience and declared, "My prison shall be my grave before I will budge one jot, for I owe obedience of conscience to no mortal man"; and in the crisis with Lord Baltimore when he says, "Can my wicked enemies yet bow? They *shall,* or break, or be broken in pieces before a year from this time comes about, and my true friends rejoice," and in another emergency, "If lenitives will not do, *coercives* must be tried." While under arrest in the tower of London he said to Sir John Robinson, Lord Lieutenant of the Tower: "I would have thee and all men know I scorn that religion which is not worth suffering for, and which is not able to sustain those who are afflicted for it. Mine is; and whatever be my lot, I am resigned to the will of God. Thy religion persecutes, mine forgives, and I desire that God may forgive you all that are concerned in my commitment. I leave you, wishing you everlasting salvation."

In the plans of government which he expressed are best exemplified his advanced ideas, many of them the best of to-day. Freedom and toleration of every kind are the rule, indeed he says, "There is hardly one frame of government in the world so ill designed by its founders, that in good hands would not do well enough," and "any government is free to the people under it (whatever be the frame) where the laws rule and the people are a party to those laws." He proposed to the Lords of Trade a plan of union or general government for the Colonies in America which is remarkable because it foreshadows the provisions of our national constitution.

He travelled in Holland and Germany as well as Pennsylvania, preaching and making many converts. Too little has been said of the human part of Penn's nature and of the lovely lady who must have been the sweet inspiration of his life. It was when he was twenty-seven years old that this tenderness fortunately came into his life to soften a spirit so beset by religious controversy, preaching, trials and imprisonments. "Gulie," or Gulielma Maria Springett, was the daughter of a gallant young Puritan officer whose widow married Isaac Penington. They lived at Chalfont in Buckinghamshire and were people of means. Quakerism brought them persecution, and it was in 1668, after their sufferings had begun, that Penn first knew them. Thomas Ellwood, Milton's friend, lived with them, and tells us that Guli was "completely comely" and that the endowments of her mind "were every way extraordinary." In 1672 they were married and settled down at Rickmansworth in Hertfordshire. "Their honeymoon lasted long; the spring and summer came and went, but Penn still remained with his young and lovely wife at Rickmansworth; neither the flatteries of friends nor the attacks of foes could draw him away from his charming seclusion." One of the best things Penn has written is his letter to his wife and children. To her he says: "Remember thou wast the love of my youth, and much the joy of my life—the most beloved as well as the most worthy of all my earthly comforts; and the reason of that love was more thy inward than thy outward excellencies, which yet were many. God knowest and thou knowest I can say it was a match of His making; and that God's image in us both was the first thing and the most amiable and engaging ornament in our eyes."

His "Fruits of Solitude" is a collection of 850 maxims which are the result of his experience in life and his contemplation of it in retirement. They contain many excellent truths and he summarizes the religion of the Quakers in the maxim, "The less form in religion the better, since God is a spirit."

We may pass over his trusteeship of New Jersey and Proprietorship of Pennsylvania which are so well known. Within a few years he has been proclaimed in Parliament as the greatest Colonial Governor England has ever had— a real tribute from a nation which governs one-fifth of the civilized world.

It was a period of intense religious opinions which were so absorbing as to control the political and indeed whole conduct of the people. The Quakers believed in the universal and direct revelation of God to each individual and that this "Inward Light" or "Spirit of Christ" could be best found and cultivated by silence and meditation without the barriers erected by outward or worldly things which they believed to be nonessential and of the senses only. They objected to a prearranged ceremony and a "man-made ministry" and thought that religion was not so much a matter of creed or dogma as of right living. They knew that worship is an experience and not a ceremony and believed that the only worship acceptable to God is that which arises from the manifestation of His Spirit in each seeking heart. They wished to revive Christianity when God revealed Himself directly to man. In their earliest history they made extreme protests against the bondage of ancient dogmas and what they considered non-religious and privileged practices. But as the sect grew and organized it became orderly while at the same time the abuses it objected to declined.

The first settlers of Philadelphia were of course English Quakers, but the absolute freedom of conscience guaranteed under the "Holy Experiment" soon attracted many other sects. Religious persecution at home as well as Penn's preaching among them brought many Germans and these, under Francis Daniel Pastorius, founded the first settlement of that nationality in America at Germantown. They resembled the Quakers very much, with less quietism. Indeed, their leader became a Quaker and was one of the most remarkable men in the whole colony. He could speak eight languages and was well read in Science and Philosophy, having studied at Basle, Strasburg and Jena and lectured at Frankfort. He was one of those who signed the first protest against slavery in this country issued by the Friends' Meeting in Germantown in 1688.

The Welsh were nearly all Quakers, with a sprinkling of Baptists and Churchmen. They took up the "Welsh Barony" west of the Schuylkill and on its other side where is now Penllyn, Gwynedd and North Wales. Here they ruled in their own way, their Quaker Meetings exercising civil authority and handing down "advice" which seems to have regulated the entire community so that all were "satisfied." All the physicians in the province prior to 1700 appear to have been Welshmen, the most prominent being Dr. Thomas Wynne, who came over with Penn in the *Welcome* and for whom Chestnut Street was originally named.

Their positions in the community at home were those of rugged yeomen of the English democracy, tradesmen and artisans, with few gentry or University men, although the Welsh Quakers had pedigrees dating back to Adam and brought them along. In seventeenth century England, from whence they came, there were few families where learning was esteemed. In his account of the country gentry Burnett writes: "They are the worst instructed and least knowing of any of their rank I ever went amongst." At the universities men were taught merely to despise all who had forsaken the church, and he found the dissenters alone well taught. Macauley says: "Few knights of the shire had libraries so good as may now perpetually be found in the servants' hall, or in the back parlour of the small shopkeeper. As to the lady of the manor and her daughters, their literary stores generally consisted of a prayer book and a receipt book. During the latter part of the seventeenth century the culture of the female mind seems to have been almost entirely neglected. Ladies highly born and highly bred were unable to write a line in their mother tongue without solecisms and faults of spelling such as a charity girl would now be ashamed to commit." Swift, writing a letter to a young lady lately married, takes it for granted that she cannot read aloud or spell. This being the condition of culture in the mother country we can easily believe from what the early settlers in Pennsylvania did and what they wrote that many of them were well bred and above the average culture. They were without advantages for the education of their children and in a wilderness three thousand miles from home and help, had to win the battle for existence before they could give much time and attention to the arts that cultivate and refine.

Nevertheless they laid out the city and built their houses with taste and skill. Fifteen thousand came between 1681 and 1700 at an average of 70 shillings per head, which amounts to 50,000 pounds they must have paid. Their purchases cost them 25,000 pounds more and as has been said they brought much useful material with them.

Penn went about the colonization of his province in a business-like way and with great advertising skill. He issued a series of immigration pamphlets in the interest of his project with a scrupulous regard for true statements and simple facts without exaggeration. He described the plentifulness of timber, game and commodities and granted all legislative power to the people and government. No law was to be made or money raised but by the people's consent. To buyers he offered 5000 acres free from any Indian encumbrance for 100 pounds and a shilling per annum quit rent for every 100 acres. To renters he offered land at the rate of one penny per acre not exceeding 200 acres and to servants he gave 50 acres to the master for every head and 50 acres to the servant at the expiration of his time of endenture. The modern advertiser may well turn for example to his descriptions of the Province aimed to attract settlers of industry and worth rather than the Cavaliers of the southern colonies.

The servants generally came over on separate ships but appear in many cases to have been of the same social rank as the masters, being bound to work for them for a few years or until the money advanced them for their passage had been repaid.

Penn appeals to "Industrious Husbandment and Day Labourers, Laborious Handicrafts, especially Carpenters, Masons, Smiths, Weavers, Taylors, Tanners, Shoemakers, Shipwrights, etc. Ingenious Spirits that being low in the world, are much clogg'd and oppressed about a Livelihood, for the means of subsisting being easie there, they may have the time and opportunity to gratify their inclinations, and thereby improve science and help nurseries of people, younger brothers of small Inheritances and men of Universal Spirits that have an eye to the Good of Posterity, and that both understand and delight to promote good Discipline and Just Government among a plain and well intending people."

It is easily seen what a sensible man Penn was and how earnestly he hoped for the success of his "Holy Experiment" without great material gain for himself. He described what to take on the journey, its cost and what is first to be done on arrival. This was serious business, a journey in a little boat for two months on a great sea to an almost unknown wilderness, and they must not delude themselves with an expectation of "An Immediate Amendment of their Conditions." Indeed, he says, they must be willing to do without conveniences for two or three years. The passage money was six pounds a head for masters, five for servants and fifty shillings for children under seven years. Live stock can be purchased there at easy rates. Finally he exhorts all to have an eye above all things to the providence of God in the disposal of themselves and not to move rashly or from a fickle mind. "In all of which I beseech Almighty God to direct us, that his blessing may attend our honest endeavour, and then the Consequence of all our undertaking will turn to the Glory of his great Name, and the true happiness of us and our Posterity."

Travelling between London and Bristol during the next three months Penn disposed of 300,000 acres of unlocated land in the new province to about 250 persons who were known as the first purchasers and were well-to-do Quakers of northern England, about two-thirds equally divided between London and Bristol. In October, 1681, he sent over three commissioners to help Governor Markham, arrived in June, organize the colony, lay out grants and settle upon the capital city. With these went the advance guards of immigrants, one from London in the Ship *John* and the other from Bristol in the *Factor*. In March, 1682, the Free Society of Traders in Pennsylvania was incorporated and in the following month the Surveyor General, Thomas Holme, sailed and the frame of government was drawn up. By the time Penn sailed in August, 1682, 600,000 acres had been sold and in the list of purchasers published in London in that year by the Committee of the Free Society of Traders there are some 600 names, a few of which

William Penn's House
Built 1682· Removed, 1883,
from Letitia Street to Fairmount Park

still survive among us. Most Philadelphians will recognize an ancestor in a list containing the names of More, Harrison, Knight, Flower, Baker, Taylor, Allen, Bond, Pickering, Jones, Bowman, Fisher, Turner, Holme, Davis, Chambers, Fox, Sharpless, Rowland, Ellis, Alsop, Barklay, Criscrin, Martindale, Palmer, Carpenter, Matlock, Thomas, Powell, Parsons, Griscom, Barnes, Lehman, Noble, Gibson, Fell, Harding, Scott, Dickson, Paschall, Sheppard, Russell, Harris, Mitchell, Dickinson, Cross, Clark, Guest, Buckley, Lyvesly, Kinsey, Hayward, Kent, Green, Loyd, Pierce, West, Welsh, White, Morris, Potter, Pusey, Jeffries, Geery, Austin, Hicks, Cope, Bacon, Jenkins, Hart, Phillips, Roberts, Warner, Nixon, Keith, Carter, Coats, Bailey, Saunders, Townsend, Andrews, Evans, Waln, Pritchard, Collins, Rogers, Mason, Wood, Price, Spencer, Murrey, Hill, Child, Miles, Stephens, Marshall, Hunt, Richards, Brock, Haines, Howell and Johnson.

The earliest immigrants arrived before Philadelphia was surveyed and did not know where it was. They stopped at Upland, now Chester, which was peopled by the Swedes and some English Quakers from Jersey. Philadelphia was located in 1682, "having a high and dry bank next to the water, with a shore ornamented with a fine view of pine trees growing upon it." In this bank they made caves to shelter their families and belongings and then went out into the wilderness with a warrant of survey to choose their land.

There was a steady stream of immigration during the first year, and more than thirty ships and several thousand settlers arrived. Penn's letter to the Society of Traders in 1683 describes his own observations in his dominion which seem to have been keen since few details are overlooked. Here is part of it:

A Letter from William Penn, Proprietary and Governour of Pennsylvania in America, to the Committee of the Free Society of Traders of that Province, Residing in London. Containing a General Description of the said Province, it's Soil, Air, Water, Seasons and Produce both Natural and Artificial.

The Natural Produce of the Country, of Vegetables, is Trees, Fruits, Plants, Flowers. The Trees of most Note, are the Black Walnut, Cedar, Cyprus, Chestnut, Poplar, Cumwood, Hickery, Sassafras, Ash, Beech, and Oak of divers Sorts, as Red, White and Black; Spanish Chestnut and Swamp, the most Durable of all. Of All which, there is Plenty for the Use of Man. The Fruits that I find in the Woods, are the White and Black Mulberry, Chestnut, Wallnut, Plumbs, Strawberries, Cranberries, Hurtleberries, and Grapes of divers Sorts. The Great Red Grape (now Ripe) called by Ignorance, The Fox Grape, (because of the Relish it hath with unskilful Palates) is in it self an Extraordinary Grape and by Art, doubtless may be Cultivated to an Excellent Wine, if not so Sweet, yet little inferior to the Frontiniack, as it is not much unlike in Taste, Ruddiness set aside, which in such Things, as well as in Mankind, differs the Case much; There is a White Kind of Muskadel, and a Little Black Grape, like the Cluster Grape of England, not yet so Ripe as the other; but they tell me, when Ripe Sweeter and that they only want Skilful Vinerons to make good Use of them; I intend to venture on it with my Frenchman this Season, who shews some Knowledge in those Things. Here are Also, Peaches and very Good, and in Great Quantities, not an Indian Plantation without them; but whether Naturally here at first, I know not, however one may have them by Bushels for little; they make a Pleasant Drink, and I think not Inferior to any Peach you have in England, except the True Newington. Tis disputable with me, whether it be Best to fall to Fining the Fruits of the Country, especially the Grape, by the Care and Skill of Art, or send for Foreign Stems and sets, already Good and approved. It seems most Reasonable to believe, that not only a Thing groweth Best, where it naturally grows; but will hardly be equalled by another Species of the same kind, that doth not naturally grow there. But to solve the Doubt, I intend, if God gives me Life, to try Both, and hope the Consequence will be as Good Wine, as any European Countries, of the same Latitude, do yield.

The Artificial Produce of the Country, is Wheat, Barley, Oats, Rye, Pease, Beans, Squashes, Pumpkins, Water-Melons, Mush-Melons, and all Herbs and Roots that our Gardens in England usually bring forth.

Of Living Creatures; Fish, Fowl, and the Beasts of the Woods, here are divers Sorts, some for Food and Profit, and some for Profit only; for Food, as well as Profit, the Elk, as big as a small Ox, Deer Bigger than ours, Beaver, Racoon, Rabbits, Squirrels, and some eat Young Bear and commend it. Of Fowl of the Land, there is the Turkey, (Forty and Fifty Pound Weight) which is very great; Pheasants, Heath-Birds, Pigeons, and Partridges in Abundance. Of the Water, the Swan, Goose, White and Gray; Brands, Ducks, Teal, also the Snipe and Curloe, and that in Great Numbers; but the Duck and Teal excel, nor so Good have I ever eat in other Countries. Of Fish, there is the Sturgeon, Herring, Rock, Shad, Cats-head, Sheepshead, Eel, Smelt, Pearch, Roach; and in Inland Rivers, Trout, some say, Salmon, above the Falls. Of Shell Fish, we have Oysters, Crabs, Cockles, Conchs, and Museles; some Oysters six inches long; and one sort of Cockles as big as the Stewing Oysters, they make a Rich Broth. The Creatures for Profit only, by Skin or Fur, and that are Natural to these Parts, are the Wild Cat, Panther, Otter, Wolf, Fox, Fisher, Minx, Musk-Rat: And, of the Water, the Whale for Oil, of which we have good Store, and Two Companies of Whalers whose Boats are Built, will soon begin their work, which hath the Appearance of a Considerable Imprivement. To say nothing of our Reasonable Hopes of Good Cod in the Bay.

He described the looks, character, language, customs, government and religion of the Indians and says he has learned their language. The settlers have had, he says, two General Assemblies which sat only three weeks and passed seventy laws without a dissent. Courts and officers are established and there are three peace-makers chosen by every court to arbitrate differences and prevent lawsuits among the 4000 settlers. Philadelphia was laid out on a strip of land a mile wide from the Delaware to the Schuylkill rivers and advanced within a year to four score houses and cottages. The office of the Free Society of Traders was on the west side of Front Street near the south side of Dock Creek at the foot of "Society Hill," so named from the location of the Company's headquarters. A Front Street along each river bank was planned, a High Street (now Market) near the middle from river to river one hundred feet broad and a Broad Street in the middle of the city from side to side of like breadth. In the centre of the city a square of ten acres was to provide at each angle for the houses of public affairs such as a Meeting House, Assembly or State House, a Market House and a School House. In addition the squares in each quarter of the city were provided for and to contain eight acres each. Eight streets were to run from Front to Front and twenty besides Broad Street from side to side, all fifty feet wide. In laying out the lots, says Penn, each purchaser "hath room enough for a House, Garden and small Orchard, to the great Content and Satisfaction of all here concerned."

Penn's design was to have a promenade on the high bank of the river front the whole length of the city, intending Front Street to have an uninterrupted view of the Delaware River scenery. Had it not been for the trickery and deceit of some of the people during his absence this wonderful plan would have given us the most beautiful city in America.

Upon his return in England in 1685 he wrote a further description of the Province, telling of the divers collection of European nations represented there. French, Dutch, Germans, Swedes, Danes, Finns, Scotch, Irish, English "and of the last equal to all the rest." There are now 357 houses, mostly large, well built with cellars, three stories and some with balconies. The tradesmen consist of carpenters, joiners, bricklayers, taylors, shoemakers, butchers, bakers, brewers, glovers, tanners, felmongers, wheelwrights, millwrights, shipwrights, boatwrights, ropemakers, saylmakers, blockmakers, turners, etc. There are two markets every week and two fairs every year. There are seven Ordinaries (Taverns) and good meal can be had for sixpence. The hours for work and meals are "fixt and known by Ring of Bell." Some vessels and many boats have been built, many "Brickerys," good cheap brick and "many brave Brick Houses" going up. These enthusiastic accounts left us by the Founder are the records of a truly remarkable development and are the best evidence of the early state of Philadelphia.

The most valuable contribution to our present conditions which this many-sided man has given us is his "An Essay towards the Present Peace of Europe" which seems almost prophetic. In it he states the blessings and reasonableness of peace, the horrors and destruction of war and advocates a system of arbitration or general government to settle all the disputes of the European nations and prevent war. He proposed a limited States of Europe, with a diet or general council, to which each state should send its representatives; and he even suggested the number each nation should send. When a nation broke the laws or refused to submit to the diet the others should combine in a police duty to enforce their mandates. This essay is a truly remarkable document so clearly does it ring down through the centuries. His treatment of the Indians is well known and was founded upon kindness and justice out of which, he said, could never come strife. It was the love of God which George Fox said took away the occasion for all wars.

His wife's death was a great trial to him and he was

beset with troubles in business and in his Province. His children who survived were by his second wife, Hannah Callowhill, and were a disappointment to him. But with all the trials, mental and physical, which came to him in his busy life, his spirit was resolute and vigorous until near the end. About six years before his death his health declined and his mind weakened, but he lived in tenderness and peace. He died at the age of seventy-four, on the 30th of July, 1718, and is buried with his family at Jordan's Meeting House, near Chalfont St. Giles, England. We may fittingly close with his own saying so typical of his character—"I know of no religion which destroys courtesy, civility and kindness."

II: Penn's Greene Country Towne

PASTORIUS says he was often lost in the woods and brush in going from his cave along the river's bank to the house of the Dutch baker Bom at the southeast corner of Third and Chestnut Streets where he procured his bread. Soon, however, the forest was all felled except a cluster of black walnut trees which stood until 1818 on Chestnut Street opposite the State House. The hills were reduced and the miry places filled. The greater part of the houses were south of High Street and north of Dock Creek, which was swampy. At the north of the creek there was a ferry at the Blue Anchor Inn for conveying passengers to the opposite bank called "Society Hill," where the Society of Traders had their office. Here was the public landing and afterwards a drawbridge which allowed ships to come up as far as Second Street. Dock Creek traversed a "deep valley" to Fourth and High Streets and on the northern side of High west of Fourth it formed a great pond, famous for its wild ducks and splatterdocks and surrounded with natural shrubbery. The Indians called the creek Coocanocon, but the first landing at its mouth, the boatyards, tanneries and lumber landing places soon gave it another name.

Just above the northern boundary of the little town was Pegg's run, now Willow Street, named by the Indians Conoqinoque and later after Daniel Pegg who owned much land in that section. At Tenth and Vine Streets it separated into two streams running further westward. There was another duck pond in the rear of Christ Church on

Second Street and another near Fifth and Locust Streets at the beginning of a stream which ran into Dock Creek at Girard's Bank. For urchins who got over the great Dock Creek there was plenty of game, fruit, berries and nuts in the woods opposite. George Warner landed in 1726 and on account of the smallpox came ashore at the Swedes' Church "far below the great towne." He stopped at the Blue House Tavern at the southwest corner of what is now Ninth and South Streets, near a great pond, and they saw nothing in all their route there but swamps and lofty forests and wild game. Removing to the Blue Anchor at the drawbridge on Dock Street he saw not one house.

There was a good-sized pond at Eighth and Arch Streets, another nearby toward Seventh, one at Race and Branch and one at Fifth and High, now Market Street.

Gabriel Thomas tells us that in 1698 there were 2000 houses, stately and of brick generally three stories high "after the Mode in London." There were many lanes and alleys from Front to Second Streets, abundance of produce, excellent climate and good wages for "Trades Men" of whom there are many of every sort. The maid servants' wages, he says, are six to ten pounds per annum and "of Lawyers and Physicians I shall say nothing, because this country is very Peaceable and Healthy." By this time there is a "Noble Town House or Guild Hall, a Handsome Market House and a Convenient Prison." Also Warehouses, Malt and Brew Houses, Bake Houses for Public Use, several good Schools and "no beggars or old maids." Paper and linen are made in Germantown and the people are mostly Lutherans, Church of England, Presbyterians, Baptists and Quakers. Thomas thinks that of the many gardens surrounding the houses that of Edward Shippen who lived in the "Great House" in Second Street north of Spruce, excels in size and quality.

Edward Shippen was a Yorkshireman and a Mayor of the city. He was a wealthy merchant, speaker of the Assembly, provincial councillor and chief justice. His house, "on the hill near the towne," surpassed his contemporaries in style and grandeur and was surrounded by a "great and famous orchard." The lawn before the house descended to Dock Creek and was the grazing place for a herd of "tranquil deer." Penn stopped with him on his arrival in 1699 for his second visit.

On the square running from Front to Second and fronting on High was the large lot given by Penn to his daughter Letitia and the house, afterwards on Letitia Street. It has been moved and is now attractively set in Fairmount Park at the western end of the Girard Avenue bridge and must present much the same appearance as it did when built. Tradition alone has ascribed Penn's residence in it.

William Frampton lived on the west side of Front Street between Walnut and Spruce. He had extensive land in the rear of Second Street by the south side of Dock Creek and on it was his brew house, bake house and an early residence rented as an inn. He probably had the greatest stock of merchandise of any in the city and owned one of the first three wharves.

Samuel Carpenter had the first "Coffee House" in the neighborhood of Front and Walnut Streets. He also had a crane, bake house and wharf. The only public landings were at Dock Street, north of the drawbridge, at the "Penny Pot House," north side of Vine Street and at a great breach through the high bank of the river at Mulberry Street, which afterward became known as Arch Street because of the arched bridge for Front Street over this breach in the hill.

Front Street was the principal street of the city for a long time, first as a residence street when all the houses were built on the western side, and afterwards as a place of trade. On the arrival of ships from England in spring and autumn, all along Front Street from Arch to Walnut, the pavements were covered with boxes and bales from the mother country. On King Street, now Water, separated from Front by a wall and an iron railing, were the warehouses and stores of the old-time merchants. Here were the India stores of Robert Morris and Thomas Willing and here Jacob Ridgway, John Welsh, Thomas P. Cope, Robert Ralston, Charles Massey, Manuel Eyre, Henry Pratt, Stephen Girard, the Walns, Whartons, Lewises, Hollingsworths and many others engaged in trade with South America, the Indies, China, and European cities, and built up great fortunes.

The wells were generally public and in the street and there were few pumps in the early days. Both seem to have been the subject of much complaint. In 1744 there was a well to every house and several in the streets with a "pump of excellent water every fifty paces."

The only pavement was near the Court House at Second and High Streets and the then short market house extending westward about half a square. Extensive building began first on "Society Hill" and particularly on the west side of Front Street with grounds extending to Second.

The earliest pavement was a narrow footwalk of bricks filled in on each side with gravel or the whole with gravel only. The rest of the street was very bad until the large pebbles or cobbles came and that was not much better.

The first street to be paved was Second from High to Chestnut because one of the Whartons on horseback was mired there, thrown from his horse and broke his leg. After that a subscription was taken up and the street paved. His experience was somewhat similar to that of one of the Johnsons in Germantown who had to saddle his horse

SALUS PER CHRISTU

Christ Church † †
Second Street near Arch
· Founded 1695 ·

after a rain in order to cross Main Street. Tales are told of how gallants, including the doughty Washington, had to carry ladies from their coaches to the entrances of houses. One Purdon, a British soldier on duty in Philadelphia, had charge of the first paving and was so useful that he was released from the army to serve the community in a better way. There was very little general effort to have the middle of the streets paved until 1761 and then only in a desultory way through money derived from lotteries. In 1782 the city was levelled and many graceful undulations destroyed. The State House at that time stood upon a little eminence about four feet higher than the surrounding streets which were unfortunately filled in. The sidewalks were protected from the traffic of the streets with posts and it was not until 1786 that the first curb-stones were introduced on Water Street from High to Arch. The biggest pebbles were always placed in the middle of the street, when the gutters were not there, and so the roughest riding was where it should have been easiest. There were a dozen bridges in the little town and six of them crossed Dock Creek.

In 1751 the Grand Jury expressed the need for watch-men and paved streets and the next year an act was passed providing for a night watch and for "enlightening the city" which had hitherto been illuminated only by private lamps. The guardians of the city were first citizens who served for a period by necessity. They went around every night before going to rest to see that all was well and such men as Joseph Shippen, Abram Carpenter, George Clay-poole and Henry Preston were in 1706 fined "for neglect to serve as constables." It was a time of small beginnings and of mutual responsibility.

Highway robberies were of such frequent occurrence that the citizens were compelled at last, with the approval of the Supreme Executive Council, to organize themselves into patrols for the protection of property and persons passing through the city at night. Says a city newspaper as late as 1787 after the mitigation of penalties which the new penal code provided:

"On Tuesday night between twelve and one o'clock, as William Hamilton, Esq., and Miss Hamilton, his niece, were returning from the city to Bush Hill, they were attacked in the neighborhood of Twelfth and Market Streets by six or eight footpads, who formed a line across the road and called violently to the postilions to stop. This not being complied with, one of the villains fired a pistol, and another a blunderbuss. One of the postilions being stunned by a ball, which struck his cap, for a moment occasioned the stopping of the carriage, and the whole band immediately closed round to seize their prey. Mr. Hamilton, putting his head out of one of the windows, called loudly for the postilions to drive on, and ordered his servants, two of whom just then came up at full gallop, to fire on the rascals, who immediately ran off with the utmost precipitation through a corn-field, which greatly favored their retreat. The servants, being soon after joined by others from Bush Hill, well armed, made diligent search after the villains until daylight, but without success."

Penn's busy colonists who had come to the new country on account of religious principles had little concern about crimes and disorder. For twelves years an ordinary frame dwelling was the only jail the town possessed, and it was oftenest empty. The stone prison at Third and High Streets was not finished, indeed, until 1723. A cage seven feet square was provided for the evildoer who was taken out with public formality to be "smartly whipped" and made to pay six shillings for each unwelcome service of this kind. The Quakers had little of the melodramatic in their natures and criminals were in little danger of the hero worship of modern days. Justice was prompt and impartial while common sense and exactness held sway over sentiment.

Offenses of the Sabbath were serious affairs and in 1702 George Robinson was fined for "uttering two very bad curses." Women were held as accountable before the law as men and their offenses punished as promptly and justly. So it is little wonder that accusations of witchcraft and of dealings with evil spirits should have had no effect upon the placid Friends. Many attempts, indeed, were made to introduce these dramatic affairs into an atmosphere of calm depreciation but all met with a mortifying indifference.

Parties of Indians frequently came to the city to trade and see the sights and excited no surprise. They often remained for several weeks and were generally quartered in the State House yard. There are at present two plots of open ground in the city which tradition says were set aside by Penn as Indian reservations for all time. One of these is in the rear of 145 South Second Street and the other back from Walnut Street near Broad, adjoining the Ritz-Carlton Hotel.

The natural opportunities of the place, the thrift and skill of the settlers and the liberality of the government soon brought wealth and growth. At the time of the revolution the city was the greatest in the country. "No other could boast of so many streets, so many houses, so many people, so much renown. No other city was so rich, so extravagant, so fashionable." Among the features which impressed visitors from a distance was the fineness of the houses and this was in large measure due to the artisans which Penn had induced to come and who had brought old world ideas as well as skill with them. As early as 1724, indeed, these composed a guild large enough to be patterned after "The Worshipful Company of Carpenters of London," founded in 1477. Penn brought over James Portius, a skillful architect, to "design and execute his Proprietory buildings," and he left his valuable collection of architectural works to the Carpenters' Company to form the basis of their present library. The book of joinery published in 1745 gives ample evidence of the source of the fine dwellings that graced the streets, as well as the presence of such able amateur architects as Doctor Kearsley, who produced Christ Church, Andrew Hamilton, who designed the State House, and Samuel Rhodes, who planned the Pennsylvania Hospital.

III: The Early City

A GLIMPSE of some of the notable dwellings and their occupants will give us some idea of what the city looked like and did during the first century of its existence when it was the scene of so many distinguished events in the nation's history and gave birth to so many useful institutions whose foundations were so well laid that they have survived in their usefulness to-day.

At the southeast corner of Norris' Alley and Second Street where now stands the Main Office of the Keystone Telephone Company Samuel Carpenter built the "Slate Roof House," noted as the city residence of Penn and his family when on his second visit to the city in 1700. Here was born John Penn "The American." On returning to England in 1701 Penn left James Logan in charge and he retained it as a government house until 1704, when it was purchased from Carpenter by William Trent, founder of Trenton, for 850 pounds. Trent improved the place and had a fine garden extending half way to Front Street and on Second nearly to Walnut. It was sold in 1709 to Isaac Norris and came finally to be a boarding house and a shop. In 1867 it was pulled down to make way for the Commercial Exchange.

David Breintnall built one of the first good houses at what is now 115 Chestnut Street, but deeming it too fine for his Quaker persuasion he let it to the Governor of Barbadoes who came to Philadelphia for his health. He used to reach its door in a boat by way of Dock Creek. Here was the first Chestnut Street bridge.

Clarke's Hall was built by William Clarke and occupied

land from Chestnut Street to Dock Creek and from Third up to Hudson's Alley. It was built of brick and had well cultivated gardens in the rear. There were only two neighbors, Governor Lloyd at the northeast corner of Third and Chestnut Streets and Mayor William Hudson near the southeast corner of the same streets. When young William Penn junior came over, James Logan rented Clarke Hall and occupied it himself with Penn, Governor Evans and Judge Mompesson. The place descended through Andrew Hamilton and John Pemberton to the wealthy Quaker Israel Pemberton and at the time of the Revolution was famous for its formal gardens and shrubbery. It was rented and occupied by Alexander Hamilton for the offices of the Treasury of the United States until 1800 and was soon after this torn down.

Joshua Carpenter was the brother of Samuel who has been mentioned as one of the earliest to improve the new city. His house fronted on Chestnut Street, being in the centre of a lot running back to the next street and from Sixth to Seventh. Here lived Doctor Graeme, son-in-law to Sir William Keith, who gave his name to that worthy's famous seat at Horsham. Graeme was the father of the celebrated Mrs. Ferguson. Governor Thomas lived in the house from 1738 to 1747 and the shrubbery and fruit trees of the garden extending to Seventh Street were visited by many. Later it was occupied by Colonel John Dickinson and General Philemon Dickinson and during the Revolution was used as a hospital for the American soldiery. After that it was taken by the Chevalier de Luzerne, Ambassador of France, who entertained lavishly. He was followed by Monsieur Gerard, likewise the Ambassador of his country, and finally it came to Judge Tilghman who sold it for "improvements" in 1826.

Parson Duché was a picturesque figure of the Revolutionary period. He was one of the first graduates of the Academy, now the University of Pennsylvania, and was an eloquent preacher. While pastor of St. Peter's Church he was asked to act as chaplain of the Continental Congress then sitting in Carpenters' Hall. This he did and delivered a remarkable prayer by which the delegates were much moved. His father built him a house in 1758 in South Third Street which was deemed quite out of town. Duché's patriotism soon waned and he tried to induce Washington to forsake the cause, for which he was compelled to flee to England. The house was later occupied by Governor McKean.

Among the residents of "Society Hill" were Samuel Powell and Joseph Wharton. The former lived at 244 South Third Street and was distinguished as Mayor of the City and as a lavish entertainer in his handsome house built in 1769. His garden and extensive grounds were beautifully laid out and the walks adorned with costly statuary. Nearby lived Thomas Willing, William Bingham and Colonel William Byrd of Westover in Virginia. Samuel Powell was a graduate of the College and a man of literary and scientific attainments. Washington was frequently a guest at his house as were many other notables. Joseph Wharton was the owner of "Walnut Grove," near the now Fifth and Washington Avenue, where the "Mischianza" was held in 1778.

Bishop White, the first Anglican Bishop in America, lived at 402 South Front Street and later in Walnut Street above Third. He was one of the most revered and trusted men in the city, a graduate and Trustee of the University, chaplain of the Congress, rector of Christ Church and intimate of Washington. Next door to the Bishop on Front Street was the handsome residence of John Stocker, an affluent merchant and a founder of the Mutual Assurance Company, the second oldest fire insurance company in Philadelphia.

John Stamper, a wealthy English merchant and the Mayor in 1760, lived at 224 Pine Street and after him Robert Blackwell, a noted minister connected with Christ Church and St. Peter's. At 322 Union Street, now DeLancey, lived Jonathan Evans, a "concerned" Friend and a prominent figure in the Separation of 1827. His Meeting was in Pine Street near Front, where that charming Quakeress, Dorthy Payne, afterwards Dolly Madison, wife of President James Madison, married James Todd.

The large house at 321 South Front Street sheltered Henry Hill, of Madeira wine fame, in 1786. Later came the McCalls and Doctor Philip Syng Physick, the father of American Surgery. Mordecai Lewis, a proficient student of the classics and a prominent merchant, lived at 336 Spruce Street. Samuel Fisher, a noted merchant and eminent Quaker, presented the house to his daughter Deborah who married William Wharton in 1817 and it became the gathering place of many Friends who opposed Jonathan Evans and his party in the schism among the Friends in 1827.

John Barclay, Mayor in 1791, built the fine old house now occupied by the Pennsylvania Seamen's Friend Society at 422 South Front Street. Its spiral stairway running to the lantern in the roof is a famous piece of architecture.

In 1790 the rich William Bingham built his "Mansion House" at Third and Spruce Streets upon a large plot of ground about which he planted Lombardy poplars, the first seen in the city. He had a high board fence about his grounds to conceal their beauty and keep the vulgar gaze from his lavish entertainments.

At the southwest corner of Third Street and Willing's Alley was the house built for Charles Willing in 1745 after the pattern of the family homestead in Bristol, England. It was "on the hill beyond Dock Creek," and was thought to be a rural home outside the town. The grounds extended from Third to Fourth Streets and had many famous oak trees. Mr. Willing's daughter married Senator Bingham who lived nearby and the whole area along Third Street to Spruce thus became one of family distinction.

Charles Norris' house on Chestnut between Fourth and Fifth Streets was one of the finest in the city at the time of its erection in 1750. Like so many others it was surrounded by a fine garden laid out formally and containing many fruit trees and a hot house, all presided over by a Swiss gardener for a quarter of a century. The plumbing of the house was above the ordinary and supplied cisterns and dairy. It furnished more lead for bullets during the Revolution than any other house in town.

"Fort Wilson," at the southwest corner of Third and Walnut Streets, was the residence of James Wilson. He was a professor in the College and the founder of its Law School in 1790, the first on the Continent. His services in the Constitutional Convention were very distinguished and he later went on the Supreme Bench by appointment of President Washington. Although he had signed the Declaration of Independence, he was one of the courageous defenders of the Loyalists accused of treason. On this account his house was surrounded by a mob in 1779 and serious times were averted for the occupants of the house by the presence of the First City Troop.

On Pemberton Street near Front, and south of Bainbridge, there is a high wall with two quaint little houses facing each other at each side of a gateway through which one gets a glimpse of a courtyard and trees. In the bricks of the wall are black headers forming the letters

"G. M." and the date "1748." This little settlement was built by George Mifflin, father of Governor Thomas Mifflin, who afterwards left it to his son John. John Mifflin sold the houses, which were used for workingmen, to John Workman of South Carolina, who added two more houses, making a court still known as "Workman's Court." Lately it has been bought by E. W. Clark and is used by the Octavia Hill Association for housing betterment.

Nearly every Philadelphian knows the Morris House on South Eighth Street, at number 225. It was built in 1786 by John Reynolds and came soon to Luke Wistar Morris, the son of Captain Samuel Morris. Effingham B. Morris has restored it to its original beauty and planted the garden about it as before. It is the best example in the city of the old-time dwelling house.

Of course the most important building of the city until the erection of the State House in 1735 was the Court House. It had two stairways uniting in front of the building facing Second Street. After the Revolution these stairways were removed and one built on the inside. Dawkin's view and Dove's caricature show the original view, while Birch's picture is of it in 1799. In all the old pictures there is seen a little balcony projecting from the second story. This was the landing to which the stairways led and from which Governors delivered their inaugural addresses, proclamations were read and speeches made. In 1739 the celebrated George Whitefield preached from this balcony to a vast concourse of people, to whom Benjamin Franklin says his voice was clearly audible. Beneath the Court House auctions were held for many years, and one of the tenants there was no less a personage than Mayor Thomas Lawrence. At one time a physician had his office on this floor.

At the northwest corner of Second and High Streets

was the home and drug store of John Speakman, Jr., a prominent Friend. Here was formed on January 25, 1812, a society which in March took the title of the Academy of Natural Sciences, that splendid institution now known all over the scientific world.

It was down Second Street and past Christ Church, the Old Court House and the Market Square that General Howe and his army made their triumphal entry into the city, when the throngs of citizens, clad in their best array, lined the sidewalks to see the grenadiers march by, steadfast and composed, splendidly equipped, and with their music sounding "God Save the King." Here, too, they listened to the wild strains of the bearded Hessians, terrible in brass fronted helmets, and suggesting plunder and pillage to the peaceful Quakers. What a contrast it was to the little patriot army which Washington had led along the same street not so long before, a sprig of green in the men's hats forming the only sign of uniformity.

In very early times a prison stood in the middle of High Street just behind the Court House or "convenient" to it as Gabriel Thomas wrote in 1698. It was soon regarded as a nuisance and was removed about 1723, the year after the stone prison was built at Third and High Streets.

At the site of the building now numbered 110 the English Bible was first published in America by Robert Aitken. He also published the first volumes of the "Transactions of the American Philosophical Society." After his death his daughter Jane brought out Charles Thomson's translation of the Bible in four volumes, the first translation attempted in the New World.

At the southwest corner of Second and High Streets there stood until 1810 the Meeting House of the Society of Friends, erected in 1712. Here the prominent Quakers of our early Colonial history worshipped, and here the tired lad Benjamin Franklin wandered after his arrival in 1723 and fell asleep on one of the benches.

On the same side of the street and to the westward were the Royal Standard and Indian King taverns in both of which the Lodge of Free Masons was accustomed to meet. John Biddle kept the latter for many years.

The Pennsylvania Hospital was first located on the south side of High Street west of Fifth. It had been the home of Chief Justice John Kinsey of the Provincial Supreme Court and was surrounded by pastures and gardens.

Near the corner of Water and High Streets dwelt Chief Justice William Allen, who was the presiding Justice over the Supreme Court from 1750 until 1754. Water Street was called King Street until the time when Kings became unpopular. Justice Allen was opulent and influential. He had been a successful merchant and a founder of the Academy and College which subsequently became the University of Pennsylvania. The fame of his coach drawn by four black horses with an English coachman on the box survived for many a day.

At 43 Water Street dwelt the famous Stephen Girard, "Merchant and Mariner," and to his house came the French Refugees, the Count de Survilliers, Field Marshal Count Grouchy and General Lallemand, especially to Sunday dinners. Indeed Girard had entertained before that Talleyrand, the Duke of Orleans, later Louis Philippe, and his brother, all of whom were émigrés at the time of the French Revolution.

It is thought that William Bradford, the first printer in the Middle Colonies, had his shop near Front and High Streets and his descendants continued the trade in the neighborhood for a full century or more. Andrew Bradford's *Mercury*, first issued 22nd December, 1719, was the first newspaper in the Middle Colonies and the second printed in this country. Until 1723 he was the only printer in the Province and being on that account a personage, secured the postmastership as an aid to the distribution of his paper. He held the position until Franklin wrested it from him on the same account.

This neighborhood was indeed the printing house square of Philadelphia until the beginning of the last century. At what is now 135 Market Street Franklin started his first printing office with Hugh Meredith and it was here in 1741 that he began the publication of the first monthly magazine in this country called *The General Magazine and Historical Chronicle for all the British Plantations in America.* Matthew Carey began business on Front below High Street in 1784 where he published *The Pennsylvania Herald.* John Dunlap, one of the founders of the First City Troop and an early Captain of it, was associated in a printing house with David C. Claypool near Second and High Streets on the south side of the latter. They published the first daily newspaper in this country and first published Washington's Farewell address. Dunlap started the *Pennsylvania Packet, or General Advertiser* in November, 1771. It was then a weekly and Claypool astonished his associate by printing it as a daily in 1784. He published the debates of Congress and Washington sent him the original manuscript of his Farewell address.

At 25 North Second Street, opposite Christ Church, was the shop of William Cobbett, widely known by the pen name of "Peter Porcupine." He was as keen a satirist as Swift and resembled him in more ways than one. Scorching invective and keen satire characterized his pamphlets and although he wrote in an age of clever pamphleteers he remained to the end the leader of them all. Just west of Grindstone Alley, on the site of the present number 219, was the clockmaker Robert Leslie whose son Charles Robert became a great painter. Next door Joseph Cruikshank, the Quaker printer and bookseller, had his shop.

As early as 1768 David Deshler lived where is now number 223. Deshler built the house on the Market Square in Germantown where President Washington lived during the yellow fever outbreak of 1793. "Honest David Deshler" was famed for his attire. He favoured olive-coloured silk, velvet knee-breeches and bright silver buckles, and astonished the plain trustees of the old Academy in Germantown when he attended his first meeting in his full dress "regalia." Next door to Deshler on High Street in 1767 lived Peletiah Webster, a former master of the Germantown Academy, now in trade. Opposite to him was Hilary Baker, the son of Hilarius Becker, the first headmaster of the same school. He became Mayor in 1796. Nearby was another Germantowner, Colonel Thomas Forrest, a Trustee of the Academy, and its President in 1799. He went to Congress for the first time at the age of 72 years.

On the north side of High Street near Fourth dwelt John and Casper Wister. The latter spelled it with an "a" and was a learned anatomist. His fame, however, rests upon his entertainments, which still linger as Wistar Parties. He was an early graduate of the medical school of the University in 1782 and in 1786 received his doctor's degree at Edinburgh, where he became President of the Royal Society of Medicine of Edinburgh. He returned in 1787 and began the practice of his profession on High Street. He soon became Professor of Anatomy in the University and gathered about him the learned men of this and other countries for delightful evenings. The famous

"Wistar Parties" were always held on Sunday nights at his later residence at Fourth and Locust Streets.

At the corner of Fifth and High Streets Israel Whelen had his office and lived at certain seasons of the year. Mr. Whelen was a fighting Quaker, although not one of the organization bearing that name. He was an authority on banking and finances and a shipping merchant of large resources. He became Commissary General in the Revolution, feeling that it was right to "resist lawless tyranny, bearing down all before it." Friends were alarmed at his digression but took him back and buried him in their graveyard at Fourth and Arch Streets. He was the head of the Electoral College that chose John Adams President and the third President of the Philadelphia Stock Exchange. In 1793 he moved to High above Eighth Street and had his place of business at the northwest corner of Fourth and High. Nathan Sellers, famed for his invention of drawn wire and wire weaving, erected the house at Sixth and High Streets.

Probably the most historic personages to reside in this vicinity lived in the house between Fifth and Sixth Streets, now numbered 526, 528 and 530. During the British occupation, this mansion being regarded as the finest in the city, was taken by General Howe for his headquarters and on its grounds was quartered the 15th Regiment of Foot. As soon as the British had evacuated the City, General Benedict Arnold, who had been placed in charge of Philadelphia, found it to his taste and so occupied it. Sometime afterward it was partially destroyed by fire, but Robert Morris built it up again with improvement and lived there for several years. It cost him £3750, and nearly at what is now numbered 510 he had his counting house. When the Capital of the Nation came to Philadelphia the fine residence so centrally located became Washington's Executive Mansion at a yearly rental of $3000. This was more than any other property in the city could command, so we are able to judge that the proximity of the Market must have been an advantage rather than otherwise. From December, 1790, until March, 1797, the President resided there except when on vacation at Mount Vernon or at Germantown during the yellow fever epidemic. At the latter place his front window again looked out upon the Market Square so that Mrs. Washington was well located for keeping the State dinners plentifully supplied.

After Robert Morris moved out to make way for Washington, he went to the southwest corner of Sixth and High Streets to live and in 1793 he moved his counting house to the same location in a back building. He got this house from Joseph Galloway, the Tory Lawyer and Speaker of the Assembly. Galloway drew up the plan for the Germantown Academy in 1759 and was a noted public character. The State confiscated his residence during the Revolution for the use of the President of the Supreme Executive Council of the State, which was the administrative body of the Commonwealth during the war. Consequently, we find Joseph Reed, William Moore and John Dickinson credited to this corner from 1778 to 1785. Dickinson was a Maryland Quaker particularly famous for his "Letters of a Pennsylvania Farmer," which told the English how the Colonies felt and secured the repeal of the Stamp Act. He opposed resistance by arms but favoured it upon constitutional grounds. His counsels prevailed in the Colonies for a long time but his opposition to the Declaration of Independence as untimely retired him to private life for a while. He proved a staunch patriot, however, and regained his influence. He was the author of the first American patriotic song, "Hearts of Oak," which appeared in Godard's "Pennsylvania Chronicle."

At what would be number 611 lived Charles Biddle between 1785 and 1791. He was the father of Nicholas Biddle, President of the Second United States Bank, and an experienced mariner. He was one of the best known men in the city and has left a most interesting autobiography. Charles Biddle was a friend of Aaron Burr and it was to his house on Chestnut Street near Fourth that Burr came after the fatal duel with Hamilton. Next door to him on Market Street lived his brother, James Biddle, who was President Judge of the First Judicial District of Pennsylvania.

On the north side of Market Street between Sixth and Seventh Streets, Dr. Joseph Priestly, the discoverer of oxygen, dwelt. Dr. Priestly is also known as the founder of Unitarianism in this country. Among the residents of this square none were better known than Elliston and John Perot. They were natives of Bermuda who had been made prisoners by the British in their conflict with Holland, and while the brothers were in business in Dominica. After coming to Philadelphia they had their first place of business in Water Street, next to Stephen Girard, for they were of French descent. Soon they took residences on Market between Seventh and Eighth Streets, where they engaged in West India trade. In 1795 Elliston lived at the present number 733 and John at 709. About 1800, however, John moved next door to his brother.

IV : The Life of the Town

THE daily life of the town was focussed at the old Provincial Hall in the Market Place at Second and High Streets. Here was the Jail and here were those much dreaded but effective instruments of correction —the Pillory, Stocks and Whipping Post. Here monarchs on their accession were proclaimed, here wars were declared and here new Governors from the balcony addressed the people over whom they were appointed to rule, and here the Royal Arms of England were displayed. Elections here took place and here the Provincial Council sat. The town bell was kept here, trade regulated and weights and measures established. But we are hurrying on too fast. Let us see how it all came about and who played the parts.

The High Street, as Market Street was originally called, was the familiar name of the principal street in nearly every English town. It was so called from the time of the Roman invasion of Britain, when they built their famous roads by laying stones so that the thoroughfare was raised somewhat above its surroundings. But if Philadelphia is indebted to England for the name of High Street nearly every American town founded since 1700 is, in turn, indebted to Philadelphia for its Market Street, which is particularly Philadelphian in street nomenclature. This, too, was due to the plan of Penn, who, long before his city was laid out or settled, had provided a wide High Street, where markets could be held on regular days of the week under certain restrictions and rules. Before that time no city or town in the Colonies had made a like provision for its inhabitants.

The markets which from very early in the city's history were characteristic of the High Street caused the inhabitants to refer to the latter as "Market Street," just as the arch over Mulberry Street at Front involuntarily led Philadelphians to allude to the street as "Arch." After the consolidation of the city the name of the street was changed to conform to usage.

The earliest recorded date of a market house in Philadelphia is 1683 when "a market place was established where butchers have movable stalls." This was at Front Street. In 1693 Robert Brett was chosen Clerk of the Market by the Councils, fees established by sixpence per head for cattle killed, two pence per head for calves and lambs, three pence for hogs and nothing for what the country people brought ready killed. Fees for the sealing of weights and measures were also fixed. In the same year rules for the regulation of the markets were drawn up by the city fathers. The market was fixed for Wednesdays and Saturdays at Second and High Streets and anything sold at any other place was forfeited, the returns to go one-half to the poor of the city and one-half to the Clerk of the Market. Nothing was to be sold until the ringing of the town bell from six to seven o'clock in the morning from April 1st to September, and an hour later during the remainder of the year. For the protection of the farmers and butchers nothing could be sold on the way to the Market and no hucksters were allowed to buy or cheapen any article until it had been two hours in the market. In 1701 the duty of the Clerk was "to have assize of bread, wine, beer, wood and other things, and to act as regulator of weights and measures."

The importance of the place as a town centre soon began to grow and in 1704 a "Watch House," sixteen by fourteen feet, was built and the Mayor and a Committee of Aldermen appointed to oversee the placing of gravel. It seems as if this was the first municipal structure and its importance is recorded in the following minutes of the Councils, May 15, 1706: "Whereas the Govr having recd an Express from the Govr of Maryland of seval vessells lately seen some few legues off the Capes of Virginia, and two of them chasing and ffiring sevall Shotts at an English vessell bound to Virginia or Maryland, which are suspected to be ffrench vessells, and pbable may have a designe upon some of the Queens Colonies. It is therefore ordered that the Watch of this City be carefully kept, and that the Constables at their pill take Care of the same, and in lease their appeare any show or danger of the Enemy, that they give the Alarm by Ringing the Market Bell and that every night one of the Aldermen see the Watch set and see that two Constables be sett thereupon till further orders."

The accommodations now began to be cramped and in November of 1708 a new market house was ordered to be built "where the stalls stand." Some delay appears and in February, 1709, a pillory, stock and whipping post were ordered to be added. To defray the cost of this extravagance the Council members were to advance the money and to be repaid with interest from the rent of stalls.

Seven Aldermen were ordered to pay double what the Common Councilmen do. As this Market House was to be of considerable importance, it is interesting to note that "Aldermen Masters and Joshua Carpenter are appointed to lay out ground and contrive the building."

By 1710 the building was under roof at the eastern end of the old market house on High Street between Second and Third Streets. There was to be a market on the ground floor and the upper floors to be devoted to public use. Built of brick and of two and one-half stories, this building is familiar to many Philadelphians by reason of the frequent publication of the old print of the "First City Hall." It was City Hall, Court House, Town Hall, State House and meeting place of the Municipal Council and Legislature as well as a market house until 1735, when the State House was built. From its balcony the early Governors delivered their inaugural addresses, the people assembled there for the discussion of public questions and at one time a speaker addressed an assemblage of six thousand persons gathered about the building. The structure contained open passageways on the first or street floor where there were market stalls, the building proper being over where the market was held. In 1714 the entertainment of proclaiming the King cost the Mayor and Aldermen thirty pounds and ten shillings.

The rent of the stalls was only to "ffreemen" at nine shillings per annum and meat was to be sold at the west end only. When rents were not paid promptly the "Beadle was ordered to pluck up the stall."

The city was growing rapidly and in November of 1718 the building of new stalls was planned. Whereupon Thomas Rodman produced a plan which the Councils approved. The stalls were to extend west of the Court House, to be the same width and ten feet to the "joice." The length of two stalls was eighteen feet with a four foot alley between them and the next two, the breadth of stall and shelter at the back to be each three and a half feet and the stalls to begin eight feet from the Court House. A fourteen foot walk down the middle posted at both sides, completed the design. Aldermen Norris and Logan offered to lend one hundred pounds each for forty-eight stalls.

The method of building the stalls was debated again and again until January, 1720, when Alderman Rodman proposed to build thirty stalls with brick pillars three feet higher than originally intended and to arch and plaster the roof for four hundred pounds. By 1722 the old stalls suffered in comparison with the new and they were ordered removed from under the Court House and west of the new ones. The butchers were put out of the old stalls between the prison and Court House and they were let for herbs, milk, butter and fish, the Cryer giving public notice of this edict. The rents were raised to three pounds per annum but all through the records we find much trouble in collecting the rents and fees. The Clerk's job was no sinecure. A curious regulation appears at this time that no person be "suffered to Smoak Tobacco in the market or Market House or in any of the stalls," in harmony with the Act of Assembly prohibiting "smoking" in the streets. A paternal government indeed was this!

A wave of reform and cleanliness seems now to have engaged the Council's attention. The killing of animals and the leaving of dirt and offal in the market was prohibited. We wonder now how a shambles could have been tolerated in the City's centre for so long a time. Mary Whiteker was employed at two shillings a week to sweep the Court House and Stalls twice weekly. Although the Councils no doubt with the best intentions passed very excellent rules, they seem to have been as much disregarded as are so many of our present City Ordinances. In 1727 there is much complaint of the hucksters buying up of provisions and selling to persons coming to Market so that the City ordinance regulating this practice was ordered published. In 1730 the killing of meat by the butchers was declared a nuisance, although prohibited in 1722.

The close of the year 1729 marked another important period in the enlargement of the Market. In January of 1730 twenty stalls were ordered built from the Court House to the river to begin one hundred feet eastward from the stairs of the Court House. This was called the

"Jersey Market" and it was customary for farmers to come two days a week from the sister Colony to expose their produce. A bell was put up at Front Street and it was the custom to have it rung when a boat of produce had put in at the wharf. From an early print by Henry Dawkins it is seen that these stalls were open to all weathers in 1764.

More objections appear in 1736. Private stalls in front of the Court House, selling goods, empty carts and the lying of horses in the Market Place were objected to. In this year a Committee of Councils recommended paving in front of the Court House, erecting posts, making new "moving stalls" to be covered with painted canvas and the exhibition of two sample stalls, all at a cost of 200 pounds. This was the first paving in the City and here also was begun the work of sweeping the City streets. Both these suggestions came from Benjamin Franklin.

In 1740 the middle of the street from the Pillory to Laetitia Court was posted or gravelled the breadth of twenty feet and new stalls erected from the Court House to Laetitia Court. These improvements brought a need for more regulations and the Councils declared that the driving of carts and carriages through the Market Place was dangerous and ordered chains to be put up to prevent it from sunrise to ten o'clock in summer and for an hour longer in winter on Market days. So we see the beginnings of street paving, street cleaning and traffic regulations to have originated in the Market Place.

No doubt the market now was crowded, for merchandise was definitely excluded and Patrick Baird was compelled to pay twenty-five pounds per annum for a stall under the Court House.

On May 20, 1745, the residents of the southern part of the City, known as "Society Hill," prayed for permission to erect a market on South Second Street from Pine to Cedar, as "an ornament and convenience." This section of the city known as the "New Market Square" was surrounded by the lands of Joseph Wharton, Edward Shippen and Samuel Powell and it was the first two who proposed to build sixteen stalls on South Second Street, eight south of Lombard and eight north of it, to be paid for out of the rents. The building which we know at Second and Pine Streets was after the design of the Court House at Second and High Streets, and it constitutes an historical evidence of past customs, the last of a type intimately associated with the early history of the City. It is an example of the town hall and market place which was the centre of civic life here as in the old world. The stone aisle has echoed to the tread of famous people and the fairest of Philadelphia's prominent families who lived nearby. President and Mrs. Washington, Dolly Madison, Stephen Girard, Joseph Bonaparte and other notables are said to have frequented the Second Street Market.

In 1759 the stalls on High Street were extended to Third Street and a vault for oil to use in the City lamps was built under the Meat Market. This was quite an extension and when we realize that the forest began at Eighth Street we will understand what a sizeable market the City had.

In 1763 repairs were necessary to the Jersey Market and stalls with brick pillars were ordered eastward of the Court House and forty feet from the line of Second Street, to be covered, and at the east end on Front Street at the top of the hill a building was to be built for a green market and exchange. Five hundred pounds was appropriated but the work was deferred until 1769. The terminal at Front and High Streets with its architectural dome remained until all were taken down in 1859. The North Second Street Market was built about 1763.

In 1764 a Fish Market was established "between the Stone Bridge in Front Street and the Wooden Bridge in King Street at the Drawbridge." This was in the middle of High Street from Water to the river. The people having complained of the offensiveness of shad and herring their sale was confined to this market and the "Public Wharffs." In front of the old London Coffee House, which stood at the southwest corner of Front and Market Streets until 1883, it was customary for the fishermen to erect a Maypole on May Day. They decorated it with greens and boughs and bright colored ribbons.

The year 1773 brought a demand for further extensions both on High and Second Streets. The Councils were agreed to go forward with the addition on High Street but the residents on that thoroughfare from Third to Fourth Streets arose in protest as one man. They objected in a "dignified and gentle address couched in terms the least offensive possible" to the further encumbrance of the street as lowering their property values and abridging their rightful liberties. The Corporation, however, resolved to go on, workmen were employed and materials collected. The objectors sought legal advice and though convinced of their rightful opposition, wishing to avoid a disturbance of tranquillity, waited upon the Mayor with another petition which met a similar fate to that of the remonstrance. Now some of the residents hired wagons and hauled away the stones intended for pillars and removed the sand and lime. They destroyed by night what the workmen did by day. Mayor William Fisher looked on at the proceedings in angry astonishment and some of the angry Aldermen gave orders to those who were interfering to stop. But the residents were determined and had their men continue to remove all material brought there and deposited on a vacant lot in the neighborhood.

This acute state of affairs continued for almost a week, during which time a rough wooden shed erected to store lime was demolished. At the end of the peaceful week's struggle the Council relented and upon petition of "the Society of the People called Quakers" to suspend on account of the agitation of the people, the work was deferred. The troublous times preceding and during the Revolution now intervened and the extension of the sheds to Fourth Street was not made until 1786.

Gradually the sheds were pushed westward until in 1816 they reached Eighth Street and later Thirteenth. In 1830 similar sheds were built in High Street from Fifteenth to Seventeenth Street. In 1859 all markets were removed from the centre of High Street, mainly on account of the demand for street car tracks, and the Fish Market was vacated in 1864.

As the rapidly expanding needs of the City required, market sheds and houses were built on Callowhill and Bainbridge Streets. In 1875 Ridge Avenue Farmer's Market, below Girard Avenue, opened for business. October 6, 1877, marked the opening of the New Farmers' Market at the northwest corner of Broad Street and Columbia Avenue. In 1885 there were Markets at Ninth Street and Girard Avenue and on Girard Avenue between Sixth and Twelfth Streets. There was one on Broad between Chestnut and High Streets. The Mercantile Library on Tenth Street north of Chestnut was formerly a Market House. Juniper and Race Streets, Fortieth north of Market and South Eleventh Street were other locations of markets, and at one time the City owned 49 market sheds on as many different streets.

Arrival of Franklin
in Philadelphia · 1723 ·
Foot of High Street

From The Autobiography of Benjamin Franklin, published by Ginn and Company

We are, however, at present concerned with the old markets in Colonial days which were so much the centre of the City's life. Watson tells us that "Fairs were held in the Market Houses, and opened with the same formalities as the business in our Courts at this time. The Fair-times were every May and November and lasted for three days. In them you could purchase every description of dry goods, millinery of all kinds, and caps, toys, confectionery, and so forth. The Stalls were principally and fancifully decorated and enclosed with well made patchwork coverlets. The place was always thronged, and your ears were perpetually saluted with toy trumpets, hautboys, fiddles and whistles, to catch the attention of the young fry, who, on such occasions, crowded for their long promised presents at Fair-time. They were finally discontinued by an Act of Legislature somewhere about the year 1787. It is really surprising they should have been adopted in any country where regular stores and business is ordinarily found sufficient for all purposes of trade."

Watson seems to have more regard for the regularity than the picturesqueness of life. How dull and hum-drum life would have been without a little gayety for the people who had so little opportunity of amusement in those days. These annual events brought mountebanks, peddlars and wanderers from all parts of the country as at no other time, to enliven the provincial folk.

On Tuesday and Friday evenings, the citizens were apprized of the next day's market by the pealing of Christ Church bells which on these occasions were known as the "butter bells." The ladies went to Market themselves and at such time of day as would shock their great-granddaughters. One gay gallant from a sister colony, having a curiosity to see the justly famous markets, tells us that early one morning he jumped from his bed, designing long before to have been at the Market Place. He got there by seven and "had no small satisfaction in seeing the pretty Creatures, the Young Ladies traversing the place from Stall to Stall, where they could make the best Market, some with their maid behind them with a Basket to carry home the Purchases. Others that were designed to buy but trifles, as a little fresh Butter, a Dish of Green Peas or the like, had Good Nature and Humility enough to be their own porters." It was the custom for the buyer to test the butter before purchasing and the farmers often brought in small pyramids of butter from which people could sample the quality. Some of the City's most prominent men would stop before a stall where butter was displayed for sale, take a coin from their pocket, scoop out an edge full and taste it. The sellers encouraged the sampling of their wares and would have a spoon or fork with them for the purpose. The markets were generally very crowded and as there were no side aisles a good deal of difficulty was experienced, especially when the women began wearing hoop skirts. Then the men had a pretty hard time when they came to market.

The farmers formed a habit of bringing frogs to market, caught in their home ponds. They would stand on the curb outside the Market and hold up the frogs for sale. The men bought them to frighten the ladies in the crowded aisle a little bit and make them fall back so as to let the men through.

Interesting as an intimate description of Colonial conditions may be, we should lose perspective if we did not stand off, as it were and view some of our affairs through the eyes of a stranger. So we can round out our ideas of the city's early life by knowing some of the impressions made upon distinguished visitors in those days.

Dr. Alexander Hamilton visited the city in 1744. He says the shops open at five in the morning. He drank tea at the Governor's Club, a society of gentlemen that meet at a tavern every night and converse on various subjects. The Governors come once a week, generally Wednesday, and the conversation when he was there was upon the English poets and Cervantes! He says the heat was excessive but there is a pump of excellent water every fifty paces. He mentions brick pavements, painted awnings and a number of balconies. There was but one publick clock which struck the hours but had neither index nor dial plate. Being in a tavern one night he makes this interesting observation—"a knot of Quakers there talked only about the selling of flour and the low price it bore, they touched a little upon religion, and high words arose among some of the sectaries but their blood was not hot enough to quarrel, or, to speak in the canting phrase, their zeal wanted fervency." He observes that the Quakers were the richest and the people of the greatest interest in the government and that they chiefly composed the House of Assembly, and then he remarks that, "They have the character of an obstinate and stiff-necked generation, and a perpetual plague to their governours."

A diary of this day testifies to the excellence of the entertainment. Here is one characteristic entry:

. . . "this morning most of the family were busy preparing for a great dinner, two green turtles having been sent to Johnny. . . we concluded to dress them both together here and invited the whole family in. We had three tureens of soup, the two shells baked, besides several dishes of stew, with bone turkey, roast ducks, veal and beef. After these were removed the table was filled with two kinds of jellies and various kinds of pudding, pies and preserves; and then almonds, raisins, nuts, apples and oranges. Twenty-four sat down at the table."

The next entry states that

"My husband passed a restless night with gout."

Peter Kalm, the Swedish traveller, speaks enthusiastically of the fine streets in 1748, particularly the market street which was one hundred feet wide. The Rev. Andrew Burnaby, A.M., Vicar of Greenwich, visited the city in 1759–60. He speaks of the public market held twice a week on Wednesday and Saturday as "almost equal to that of Leaden Hall," and says there is "a tolerable one every day besides." The streets are crowded with people and the river with vessels. He notes the expense of house rent as one hundred pounds per annum and that lots 30 × 100 sell for 1000 £.

In that interesting diary compiled by Jacob Hiltzheimer he tells of the ringing of the town bell for fires and that on June 4, 1766, "Being the King's birthday, dined on the banks of the Schuylkill in company of about 380 persons, several healths were drunk, among them Dr. Franklin, which gave great satisfaction to the Company."

Perhaps the custom of the ladies themselves going to market may have been caused in a measure by the condition described in 1769 by a newly arrived Englishman writing home. He says:

"You can have no idea of the plague we have with the servants on this side of the water. If you bring a good one he is spoilt in a month. Those born in the country are insolent and extravagant. The imported Dutch are to the last degree ignorant and awkward. The negroes are stupid and sulky and stink damnably. We have tried them all round, and this is the sum total of my observations: the devil take the hindmost!"

Johann David Schoepf mentions in this Travels in the Confederation 1783–4 that "Going from Philadelphia one passes the Schuylkill, at the middle ferry, by a floating bridge consisting of great logs joined together by cramp irons. In order that the bridge may rise and fall with the ebb and flow of the water, there have been fixed at suitable distances stout iron turning joints in the longitudinal timbers." There are 2400 houses, he says, and no streets west of Seventh, Vine and Pine being the north and south limits. The market buildings are two long open stalls from Front to Third and later further with the upper part of the Court House. Lanterns are placed on posts and night watchmen call out the hour and weather. "Christ Church has a beautiful chime of bells, which makes a complete octave and is heard especially on evenings before the weekly markets and at times of other glad public events. Eight notes of the octave are struck singly several times, descending rapidly one after the other—and then the accord flows in tercet and quint, ascending, and so repeated." He describes the taste in dress as English, of the finest cloth and linen. Every year dressed dolls are brought the women from Europe which give the law of the mode. To be industrious and frugal, at least more so than the inhabitants of the Provinces to the south, is the recognized and unmistakable character of the Philadelphians. He is astonished at the extraordinary stores of provisions in the markets, at the cleanliness and good order in which the stock is exposed for sale. On the evenings before the market days, Wednesday and Saturday, all the bells in the city are rung and people from a distance come into the city in great covered wagons loaded with all manner of provender. Meat costs four pence while in 1778 it was four shillings. He notes that the war left no trace of want but the same exuberant plenty. The inhabitants are well clothed, well fed and better than their betters in Europe. He saw fine wheat bread, good meats and fowls, "cyder" beer and rum. Instead of a Bourse, the people use a Coffee House where most persons engaged in business affairs meet together at mid-day to get news of entering or clearing vessels and to inform themselves of the market. Hats especially are made in Philadelphia from beaver skins and are preferred to any European make.

Ann Warder has an interesting entry in her diary under date of Sixth month, 11th, 1786. She says the Market Street Meeting is double the size of Gracechurch Street in London, that there are five doors and one each side of the Minister's gallery. The dress of the women Friends differs from England in that there are no white frocks but blue and yellow skirts with handkerchiefs close up to throats with a frill around the neck. A man in the Quaker gallery wore a mulberry coat, nankeen waistcoat and breeches with white stockings. Table dishes consisted of roast turkey, a tongue laid in mashed potatoes, whipped silly bubs, oyster-pie, boiled leg of pork, bread pudding and tarts. Provisions are cheap, she says, and the greatest luxury is the abundance of fruit. Pineapples, strawberries, apples, cherries and peas abound. The heat is violent.

Dr. Mannaset Cutler of New England was in Philadelphia in 1787. One of his notable pleasures was his view of High Street—the present Market Street—at an hour of a summer morning when it was still so dark that he could not distinctly see a man a few rods away, but when, to his astonishment, he found more than one hundred persons in the market house and crowds going into it from every street. The market building, considered by many as "the greatest curiosity in the city," was one story high, was supported by brick pillars and was nearly half a mile in length in the centre of the highway. Some parts were used for fish, other parts for meat, and others for butter, vegetables and fruits, and everything was as neat and clean as a dining hall. The crowds of people were of every rank and condition of life, of every age and of every color, and there seems to be some of every nation under Heaven; there was buzzing murmur of voices that resounded through the markets, but no clamor nor crying of wares. Again Cutler was impressed as he had been at Elbridge Gerry's, with the early hours in which the people of this city moved about in beginning their affairs for the day. It was difficult for him to reconcile this habit with the comparatively belated hours of breakfast in his own city, and the presence of the women on the streets so early seemed to have struck him at first as something that might be wanting in delicacy. "The ladies, indeed," he said of the High Street market, "are the principal purchasers, and are in a dress not easy to be known by their most intimate acquaintances and are always attended by a servant with a basket. What would the delicate Boston ladies think if they were to be abroad at this hour?" Another traveller writing under a nom-de-plume says that "One of the local institutions that had more than local celebrity was the High Street Market." Beginning at Front Street it had been built at that time as far to the west as Eighth Street; it consisted of a series of colonnade sheds in the middle of the street; the columns were of brick, and the roofs, which were shingled, were arched underneath. It was impossible, according to "Prolix" to say too much of the excellence of the beef, mutton and veal, and at no other place under the welkin was there sold such butter and cheese. "They are," he said, "produced on dairy farms and by families near the city whose energies have, for several generations, been directed to this one useful end and who now work with an art made perfect by the experience of a century."

Of course we can expect something enthusiastic from John Adams. He speaks of a dinner at Mr. Chief Justice Chew's house on Third Street: "Turtle and every other thing, flummery, jellies, sweetmeats, of twenty sorts, trifles, whipped sillabubs, floating islands, fools, etc., and then a dessert of fruits, raisins, almonds, pears, peaches, wines most excellent and admirable. I drank Madeira at a great rate and found no inconvenience in it." What more glowing tribute to Philadelphia hospitality could we have than this out of New England!

J. J. Brissot de Warville records in his travels in 1788, that the market day suggests a town well managed and wealth, science and virtue, the children of Industry and Temperance are the achievements of the inhabitants. The market is one of the finest in the universe, "variety and abundance in the articles, order in the distribution, good faith and tranquillity in the trader, are all here united." Cleanliness is conspicuous in everything, articles and sellers. The women from the country are dressed decently, the articles neatly arranged and everything is assembled—both products of country and of industry. A multitude of men and women are moving in every direction without tumult or injury. A market of brothers, a rendezvous of philosophers. Silence reigns without interruption; there are no cries, the carts and horses are peaceably arranged in the next street and when disengaged move off in silence. No quarrels among porters, no fools or macaronies galloping in streets. "Habit inspired by Quakers, who planted morals in this country, a habit of doing everythink with tranquillity and with reason; injuring no person and having no need of the interposition of the magistrate." Two clerks of the police walk in the market. If they suspect a pound of butter of being light, they weigh it, if light, seized for use of hospital. Price of bread /1

to /2 the pound, beef and mutton /2 to /4, veal /1 to
/2. Hay 20/ to 30/ the ton. Butter /4 to /6 the pound.
Wood 7/ to 8/ the cord. Vegetables abundant and cheap.
Wines of Europe cheap except in taverns. Hair dressing
/8 a day or 12/ a month. One horse chaise 3 days—3
louis d'ors. Philadelphia is the metropolis of the United
States; the finest and best built town, most wealth though
not most luxurious. There are more men of information,
more political and literary knowledge and more learned
societies. At 10 P. M. all is tranquil in the streets, which
are lighted by lamps placed like those of London. Few
watchmen. Footways are of brick, gutters brick or wood.
Strong posts to prevent carriages on footways. Public
pumps in great numbers. Families sit in evenings to take
fresh air on two benches placed at the door of each house.
Many handsome wagons long, light and open, chairs and
sulkeys. There are no fine horses. The streets are not
inscribed nor the doors numbered. The shops are re-
markably neat.

These contemporary portraits, thumb-nail sketches
though they are, serve to give us a glimpse of the peace
and good-living of our forefathers, no little of which came
from the care that they bestowed upon their markets
as the civic centre of the community. Undoubtedly it
was brought about by the interest and participation of
the best people in the place.

This is the picture of Penn's "greene country towne"
with its "many Brave Brick Houses" surrounded by gardens and orchards "to the great Content and Satisfaction
of all here concerned" with its streams and duck ponds and
expanse of lovely river front. The earliest traces of it
all are gone but there are a few reminders in similar old
streets given over to the unappreciative. There are some
front cellar doors on the sidewalk, numerous old fire in-

surance marks, a few footscrapers and old knockers, while the famous Philadelphia marble steps kept so scrupulously clean have not yet vanished.   Architects are building houses after the old style and we are thinking of an open river front with the esplanade which William Penn hoped and planned for.

V: Early Government

THE first Assembly met at Chester, December 4, 1682, and then at Philadelphia March 12, 1683, probably in the "boarded meeting house" which was replaced in 1684 by the Bank Meeting House on the bank of the river, Front Street above Arch. Here the Assembly probably convened for some years. In 1695 it met in the principal room of Richard Whitpain's great house on the east side of Front Street between Walnut and Spruce Streets. The next year it met at the house of Samuel Carpenter on the west side of King (Water) Street above Walnut, then at Isaac Norris' in 1699 and again at the Whitpain house in 1701, then owned by Joseph Shippen. With no permanent home yet erected they continued to roam and settled next in the school room of Thomas Makin, their clerk. After this the new Friends' Meeting House on the southwest corner of Second and High Streets, which was built in 1695, was their home until 1707, when they moved into the Court House in the middle of High Street at Second. In 1728 they became restive again and requested the Governor and Council to make an order for a meeting place most convenient for the despatch of business because of "indecencies used towards members of the Assembly" where it had been sitting. No doubt the Town House and Markets was too public a place and the busy stir of varied things and people probably interrupted the grave deliberations of the Assembly. The Governor and Council did not see fit to grant the request for the Assembly moved to the house of Captain Anthony Morris, on Second below Walnut Street.

In 1729 an act was passed providing for a State House and appointing Thomas Lawrence, Andrew Hamilton and John Kearsley for the building and carrying out of the same. Hamilton and Kearsley both presented designs and Lawrence cast the deciding vote for Hamilton's plan. The matter was carried to the floor of the House which approved the recommendation of the committee and the work was begun in 1735 on Chestnut Street where we still admire its completion. William Allen bought the square from the Welsh Friends of Radnor Township who had received the lots there from Penn to accompany their country purchases.

The whole of the ground between Chestnut and Walnut Streets was not taken up at first and the sides on Fifth and Sixth Streets extended farther south than did the centre. The ground lying to the southward of the building was, however, "to be enclosed and remain a public green and walk for ever." In this square to-day stand the most interesting and complete group of Colonial buildings in America. In importance of association with great events they are of course unique. They have been used for many sorts of purposes and much has been written about the assemblages, events and people of the buildings and grounds. Many dinners and balls were given in the new building and many notable persons entertained.

Mayor William Allen seems to have opened the series of social events by a feast on the 30th of September, 1736, the "most grand and the most elegant entertainment that has been made in these parts of America" as described in Franklin's *Pennsylvania Gazette*. Governors entertained and were dined in the long room or banqueting hall on the second floor and the State House seems to have been the principal place for such events until September, 1774, when the gentlemen of the city gave a dinner for the members of the Continental Congress. After that only private dinners took place there.

The first occupancy of the State House by the Legislature was in October, 1736, when Andrew Hamilton was elected Speaker for the seventh term, and Benjamin Franklin was clerk. The building was still unfinished in 1741, and in the summer of that year the Assembly insisted that at least the plastering and glazing should be finished for the next session, and that "the whole building with all its parts should be finished without delay."

In 1745 the finishing touches were given to the Assembly Room—the east room—and a handsome silver inkstand (the one which was later used in signing the Declaration of Independence) was provided for the Speaker's table, at a cost of £25 16s.

The second room prepared for use was the western or Judicial Chamber, on the first floor. In 1743 it was ordered to be finished upon a plan corresponding in style with the Assembly Room.

In October, 1748, the Governor's Council took possession of the western chamber in the second story, which thereafter became known as "the Council Chamber."

The staircase leading to the Council Chamber, and to the other two rooms on this floor, the Banqueting Hall and the room of the Clerks of the Assembly, was completed as early as 1741.

In 1740 the Assembly ordered the tower to be carried up, "to contain the staircase, with a suitable place thereon for hanging a Bell," and in June, 1753, Isaac Norris, the Speaker and a Quaker Minister, ordered Pass & Stow to place in position in the State House steeple a "new great Bell, weighing 2080 lbs. with this motto:

'Proclaim Liberty throughout all the Land unto all the inhabitants thereof—Lev. xxv: 10.' "

Pass & Stow were paid in September following £70 13s 5d.

In 1752 a clock was ordered, and in 1759 it was in place and paid for. The State House was practically completed at this time.

Of the notable events that have taken place in the Old State House the following are of especial interest:

On June 16, 1775, Washington accepted his appointment as General of the Continental Army in the east room (Declaration Chamber).

On July 4, 1776, the declaration of the Colonies that they were and of right ought to be free and independent States was made in the east room (Declaration Chamber).

The Convention to form a new Constitution for Pennsylvania met in the west (Supreme Court) chamber July 15—September 28, 1776. This Convention unanimously approved the Declaration of Independence, and on July 20, 1776, elected to Congress the delegates who were the Signers in behalf of Pennsylvania of that document.

The American officers taken at the Battles of the Brandy‚ wine (September 11, 1777) and Germantown (October 4, 1777) were held in the Declaration Chamber by the British as prisoners of war.

Congress, which had left Philadelphia in December, 1776, reconvened in the east room March 4, 1777; they left again September 18, returned July 2, 1778, and continued to sit here until the close of the Revolution.

On July 9, 1778, the Articles of Confederation and perpetual union between the States were signed in the Declaration Chamber by eight States. The five remaining signed later, the last (Maryland) on March 1, 1781.

The Federal Convention to frame a Constitution for the United States met in this chamber May 14—September

17, 1787, and, after final action and engrossing of the Constitution, those present affixed to it their signatures.

The Convention for the State of Pennsylvania ratified the Federal Constitution here on December 13, 1787. The Convention to frame the Constitution of Pennsylvania of 1790 met in this chamber also.

In 1802 the whole of the second floor of the State House was used as the Peale Museum, Charles W. Peale, the portrait painter, having been granted the use of it by the Legislature rent free. The Museum contained a number of portraits of distinguished persons, painted from life, chiefly by Peale himself and his son, Rembrandt Peale. There was a collection of birds, with the scenery appropriate to each—mountains, plains, water, etc. Insects were also exhibited. The Marine Room contained many amphibious animals, as well as a variety of fishes. Minerals and fossils were also displayed. There was, too, a perfect skeleton of a mammoth.

In 1824 Lafayette visited Philadelphia, and was given a reception in Independence Chamber.

While the body of John Marshall, Chief Justice of the United States Supreme Court, was being removed from the house on Walnut Street in which he died, to Virginia for burial, the Liberty Bell was ordered tolled in honor of the great jurist. This was on July 8, 1835, and it was while being thus tolled that the Bell became cracked.

The bodies of Henry Clay (1852) and Elisha Kent Kane, the Arctic explorer (1857) and Abraham Lincoln (1865) were among those which lay in state in Independence Hall.

While the constructive work of Andrew Hamilton embraced only the State House and adjoining offices, he had recognized that the city and county would require better accommodations, and he had created a trust in the two pieces of ground on which stand Congress Hall (the County Building) at the corner of Chestnut and Sixth Streets, and the old City Hall, on the corner of Fifth Street. In order to bring the whole façade into one general effect Mr. Hamilton had stipulated that the buildings should be of like form, structure and dimensions.

The County Building was begun in 1787 and finished in 1789. The City Hall Building was begun in 1789 and finished in 1791.

The Congress of the United States occupied the County Building from the beginning of its third session, December 6, 1790, until the seat of government was removed to Washington, District of Columbia, in 1800.

Washington was inaugurated in this building for his second term as President of the United States (March 4, 1793) and John Adams was inaugurated here on March 4, 1797. The House of Representatives occupied the lower floor; the Senate occupied the second floor.

The Supreme Court of the United States held its first session on the second floor of the City Building, beginning February 7, 1791, and continuing until August 15, 1800. The Supreme Court of Pennsylvania sat on the second floor of this building also.

The Mayor, Aldermen and Common Council men sat as one body in the large back room on the first floor. Adjoining, on the west side, was the Mayor's office, which was so used until March 27, 1895, when the office was moved to the new City Hall.

The Committee for the War of 1812 and that for the Civil War sat in this building.

In March, 1812, Philadelphia got permission from the Legislature to remove a portion of the wings of the building, including the arcades, and to construct buildings for the public use of the day.

The new buildings were carefully planned, and erected by Robert Mills, the architect.

In 1816 the City of Philadelphia became the actual owner of the entire property. The deed of sale was formally executed June 29, 1818, for and in consideration of the sum of $70,000.

Several changes seem to have taken place at this time. Congress Hall was fitted up for the Supreme Court of the State, which since 1802 had been sitting in Independence Hall.

In 1854 the second story of the State House was fitted up for the use of City Councils, which continued to meet there until 1895.

Some years later the whole group of buildings was restored, and now Independence Chamber is kept as nearly as possible in its original state, as a memorial of the year 1776 and its associations.

The building at the corner of Chestnut and Sixth Streets (Congress Hall) was restored in 1913, and the City Building at Fifth Street in the same year.

When Philadelphia was incorporated on October 25, 1701, with boundaries from Vine Street to Cedar, now South Street, and from river to river, the territory of the county was very different in area from the present time. The land of the county outside the city was partly known as the "liberties" and under much less control. North of Vine Street was called the "Northern Liberties," west of the Schuylkill River the "Western Liberties," and south of Cedar Street the "District of Southwark."

The settlement of the city did not follow the city lines as had been expected but was prompted by commerce. Thus, the Delaware River front first became the built-up portion and was the base of a triangle, about the middle of the eighteenth century, with the apex within the city proper but east of Broad Street.

The incorporation of the local governments was a privilege of the Legislature and was not always wisely or honestly done. One by one a large number of these independent jurisdictions sprang up, such as Moyamensing, Spring Garden, Kensington, Penn, Richmond, West Philadelphia, Belmont and others in more outlying districts. As the population increased the police control became more and more difficult. The conflicting jurisdictions and the limitations of the police practically to their own districts seriously interfered with maintaining public order and it was said, indeed, that the criminal classes were better informed as to the limits of the different districts than many of the officers. Riots and general abuse finally moulded public opinion to such an extent that the Legislature passed a bill in 1854 which welded into one municipality the twenty-seven jurisdictions of the City, Southwark, Northern Liberties, Moyamensing, Spring Garden, Kensington, South Penn, Richmond, West Philadelphia, Belmont, Manayunk, Germantown, Whitehall, Frankford, Bridesburg, Aramingo, Passayunk, Blockley, Kingsessing, Roxboro, Penn, Oxford, Lower Dublin, Delaware, Moreland, Byberry and Bristol.

The first local government outside the City appeared in Southwark, named after one of the suburbs of London. It lay southeast of the City beyond the boundary of South Street and extended about a mile along the Delaware River, including the old Swedish settlement of Wicaco. It was erected into a municipality in May, 1762, and became a corporation in 1794. Northern Liberties had a commission in 1771.

The Swedes were a peaceable, religious people and were anxious to aid the colonists in every way. Penn wrote of

The State House · ·
as it was at the time of
The Declaration of Independence

From The Autobiography of Benjamin Franklin, published by Ginn and Company

them, "The Swedes for themselves, deputed Lasse Cock to acquaint him that they would love, serve and obey him with all they had, declaring it was the best day they ever saw."

Southwark had always been the home of many industries. In Colonial days Wharton's still-house, for distilling rum from molasses, was on the wharf near Old Swedes' Church and on Front Street was the nitre works of William Brown. The first china works, founded by Gousse Bonnin and George Anthony Morris in 1769, was near Front and Prime Streets. It was the only factory making white ware in this country but did not last long. A later enterprise was the Shot Tower founded in 1808 by Bishop and Sparks at Front and Carpenter Streets for the purpose of making shot for sportsmen. When the War of 1812 broke, Bishop, who was a Friend, withdrew but the business was continued for many years.

Old Southwark was the scene of the beginning of the Mason and Dixon's line, which is perhaps the most mentioned of any boundary line in this country. In 1763 Jeremiah Dixon and Charles Mason, two English surveyors, were sent out to survey and establish the boundary line between Pennsylvania and Maryland which had been the cause of frequent controversies and even bloodshed. Their first duty was to determine exactly the most southern part of Philadelphia, which they decided was "the north wall of a house occupied by Thomas Plumstead and Joseph Huddle." To find its latitude they built an observatory, which was the first structure of the kind ever built in America for scientific purposes. It was probably very near the Plumstead house which now stands at number 30 South Street. They traced their line two hundred and forty-four miles until stopped by Indians, so that it was not completed until 1782. One hundred and thirty miles of the original line were marked with mile stones, every fifth one bearing the arms of Lord Baltimore on one side and those of William Penn on the other.

The Meschianza given by the British officers upon the departure of General Howe has been frequently described but very little has ever been said about its locality except that it was the Wharton place in Southwark. "Walnut Grove," the family estate of the Whartons, was situated near what is now Fifth and Washington Avenue. The original owner was Joseph Wharton, a wealthy cooper, who had married Hannah Carpenter, granddaughter of Samuel Carpenter, prominent among the early settlers as we have seen and the wealthiest man in the colony. Shortly after his marriage Joseph Wharton bought from Charles Brockden an estate of eighteen acres in Wicaco, and upon it, about 1735 built his residence. It was plain and comfortable with an unusually large number of rooms, and the grounds sloped down to the river. Joseph Wharton was a man of dignified manners and was called "The Duke." He had been dead but a short while when the British occupied Philadelphia and it is supposed that Walnut Grove was empty at the time, otherwise the festivities which took place there would not have been countenanced, as the Whartons were Quakers.

The district of the Northern Liberties was almost rural until well into the nineteenth century. There were no wagon pavements in any part of it until about 1840 and several streets were not even run. Old Fourth Street was the principal street and the oldest. It was called the York Road before the Revolution. At the corner of Green Street was a famous skating pond. In 1813 Friends built a large meeting house at this corner and here was enacted many of the stirring events which led to the Separation in the Society in 1827. The Hicksite branch had its birth at that time in this house and meetings were held twice a week there until after the celebration of the one hundredth anniversary, when Friends, having removed from the neighborhood, gave it over for neighborhood work among the foreign population of the district.

Near Third and Brown Streets was Coates' wood of some five acres, cut down by Colonel Coates for pocket money when he was young. The Northern Liberties district was famous for its rioting and disorder. The ship carpenters from Kensington and the butchers from Spring Garden used to engage in many a fracas and fighting was common every Saturday night. The spirit of unrest and disorder in the Northern Liberties found its height in the Native American riots of 1844, when the military were called out and many lives lost.

VI: The First Roads

NEITHER the Dutch nor the Swedes were road-builders and the Delaware River was the only great thoroughfare until the settlements began to grow back into the country from its banks. The first roads were mere paths through the woods made by the Indians and only pack horses were used for a long time in the conveyance of goods. Conestoga wagons came in 1760. The marketing going to the city was carried on horseback with side panniers and hampers and most of the horses were ridden by women.

In 1686 the Council appointed a committee to inspect all the business of roads and to order them to be laid out in the most proper and convenient places. The committee and surveyors were ordered in that year to lay out a more commodious road from the Broad Street in Philadelphia to the Falls of the Delaware, where Trenton now stands. This road really went out Front Street through Frankford, Bristol and Trenton as we now know them. During the session of the Council in 1697 numerous roads were laid out such as from William's Landing on the Delaware in Bucks County into the King's Great Road to shorten the post-road to New York, the Gray's Ferry Road and the Darby Road to Hertford. Perhaps the two best known roads were the York Road and the Lancaster Pike.

The Council was petitioned in 1711 to lay out the York Road and the course is described in the order of the Council thus:

To begin at the side of the River Delaware opposite to John Reading's landing, from thence by the most direct and convenient course to Buckingham meeting house, and from thence the most direct and convenient course through the lands of Thomas Watson, and from thence ye most direct and convenient course to Stephen Jenkins on the west side of his house, and from thence the most direct and convenient course by the house late of Richard Wall, now in possession of George Shoemaker and so forward by the most direct and convenient course to Phila.

The turnpike from Philadelphia to Lancester was begun in 1792 and finished in 1794 at a cost of $465,000. It was the first stone turnpike in the Union.

The roads were very bad until these turnpikes were constructed and all farmers commended and used them until the benefactors who built them were forgotten and they were shunned, leaving the stockholders to get half an income. If none had been built the roads would have mostly become clay pits and a serious condition ensued.

In July, 1718, a road was ordered laid out between Philadelphia and the Wissahickon mills. Part of the Ridge Road was made in 1698 for carting lime to the City from the kilns at Plymouth. There followed the road from Germantown to Perkiomen in 1801, from Cheltenham to Willow Grove in 1803, the Chestnut Hill and Springhouse Turnpike in 1804, the Philadelphia, Bristol and Morrisville road in 1904, the Philadelphia, Brandywine and New London road in 1810, the Perkiomen and Reading Turnpike in 1811, the entire Ridge Road in 1812, and the Spring House and Bethlehem Turnpike in 1814.

Penn established a weekly post route between Philadelphia, Chester and New Castle in 1682 and the letters were carried by travellers, traders or special messengers. The first public conveyance for passengers was the stage between Burlington, New Jersey and Amboy in 1732. It connected at Amboy with New York and at Burlington with Philadelphia by boat. The stage between Philadelphia and

New York was not set up until 1756 and made the run in three days at two pence a mile. On summer days the stages usually made forty miles, but in winter, when the snow was deep and the darkness came on early in the afternoon, rarely more than twenty-five. At one season of the year the traveller was oppressed by the heat and half choked by the dust, while at another he could scarce keep from freezing. Generally put down at an inn about ten at night, cramped and weary, he ate a frugal supper and betook himself to bed, with a notice to the landlord that he would be called at three the next morning. At this time, rain, snow, or fair, he was forced to rise and make ready by the light of a horn-lantern or a farthing candle for another eighteen-hour ride, when horses were changed. Sometimes, too, he was forced to get down and lift the coach out of a quagmire or a rut. Thomas Twining, travelling in America in 1795, says that the wagon in which he rode was a long car with four benches holding nine passengers and a driver. The light roof was supported by eight slender pillars and from it hung three leather curtains rolled up at the pleasure of the passengers. There was no place for luggage except in front of the passengers and no backs to the benches, which made the riding very uncomfortable.

In 1757 a boat left Whitehall wharf in New York on Tuesday to the Blazing Star in New Jersey. The passengers went thence by stage to New Brunswick, by another stage to Trenton and by still another to the Sign of the George (the St. George and the Dragon) at Second and Arch Streets, arriving on Friday afternoon. Another route was from the Sign of the Death of the Fox in Strawberry Alley, Philadelphia, to Trenton Ferry, a stage through Princeton and New Brunswick to Perth Amboy and by boat to New York. In 1759 there was a stage

Benjamin Franklin ··
in Keimer's Printing House

From The Autobiography of Benjamin Franklin , published by Ginn and Company

line set up from Cooper's Ferry, opposite Philadelphia, through Mount Holly and Monmouth County to Sandy Hook, thence to Middletown and by boat to New York. In 1771 John Barnhill set up a stage called The Flying Machine, which made the run in two days and a half.

The route to Baltimore was by boat to New Castle, Delaware, then across the country by stage to the head of the Elk River and so by boat to Baltimore.

In 1796 there were four daily stages to New York, one to Baltimore and one once or twice a week to Lancaster, Bethlehem, Wilmington, Dover, Harrisburg, Reading and Easton. The ride to Lancaster took three days for the round trip and it took two days to get to Reading. The roads to Baltimore were perhaps the worst of many bad ones. Chasms ten feet deep were frequent and it very often took five days to make the trip. Coaches were overturned, passengers killed and horses destroyed so that one can easily see how small the world was for the early settlers. Sometimes there was no stage for two weeks.

The first through line of stages to Pittsburgh was in August, 1804, and it took seven days to get there.

Later canal boats were brought by canal through the Allegheny Mountains from Pittsburgh to Columbia, then by the Pennsylvania Railroad to Philadelphia, entering through Fairmount Park. They were taken down Willow Street on trucks drawn by horses to warehouses on Delaware Avenue, where they discharged and loaded their freight.

VII: The Old Taverns

IT is a great leap of the imagination to picture the old inns of the City. We are so used to the luxurious appointments and spacious dimensions of our present hotels that we can hardly comprehend the little Blue Anchor Tavern twelve by twenty-two feet and of two stories which was equally popular in its day. These early inns accommodated man and beast and the jolly landlord and bright-eyed barmaid were a large part of their attractions. The table was clean and groaned under a weight of wholesome viands. Hot punch or a tankard of foaming ale in a cosy corner of the tap room or before a roaring fire were features which we can perhaps count a loss to-day. The healthy out-door life of our ancestors did not call for a varied menu with French names or wines with high sounding titles. The beds were hard but clean in small rooms with bare floors, white-washed walls and small windows with plain curtains. Men frequented the taverns to meet their neighbours and discuss the news and business of the day, while enjoying a quiet glass or pipe. The large influx of immigrants and the continued stream of strangers in the early days caused the setting up of a great number of taverns in Philadelphia. These people had to be provided for as well as a substitute for our present clubs and business exchanges. It was a paying business and many embarked in it. Complaints were made in the Councils and public prints of the nuisances of intemperance but not more, indeed not as many, as might have been expected in a time of hard drinking. Many important events and illustrious personages are connected with the old inns and not a little of early history was made in them. Their quaint signs and rhymed sentiments awaken many interesting memories.

As Penn came up the river from Chester in a barge he was much attracted by the "low and sandy beach" at the mouth of the once beautiful and rural Dock Creek. The little party came to the shore by the side of Guest's new house, then in a state of building, which appropriately enough was to become an inn, known in the earliest records as "The Blue Anchor Tavern." All the earliest keepers of the inn were Friends: Guest, Reese Price, Peter Howard and Benjamin Humphries. It was in front of this inn that Penn is said to have mingled most intimately with the Indians, at once introducing himself and ingratiating himself into their confidence. He walked with them, sat down on the ground with them and ate their roasted acorns and hominy. Soon they jumped up and leaped about in an expression of joy and satisfaction. Penn had been an athlete of no mean repute while at Oxford and was now only 38, so that he was able to beat them all at their exercises and thus gain another point in their admiration. This incident recalls that some Friends thought William was too prone to cheerfulness and gayety for a grave "public Friend."

The Blue Anchor Tavern became, as so many of the later inns also did, of much consequence as a place of business. It was the key to the City and really at first the only public building. Vessels with building timber from Jersey, where the earlier settlers had set up mills, or with traffic from New England, made a landing at Dock Creek where was the only public wharf. Here was the public ferry where people were put over to Society Hill before the bridge at Front Street was built, and to Windmill

Island in the Delaware and Jersey further on. The Blue Anchor Tavern is supposed to have been the first house built in Philadelphia and the furthest advanced upon Penn's arrival. Some of its timbers were thought to have come over in the first ships as were those of other houses, to expedite the building. The structure was timbered, filled in with small bricks and had the dimensions of twelve by twenty-two feet with a ceiling of about eight and half feet in height. It was situated at what is now the northwest corner of Front and Dock Streets and was subsequently called the "Boatman and Call." The present Blue Anchor Tavern near this spot is the third of the name.

The Penny Pot House and Landing at Vine Street was on land ordained by Penn in 1701 to be "left open and common for the use of the City." It was famed for its beer at a penny a pot and was a two-story brick house of good dimensions. Vine Street lay along a vale and was first called Valley Street, where it was not so difficult to land lumber or goods. So as in the case of the Blue Anchor Tavern this became a "port of entry" and an advantageous location for an inn. The roads about it, however, presented a different condition than the river and were almost impassable. The Council frequently protested against their dangerous condition in early times. The Penny Pot House stood well into the nineteenth century and went by the name of the "Jolly Tar Inn."

It was in the Old London Coffee House that much of the early business was done. This picturesque old building, which was removed about 1883, was built in 1702. It stood on a part of property patented by Penn to his daughter, Laetitia in 1701. She sold the corner of Second and High Streets to Charles Reed, who erected the building. At the death of Reed his widow conveyed it to Israel Pemberton, a wealthy Quaker, who willed it to his son John in 1751. In 1754 William Bradford, a grandson of the first printer of that name, removed his print shop from Second Street next door to the old house which he opened as a house of entertainment. Under his management it became the busiest place in the City. It was a kind of Merchants' Exchange, and at times, it is said, slaves were sold before its doors. Gifford Dailey had it in 1780 but after a time the owner, John Pemberton, prohibited the dispensing of strong drink there and let the building to John Stokes to be used as a dwelling. During the sessions of the Continental Congress and during the British occupation the London Coffee House was the centre of much gayety and entertainment by prominent men. Colonel Eleazor Oswald, a gallant artillery officer of the Revolution, succeeded Dailey as host and next door published the *Independent Gazeteer* and the *Chronicle of Freedom*. When John Pemberton died the property went to the Pleasant family and in 1796 was sold to Stokes. Bradford's petition to the Governor for a license shows that coffee was ordinarily drunk as a refreshment then as spiritous liquors are now. Indeed the petition mentions briefly and merely casually that there may sometimes be occasion to furnish other liquors besides coffee. The house was long the centre of attraction for genteel strangers and the Governor as well as other persons of note, ordinarily went at set hours to sip their coffee and some of these had their known stalls. The general parade was in front of the house under a shed of common construction and as it was the most public place adjacent to the market, the people brought all sales of horses, carriages, groceries and other goods there. It was a sort of bourse or clearing house for trade. Pemberton required the Proprietor to preserve decency, prevent profane words, close it on the Sabbath and prevent card playing, dicing and back-gammon. For such conditions to prevail in the principal public house of the City was an indication of the marked moral feelings of the town. *The Pennsylvania Journal* of January 31, 1760, contained this:

Notice is hereby given that I, John Cisty, being employed by a number of gentlemen, intend to ride as a Messenger between Baltimore town in Maryland and Philadelphia, once a Fortnight during the Winter and once a Week in Summer. Any Gentleman having letters to send, then by leaving them at the London Coffee House, may depend they shall be called for by their humble servant,

John Cisty.

There was an earlier "London Coffee House" of less success built by Samuel Carpenter upon some of the ground near Walnut and Front Streets and kept by his brother Joseph. Here the ship captains and merchants congregated to discuss the commercial and political news.

On Chestnut Street opposite the State House stood Clark's Inn with its sign the "Coach and Horses." It was rought-cast, of two stories and bore the date mark of 1693. In front the little space to the road was filled with bleached oyster shells so that it looked like a sea-beach tavern. It was an "out-town" tavern in Penn's days and the Founder himself frequently refreshed himself on the porch with a pipe for which he paid a penny. The innkeeper was noted for his cooked meat prepared by dogs! As cooking time approached it was no uncommon thing to see the cooks running about the streets looking for their truant laborers. These little bow-legged dogs were trained to run in a hollow cylinder, like squirrels, and so give the impulse to the turn-jack which kept the meat in motion suspended before the kitchen fire. Here was the last vestige of the noble forest of primitive days. A fine grove of walnut trees remained to serve as distant pointers to guide the strangers to the State House, itself beyond the verge of common population. This little inn for a long time gave all the entertainments to the Court-suitors and the hangers-on of the Colonial Assemblies and early Congress. After the Revolution it was known as the "Half Moon" kept by Mr. Hassell, whose only daughter Norah, "passing fair," was part of the attraction. The location of the house gave it an unusual distinction through the patronage of Governors, Assemblymen, Judges and patriots.

Enoch Story's Inn at the sign of the Pewter Platter was the scene of many a revel by the young bloods of the town. Here young William Penn, Jr., and his companions got into the fight which led to their being presented by the Grand Jury. It was at Front Street and Jones' Alley but poor Jones soon lost the distinction on account of the prominence of the inn and oddity of the sign.

The Crooked Billet Inn, on the wharf above Chestnut Street, was the first house entered by Benjamin Franklin in 1723 but he gave more distinction to the Indian King Tavern, in High Street near Third, when he selected it as the meeting place of the Junto. Afterward it met in Robert Grace's house, in Jones' Alley, west from 14 North Front Street.

Mrs. Jones' Three Crowns Taverns in Second Street and Mrs. Mullen's Beefsteak House on the east side of Water Street were famous for their table and entertained many Governors. Governor Hamilton held his Governor's Club at Mrs. Mullen's and the Free Masons and other societies had their meetings there.

The successor to the London Coffee House was the City Tavern, finished in 1773, in Second Street near Walnut. Here Monsieur Gerard, the first accredited representative of France to the United States, gave his grand entertainment in honour of Louis XVI's birthday.

Harry Epple's Inn, in Race Street, was a fashionable resort during the Revolutionary period and an Assembly Ball was given there. Washington and Louis Philippe d'Orléans were guests there.

St. George and the Dragon, better known as the George Inn, at the corner of Second and Mulberry, now Arch Street, was the stopping place of the New York and Baltimore stage coaches. It was appropriately kept by John Inskeep, at one time Mayor of the City.

At frequent intervals on the roads, houses of public entertainment served for the places where elections were held and for neighborhood merry-making. It was around them that homes were built, the villages being frequently known by the tavern sign until they were large enough to have a name of their own. In early times travellers secured entertainment at private houses and an account of John Galt in 1738 tells us that in the houses of the principal families in the country, unlimited hospitality formed a part of their regular economy. He says, "It was the custom of those who resided near the highways, after supper and the religious exercises of the evening, to make a large fire in the hall, and to set out a table with refreshments for such travellers as might have occasion to pass during the night; and when the families assembled in the morning they seldom found that their tables had been unvisited."

William Hartley of Chester County in 1740 petitioned for a license because his house is "continually infested with travellers who call for and demand necessaries, and that he has been at great charges in supplying them with bedding and their horses with proper provender without any payment."

And so we might run on for many pages with a recital of more or less important houses with picturesque names, all of which have now disappeared, except the Black Horse on Second Street, near Callowhill which was dismantled about five years ago. It later years it was hardly recognizable as an inn on the front, but the arched entrance led into the old yard which suggested the busy times of its ancient history. The Black Horse goes back to 1785 at least. Even as late as 1845 it was a common thing to see teamsters and farmers take their beds and lodge on the floors. William J. Buck says he has seen frequently as many as one hundred lie down in that way. In 1805 two live porpoises were exhibited at the Black Horse and the following year the learned African Horse "Spottie" which had a tail like an elephant's and a knowledge of arithmetic. The same year two royal tigers from Surat in Asia and a living sea-dog, taken on the Delaware River near Trenton, were shown.

VIII : The Churches

THE first Friends' Meeting was held at Shakamaxon, in the now Kensington district of Philadelphia, at the house of Thomas Fairman, opposite the Treaty Elm, in 1681. The settlement of the city rendered this place inconvenient and Richard Townsend, who came with Penn in the Welcome, says in his "Testimony" that one boarded meeting house was set up where the city was to be, so that this structure must have been the first concern of the settlers, even before their dwellings, and while the caves were yet in use.

On the 9th of the First Month, 1693, a meeting of Friends was held in Philadelphia and Thomas Holme, John Songhurst, Thomas Wynne and Griffith Owen were selected to make the choice of a site for a meeting house and build it. In August of the next year the Quarterly Meeting directed the building of a house in the Centre Square where now the City Hall stands, to be fifty by forty-six feet and of brick. At the same time another meeting house was projected for the Evening Meetings up on the river bank on Front above Sassafras Street. Sassafras was later called Race, because it led to the place where the races were held. This house was fifty by thirty-eight feet, and was but a temporary affair of frame, being replaced by another of brick in 1703 which stood on the west side of Front above Race. Some of the timbers from this ancient Bank Meeting House are to be found in the present Friends' Meeting House on Twelfth Street below Market.

The meeting place at Centre Square proving inconvenient on account of its being so far out of town, a large house was built in 1695 at the corner of Second and High Streets, on ground given by George Fox, the founder of The Society of Friends. This house had a four angled roof surmounted in its centre by a raised frame of glass work, so constructed as to let light down into the meeting below. This house of course became the centre for Friends and their affairs. Governor Penn and his council met in it, as well as at the founder's residence, and beneath its roof were decided the destiny of the province until the building was taken down in 1755, when another was erected in its stead. This served until 1804, when, because of cramped quarters, the large house at Fourth and Mulberry, now Arch Street, was built on ground granted to Friends by William Penn for a burial place and so long as they "shall be in fellowship with the Yearly Meeting of said Friends in London."

The Welsh Friends built several Meeting Houses across the Schuylkill at an early time and their house at Merion, built in 1695, is the oldest Meeting House of the Society of Friends now standing in Pennsylvania. One of its founders was Thomas Wynne, "chirurgeon," and one of its frequent attenders was William Penn, who rode out on horseback on a Firstday Morning to preach. The wooden peg upon which he was wont to hang his hat is still used and until recently a Thomas Wynne sat at the head of the well kept Meeting. At Frankford, Germantown and Fair Hill there were early meetings established and houses set up where still Friends assemble for worship and discipline. Thomas Lloyd, in writing a letter to the Friends' Meeting at Dolobran, in Wales, dated the second of sixth month, 1684, tells them that there were then 800 people at meeting in Philadelphia.

In 1691 James Dickinson held meetings out of doors, sometimes in deep snow, the meeting houses not being large enough to contain the people. James Logan and Gabriel Thomas think that there were about 20,000 Friends in the province about 1700 and when Franklin testified before a Committee of the House of Commons in 1766 he estimated the number of Quakers in Pennsylvania at 53,000, one-third of the total population. As no census was ever taken, Franklin's guess was probably based more upon the influence of Friends than their actual numbers, although journals of the period frequently speak of an increase in numbers and the establishment of many new meetings and enlargement of old houses of worship. Samuel Fothergill says in 1754 that the meetings in Philadelphia are "exceedingly large and all sorts and ranks of people flock to them."

So we can easily see why our customs and institutions are so well defined in their heritage of Quaker ways and principles, peculiarities which have given advertising value to the name for more than a hundred commodities of to-day. For a time Friends were in absolute control of the government, but it was not long, with the influx of population of other sects and lands, before trouble began for the dove in controlling the eagle. Thus there arose a powerful party opposed to the control of the Friends in the Assembly, particularly on account of their peace principles. The character, influence and historic claims of the Quakers, however, constituted the potent social and political forces of the State and indeed after they became a small minority of the population and had pretty well withdrawn from politics on account of religious scruples, such was the confidence reposed in them that even in the back districts where but few Friends resided, these were generally chosen by the votes of others who were not conscientiously opposed to war.

Perhaps the most accomplished Quaker leader of the early city was James Logan, Penn's young secretary. For half a century he was a potent factor in provincial affairs. He was scholarly, genial and vigorous, believed in a defensive war and was intolerant of the narrow distinctions of his sect. Perfectly faithful to the Penn family, he managed Indian affairs with great skill and quite in the spirit of the founder. His seat at "Stenton" was and still is one of the most stately of mansions. Here he entertained Indians and distinguished visitors with a free hand and pursued the muses to his heart's content, never allowing his business to interfere.

Writing to Thomas Story in England in 1724 Logan gives us a picture of his daughter Sarah.

"Sally, besides her needle, has been learning French, and this last week, has been very busy in the dairy at the plantation, in which she delights as well as in spinning; but is this moment at the table with me (being first-day afternoon and her mother abroad), reading the 34th Psalm in Hebrew, the letters of which she learned very perfectly in less than two hours' time, an experiment I made of her capacity only for my diversion though, I never design to give her that or any other learned language, unless the French be accounted such."

Speaking of her sister Hannah, William Black, the young Virginia secretary of the Indian Commission en route to make a treaty with the Iroquois at Lancaster, writes in 1744——

"I was really very much surprised at the Appearance of so Charming a Woman, at a place where the seeming moroseness and Goutified Fathers Appearance Promised no such Beauty, tho' it must be allow'd the Man seem'd to have some Remains of a handsome enough Person, and a Complexion beyond his years, for he was turned of 70; But to return to the Lady, I declare I burnt my Lips more than once, being quite thoughtless of the warmness of my Tea, entirely lost in contemplating her Beauties. She was tall and Slender, but Exactly well Shap'd, her Features Perfect, and Complexion tho' a little the whitest, yet her Countenance had something in it extremely Sweet. Her Eyes Express'd a very great Softness, denoting a Compos'd Temper and Serenity of Mind, Her manner was Grave and Reserv'd and to be short she has a Sort of Majesty in her Person, and Agreeableness in her Behaviour, which at once surprised and Charmed the Beholders":

James Logan held many of the highest positions of public trust, was a founder of the Academy now the University of Pennsylvania, and the possessor of the most extensive library in the Colonies, which he left to the Library Company of Philadelphia. He was followed by a long line of capable and distinguished descendants, some of whom lived at "Stenton" until recent years when it passed into the possession of the city.

A leader of more rigid Friendly principle was David Lloyd, a Welshman of remarkable ability and the first political "boss" of the State. His shrewdness and championship of popular rights gained many prerogatives for the people. Thomas Lloyd and Isaac Norris, both ministers among Friends, were very prominent in the government of the province, and John Kinsey, Clerk of the Yearly Meeting, became Speaker of the Assembly and Chief Justice, thus combining leadership in Church and State until his death in 1750. He was the last of the prominent Friends in public life and the leadership of the "Quaker Party" passed strangely enough to Benjamin Franklin. It had always been the liberty party of the province and he happened to be the popular leader. The only Friend who seems to have remained prominently in public life after this time was John Dickinson, who was the most conspicuous person in the service of the State from 1760 until 1785. From the meeting of the Stamp Act Congress until his death he was a prominent figure in national history. He was the first to advocate resistance, on constitutional grounds, to the ministerial plan of taxation, and for a long period after the enforcement of the Boston Port Bill he controlled the councils of the country. He courageously maintained that the Declaration of Independence was inopportune and so sank at once from the position of a leader to that of a martyr to his opinions. However, after it was found that compromise was impossible and the step was taken he proved his patriotism and remained firm in the defence of the cause. He is perhaps best known for his "Farmer's Letters" published in the *Pennsylvania Chronicle* and addressed to the people of Great Britain, which did most to secure the repeal of the Stamp Act, but he prepared many of the important state papers for the Continental Congress and took a distinguished part in the Convention which framed the Constitution of the United States.

He is thus described by a contemporary: "I have a vivid recollection of the man, tall and spare, his hair white as snow, his face united with the severe simplicity of his sect, a neatness and elegance peculiarly in keeping with it; his manners a beautiful emanation of the great Christian principle of love, with that gentleness and affectionateness, which, whatever may be the cause, the Friends, or at least individuals among them, exhibit more than others, combining the politeness of a man of the world familiar with society in its most polished forms with conventional canons of behaviour. Truly he lives in my memory as the realization of my beau-ideal of a gentleman."

In a community of Quakers there were of course very many prominent ones but these glimpses of those generally distinguished will give a sufficient picture of the sect which founded Philadelphia and gave character to the city and its institutions. As is often the case, a few radical ones because of their grotesquesness have too often led people to misjudge the whole and believe them to be a hard, rigid, ascetic people. Their dress generally was simply the dress of everybody with the extravagance left off or, as William Penn told King James, when asked by that monarch to explain the differences in their faiths: "The only difference lies in the ornaments that have been added to thine."

An account of the marriage of Isaac Collins, of Burlington, to Rachel Budd, of Philadelphia, at the Bank Meeting in May of 1771 gives us an idea of a Quaker wedding. "His wedding dress was a coat of peach blossom cloth, the great skirts of which had outside pockets. It was lined throughout with quilted silk. The large waistcoat was of the same material. He wore small clothes, knee buckles, silk stockings and pumps. A cocked hat surmounted the whole. The bride, who is described as 'lovely in mind and person,' wore a light blue brocade, shoes of the same material, with very high heel not larger than a gold dollar, and sharply pointed at the toes. Her dress was in the fashion of the day, consisting of a robe, long in the back, with a large hoop. A short blue bodice, with a white stomacher embroidered in colors, had a blue cord laced from side to side. On her head she wore a black mode hood lined with white silk, the large cape extending over the shoulders. Upon her return from meeting after the ceremony, she put on a thin white apron of ample dimensions, tied in front with a large blue bow." Wigs were generally worn by genteel Friends, as by other people, and Ann Warder tells in her diary of a minister in the gallery at Market Street Meeting, where she attended sixth month, 11th, 1786, with a mulberry coat, nankeen waistcoat and breeches and white stockings. She says the women wore blue and yellow skirts with handkerchiefs close up to the throats with a frill around the neck. Another letter mentions a bride's dress in meeting as a "lilac satin gown and skirt with a white satin cloak and bonnet."

Penn's Manor of "Pennsbury" on the Delaware, was a model for any architect. Its size and furnishings were on a luxurious scale. The ground was terraced and the lawns and gardens extended all around the house. Vistas were cut through the trees to give views up and down the river, and many English trees of great beauty had been sent over and planted, as well as shrubs from Maryland.

The house was furnished with pewter, silver, chinaware and much handsome furniture. The curtains were of satin. The cellar was well stocked with sherry, Madeira, canary and claret, and with six large cisterns of beer. His coach, calash, sedan chair and barge were as handsome as the day furnished, and his stable was full of good horses brought from England. Nor were Friends so neglectful of art as has been supposed, for in the case of Benjamin West his parents did not reprove his passion for painting, but encouraged him in it and helped him to the best of their ability. He lived to become a founder and the President of the Royal Academy.

The Quakers' flow of wit is no less in evidence than their appetites, which are proverbial, the natural outcome of industry, thrift and a notorious cuisine. The idea that they were a sour visaged lot which the "world's people" seem to have and which has been advanced in books is about as reasonable as calling a landscape red, because the little red barn in the foreground was of that colour. So it is that peculiar and literally rigid members of a sect often give the colour to the whole body in popular estimation.

Nicholas Waln was at one time the most prominent Friend in Philadelphia and distingushed for his piety and virtue. He was the most successful lawyer in the Province and rode about in a canary colored coach to and from his mansion which is still standing at 254 South Second Street, Philadelphia. In 1772 he forsook the law and declared in Meeting that he would consecrate his life to Friendly concerns. However, nothing could keep his tongue quiet when something witty popped into his head. Once when chidden for some of his rallies he said that if his dignified friends only knew how much of his mirth he did suppress they would not think so ill of him. One day while walking along the street in his plain clothes he met a dandy of the town offensively fripped out in the extreme fashion of the period. He had on a well-fitted topcoat surmounted at the shoulders by a collection of little capes each a bit smaller than the one beneath. Walking up to the festive youth, Nicholas took hold of the lowest cape and said, "Friend, what is this?" The facetious youth replied, "That is Cape Henlopen." Touching the cape next above, Nicholas inquired, "And what is this?" "That," said the young popinjay, "is Cape Hatteras." "Then," said Nicholas, touching the jack-a-dandy's head with his finger, "this must be the lighthouse!"

On another occasion, as Nicholas was going along the street, he noticed a house where a pane of glass had been broken and a sheet of paper pasted over the aperture till new glass was set in. Seeing the mistress of the house at her knitting in the back part of the room, Nicholas jammed his walking-stick through the paper, and, putting his mouth to the hole he had made called in "Sham pane and no glass!" It was while living in the South Second Street house that he was much annoyed by repeated depredations on his woodpile. He not only suspected his next door neighbor of stealing the wood, but satisfied himself of the circumstances before acting. He then bought a cartload of wood and sent it to the offending neighbor with his compliments. The man was enraged as he had no notion that he was even suspected. He went to Nicholas in a temper and demanded to know what such a thing meant. "Friend," said Nicholas, "I was afraid thee would hurt thyself falling off my woodpile."

On one occasion Nicholas so shocked Friends that a deputation of "Weighty Friends" was sent to labour with him notwithstanding his exalted position among them. It seems he was a nervous and fidgety man and could not stand the extreme deliberation practised by some Friends in preaching. Upon one occasion a visiting minister arose in meeting, looked about him, cleared his throat and began, "I feel"— Then followed a long pause, more throat clearing, and, after another survey of the assembly, the speaker solemnly repeated, "I feel'— Again pausing and casting his eye over his hearers, he reiterated for the third time, "I feel—" This was too much for Nicholas' impatient spirit; he felt that something must be supplied to feel. In a tone louder than a whisper he burst out in his high penetrating voice, "a louse!" Nicholas knew that he was to be waited on for this indiscretion and he likewise knew when they would seek an opportunity with him. On the evening when Friends went to his house, the windows were all dark and no answer was returned to their oft repeated rappings. Finally concluding that Nicholas must be away, they were turning from the door, when a window on the second floor went up and Nicholas' head, arrayed in a night-cap, came out. "Friends," said he, "you needn't come in. The Lord's been here before you!" A print representing this incident is still in existence.

Nicholas died in 1813 universally loved and respected. Even on his death bed he could not refrain from joking. Almost with his last half-drawn breath he said, looking up, "I can't die for the life of me." Young William Evans was walking one day past 254 South Second Street, when he was called in by Nicholas Waln who was seated upon the front steps. Going into the house, he brought forth a bundle of church-warden clay pipes which he handed to William Evans with the remark, "Take them home to thy father, he will need them at Yearly Meeting time." The "father" was the noted Jonathan Evans of "Separation" fame, but in this instance, at least, he appears in no more rigid light than the Friends who stored ale in the cellar at Fourth and Green Streets and served beer there when the Yearly Meeting met in that house.

One can hardly pass the Evans family without mentioning a recent happening to one of them, a worthy representative of a family long faithful to Friends' principles. This Friend was charged with the good order of his meeting and found it necessary to seek an opportunity with another Friend whose preaching was not acceptable. His labour seemed to be unavailing and finally it became necessary to exclude the offending Friend from the meeting. Whereupon he obtained access to the cellar and one First-day morning during the silence of the meeting his voice was heard crying up through the register, "Friend Evans is a speckled bird." Friend Evans at once left his seat and went to the cellar from whence soon came muffled sounds and then "Thou shalt not put thy hand in the lion's mouth." Other Friends going below found the faithful elder wringing his lacerated hand with which he had tried to stop the obnoxious remarks.

Samuel Willets was a prominent leather and oil commission merchant in company with his brothers Robert and Amos. He gave the first large sum to Swarthmore College of which he was one of the founders. A customer once felt aggrieved about a bill of goods he had bought from the firm and felt that he had been cheated. He remonstrated with the calm Samuel about it and grew more indignant as he proceeded. He could get nothing but calm and patient replies so finally he denounced Samuel Willets with much warmth as the meanest man he had ever met, to which Samuel replied, "I guess thee has never met my brother Amos."

Isaac T. Hopper, whose picturesque portrait hangs on the wall at Swarthmore College, was well known for his humour. He frequently went into undertaking establishments and got into the coffins to "try them on." One day at the seashore he was walking along the beach in old clothes when he was asked by a visitor, looking for a sailing boat, if he was a skipper. "No," he replied, "I am a hopper."

Isaac Potts of Abington Meeting had a farm and according to the custom of the time had a large gathering of neighbors to help him with the flax pulling. It was customary for farmers, not Friends, to have fiddling and a general lively time upon such occasions and some one maliciously circulated the report that Isaac Potts had two fiddlers at his flax pulling. The next First-day he was sharply taken to task after meeting by George Williams, an elder, for having two fiddlers at his flax pulling. He replied "Dost thou not think one would have been enough?"

John Hunt and Samuel J. Levick, two eloquent ministers, were once attending Abington Quarterly Meeting held at Gwynedd in Eighth month. After meeting where both had had acceptable service they were at a large dinner at a Friend's house and being fond of a good cigar afterward, stole away to the back porch to enjoy a smoke where they thought they would not be detected. However, some Friends found them and took them sharply to task. "Yes, Friends," said John Hunt, "it is a vile weed and Samuel and I are burning it up just as fast as we know how."

Joseph Whitall is said to have discovered a burglar in

his room one night. Taking his pistol in hand he said, "Friend, I wish thee would move to one side, I am about to shoot where thee is standing."

As time wore on and the Quakers became wealthy through thrift and industry, they acquired the characteristics of nearly every important religious and political organization. Their zeal for their original message waned and their precious lives were occupied with the taking care of their property and the maintenance of their organization. Rigid dispensation of discipline and the loss of their missionary zeal depleted their numbers and the acquisition of many fads divided their strength into many groups whose opinions sharply differed. Thus with divided purposes in the press of affairs and the complexity of modern life their system of transacting the business of the Meeting by "unity" broke down their hitherto effective organization. The official Meetings are still carried on in the old way and are interesting as a quaint survival of seventeenth century customs. This does not by any means mean, however, that the Quakers or their message are dying out. There has been a spontaneous revival of their original message among many members which has spread all over the world, strangely enough without the inspiration of the Society officially or its Meetings, and this is firing great numbers to a return of the former zeal of the founders brought into modern form. It is healing the divisions of the past and bids fair to unite all in a common cause.

The Church of England men were at first few in numbers and no petition for a parish in Philadelphia was made until 1695, thirteen years after the founding of the colony. What they lacked in numbers, however, they made up in quality and in sustained hostility to the Quakers. With Christ Church and the College under Dr. William Smith as rallying points they increased and became powerful as a party. They were very friendly with the Lutheran Swedes and gradually absorbed them, as they did many of the Keithean Quakers. They were not used to and did not like religious equality and wanted their faith established by law. They had been accustomed to snubbing the Quakers at home and objected to this being a penal offense, sending long complaints to the home government asking that the colony be taken from the Quakers and made a royal province. When they gained control later they reversed this position. It was a new situation for them where they were looked upon as dissenters and where those not of their faith were the most prominent in governmental and civil life. So they held aloof in a compact way which gave them much force and built a church of great extravagance for the time and a thing of beauty forever. It was the outcome of a church built in 1695 under the ministry of the Reverend Mr. Clayton. This was a frame structure with the bell set in the crotch of a tree nearby. In 1710 it was enlarged while the Reverend Evan Evans was pastor and in 1727 the present structure was begun under the rectorship of the Reverend Mr. Cummings. This was made possible by two lotteries projected by the vestry, the tickets for each selling at four dollars apiece. One of them, known as the "Philadelphia Steeple Lottery," was drawn as late as March, 1753, and paid for the steeple, nearly twenty years after the body of the church was built. The church was designed by Doctor John Kearsley, an eminent physician who directed its building by Robert Smith, carpenter. The steeple cost £2100 and the eight bells purchased in England cost £900. They weighed eight thousand pounds and were the cause of much favorable comment. When rung the night before market, people would go all the way from Germantown to hear the tunes. They were rung for the first time at the funeral of Governor Anthony Palmer's wife, the mother of twenty-one children, all of whom died with consumption, and the ringing caused the death of one of the ringers! On the mitre surmounting the steeple, one hundred and ninety-six feet eight inches from the ground, is engraved the name of Bishop White, the first bishop.

From the time this "ring of bells," the first in the colonies, was first hung, they were kept busy. The bells were always being pealed and the German traveller, Doctor Schoepf, says that you would think you were in a papal or imperial city from the number of times the bells were rung.

There was probably no man in the city more revered and trusted than Bishop White. He was not only a churchman of distinction but was prominent in many useful public endeavors. His hospitality was famous and he was fond of good eating, with preferences for mince pies, butter and tea. Like many other citizens, the bishop took an active interest in the Hand-in-Hand Fire Company and he was a Chaplain to the Continental Congress. His interest in the College, of which he was a graduate, was very great and while sitting upon its Board of Trustees he lacked but one vote of being chosen Provost. An interesting story is told of how "Billy" White and Francis Hopkinson cultivated the acquaintance of Benjamin West while studying at the College, how they used to stroll out to the sylvan banks of the Schuykill and read the classics to him, so as to give him inspiration for his great talent, and how they, with the connivance of Benjamin Franklin, spirited his sweetheart away by a ladder in the night, and sent her to him in England, where her brother could not interfere with their marriage.

Judge Francis Hopkinson was for a time organist and there is a minute of the vestry directing that only plain and

 GLORIA DEI

Old Swedes' Church
929 South Water Street, Philadelphia
◆ Built 1700 ◆

familiar tunes be sung and that there be no frequent changes. The singer, or clerk, used to stand in the organ gallery and make the whole church resound "with his strong, deep and grave tones."

The people of Christ Church from the earliest times formed the gayest and most aristocratic set in the city. They were the best dressed, arriving for worship in damasks and brocades, velvet breeches and silk stockings, powdered hair and periwigs. They came afoot, in chairs or in the ponderous coaches of the day, that of Washington with six cream-coloured steeds adding the final touch to the imposing spectacle. As time went on, both the proprietors and governors added the weight of their influence to the Anglican party, in a ceaseless conflict with the Quaker Assembly, and the combative little church on Second Street held within itself a large proportion of the ability, energy and learning of Philadelphia. Franklin found the aid he needed for the founding of the "College and Academy of Philadelphia" in the Anglican party and four-fifths of its first trustees were church members, while that ablest of college Presidents, the Reverend Doctor William Smith, was chosen its first Provost.

At the southwest corner of Third and Pine Streets is the second Episcopal church erected in the city limits. This was in the district where many of the best families lived and when Christ Church began to be crowded a request was made for another building. This was begun in 1758 under Dr. Kearsley's care and was opened on September 4, 1761, by the Reverend Doctor William Smith, Provost of the College. Christ Church and St. Peter's were called the United Churches and were under one Rector until 1836, when the Reverend William H. DeLancey became rector of St. Peter's. Later he became Provost of the University and Bishop of Western New York. St. Paul's on the east side of Third Street below Walnut came next and was opened in 1761, three months after St. Peter's.

Two churches now belonging to the Episcopal Church but which originally belonged to another sect are old Swedes' on Swanson Street and Trinity Church, Oxford, on the Second Street Pike. Five years before William Penn started his colony the Swedes worshipped in a log building, or block-house, on ground given to the church by the widow of Swan Swanson. On the site of this primitive chapel they built a brick church in 1700 costing twenty thousand Swedish dollars. Poor and few as these earnest settlers were, they gave fifteen thousand dollars before the first stone was set and left the belfry unfinished "in order to see whether God will bless us so far that we may have a bell and in what manner we can procure it." Thus with the simple, sincere faith of children, by whom we are told wise men shall be led, the Swedes erected "Gloria Dei," which shares with Christ Church to-day the most interest of churchly buildings in Philadelphia.

Trinity Church, Oxford, on the Second Street Pike, was once a meeting place for the Quakers in a log building where a school was also kept but in 1698, at the time of the Keith schism, it was transferred to the Episcopal Church and the present brick building erected in 1711. Its pulpit was shared by the rector of the United Churches and of the Swedes' Church and we find that energetic man, Doctor William Smith, officiating there also. It is more like an old English rural parish church than any other in the diocese and the curious inscriptions on the burial stones are well worth inspection.

Out on the Darby Road is the church of St. James, Kingsessing, built in 1760 and united with Gloria Dei until 1842, and at Radnor is old St. David's, built by the Welsh churchmen more than two centuries ago. In the latter lies buried the remains of that most romantic of American soldiers, Major General Anthony Wayne.

The Scotch-Irish Presbyterians from the north of Ireland came to Pennsylvania during several decades prior to the Revolution in thousands. Most of them settled upon the frontiers, but they gave the peaceable Friends enough trouble at the centre of government. They had no patience with tolerance, were strong, vigorous, and steadfast. They brought a hostile and arrogant spirit to the Indians and promptly antagonized them by rough and quarrelsome treatment. "Why should these heathens," they said, "have lands which Christians want?" In habit of thought and life, in doctrine and testimony, they were the direct opposite of the Friends, whom they despised. Thus in really serious and sustained action they were until the Revolution the rival political force of the province. The war was three parts out of four a Scotch-Irish movement in Pennsylvania, says Isaac Sharpless, and we may well believe it. The first church of the Presbyterians in Philadelphia was organized by Francis Makemie in 1692 among the English, Welsh, Scotch and French settlers of that faith who met with a few Baptists in a storehouse situated on Second Street at the corner of Chestnut. The Reverend John Watts, a Baptist minister of Pennepeck, agreed to preach to them every other Sunday and visiting Presbyterian ministers occasionally officiated. In this way they worshipped together in peace for three years, until the Presbyterians called the Reverend Jebediah Andrews from Boston. He arrived in 1698 and soon after the Baptists withdrew and left Andrews and his flock in sole possession of the storehouse. In 1704 they built a church on the south side of High Street between Second and Third Streets. It was surrounded by some fine sycamore trees and was called the "Buttonwood Church." Franklin was a pew-holder in this church, but so he was in Christ Church and the Quakers also claimed him. He has left a statement of his faith so that anyone can decide for himself where he belonged.

The First Presbyterian Church increased in numbers and the building was enlarged twice before 1794 when it was taken down and a new and commodious structure built of handsome appearance. This was used until 1825, when the congregation moved to their present quarters on Washington Square.

In November, 1739, George Whitefield came from England to Philadelphia and created a sensation. He was eloquent, bold and denunciatory and had a fine voice. He stirred people to the depths and appealing mostly to the senses created a fever of enthusiasm in the quiet town, the like of him never before having been heard there. He began preaching in Christ Church but soon all the churches were denied to him and he preached from the balcony of the court house in High Street, the public squares and the fields. Indeed, wherever there was an open place for the populace Whitefield gave vent to his controversial preaching. Finally the people put up a building for him on Fourth Street near Arch and this in time became the home of the Academy and College of Philadelphia which developed into the University. The Presbyterians used this building until 1749, when it was given over wholly to the College, and then they erected a church at the northwest corner of Third and Arch Streets, with Gilbert Tennent as their minister. This became the Second Church and sheltered many prominent Philadelphians—such men as Peter S. Duponceau, Charles Chauncey, Thomas Bradford, Ebenezer Hazard, Josiah Randall, Thomas Leiper, Isaac Snowden, Andrew Bayard, Samuel Stille, Alexander Henry and Matthew L. Bevan. The Third Church, or "Old Pine Street Church," on Pine Street below Fourth, was first occupied in 1768, although not finished. William Rush, James Craig, George Bryan and Samuel Purviance, Jr., of the First Church, were the building committee and Robert Smith the architect. The Reverend Samuel Aitken was the first minister. Among the most prominent Presbyterian ministers of the early time were Francis Allison, who was a professor and Vice-Provost of the College, and John Ewing, who became Provost of the University.

After the Baptists stopped meeting with the Presbyterians in 1698 they met in Anthony Morris' brew-house, under the bank of the river, near Dock Creek. The Philadelphia Church was considered a part of the church at Pennepeck and the same pastors supplied both until 1746. Evan Morgan, Samuel Jones, Jenkin Jones and William Kinnersley were the prominent ministers during this time and the Reverend Morgan Edwards who arrived from England in 1761 was really their first pastor. He was a remarkable man and the prime mover in the establishment of the Baptist College in Providence, Rhode Island, now Brown University. The Lutherans had two substantial churches in the old city, one in Fifth Street extending north toward Appletree Alley and the other at the southeast corner of Fourth and Cherry Streets. The first was built in 1743 and called St. Michael's, the second in 1766 and called the Zion Church.

The Roman Catholics had about as hard a time at home as the Quakers and were glad to find a refuge under Penn's tolerant government. Even in Philadelphia they were compelled to worship quietly so as to give no offense and create no disturbance for the Anglican party was prompt to protest against them and coupled this with their objections to the peace policy of the Quakers. Thus we cannot surely tell just where the first place of worship for the Roman Catholics was, but St. Joseph's Church in Willing's

Alley was built in 1733 and this was so carefully tucked away that it could give offense to no one. At any rate, after that the Catholics did not have to meet in dwelling houses and shops beyond the city limits for fear of molestations by the "Church Party." When Whitefield came the breach was widened. "He strikes much at priestcraft, and speaks very satirically of Papists," writes James Pemberton, an eminent Friend in 1739, adding with serenity, "His intentions are good, but he has not yet arrived at such perfection as to see so far as he yet may."

Friends, however, remained calm (a habit they had) under the lashing of the Christ Church party which called the colony a "nursery of Jesuits" and William Penn "a greater Antichrist than Julian the Apostate." St. Joseph's was built under Father Greaton and he was succeeded in 1741 by Reverend Robert Harding, who built St. Mary's on Fourth Street below Walnut in 1763.

Perhaps one of the most distinguished and best loved prelates of the Roman Catholic Faith in Philadelphia was Archbishop James F. Wood, who was born at Second and Chestnut Streets in 1813. He had some commercial training, after a good education in England and in Philadelphia, and brought the finances of his church into such splendid shape as to complete the cathedral on Logan Square, which was dedicated in 1864. It is said that he always claimed to be a member of the Society of Friends, saying that it was a "society and not a religion."

The Methodists began in a sail loft on Dock Creek near the river in 1768, where Captain Thomas Webb officiated. Francis Asbury, whom Wesley had sent, was the apostle of Methodism in America and really the first organizer. He became their bishop. The first church was named St. George's and was in Fourth Street near New. Here the singing was especially good and the dress of the congregation plain. They did not insist upon an educated ministry and "Black Harry," who accompanied Mr. Asbury as his servant, frequently preached, although he knew not a letter.

Little record of the Jews in Philadelphia is found prior to the Revolution, although it is supposed they had a congregation thirty years before that time. Between 1747 and 1775 they are believed to have worshipped in a small house in Sterling Alley, which ran from Race to Cherry Streets, between Third and Fourth.

After that they built a plain brick building in Cherry Street, west of Third, which seated about two hundred persons. Among the prominent early Hebrew families were Gratz, Franks and Saloman, Haym Saloman was a remarkable man. A banker from Poland, he was confined in a dungeon when the British took New York but escaped to Philadelphia and gave valuable assistance to the young republic. He negotiated the war securities from France and Holland on his own personal security without the loss of a cent to the country and required a commission of only one-quarter of one per cent. for his invaluable services.

Although the religious controversy of the time was spirited in Philadelphia from the beginning, it took the form of pamphlets and preachments rather than the riots and bloodshed which occurred in some of the other colonies and this was due to the peaceable principles of the Quakers which some of the sects most benefited objected to, and to their insistence upon freedom of conscience for every man.

IX: The Play Houses

IN John Smith's manuscript *Journal* is the following entry under date of Sixth Month, 22d, 1749:

"Joseph Morris and I happened in at Peacock Bigger's and drank tea there, and his daughter being one of the company who were going to hear the tragedy of "Cato" acted, it occasioned some conversation, in which I expressed my sorrow that anything of the kind was encouraged."

From whence this little troupe of players came and just where they performed is not known but they gave to Philadelphia the honour of seeing the first Shakespearian representation in America. They were managed by Murray and Kean and must have found encouragement, for they remained until 1750, as is shown by a minute of the Common Council on the 8th of January of that year as follows:

"The Recorder reported that certain persons had lately taken upon them to act plays in this City, and, as he was informed, intended to make a frequent practice thereof, which, it was to be feared, would be attended by very mischievous effects, such as the encouragement of idleness and drawing great sums of money from weak and inconsiderate persons, who are apt to be fond of that kind of entertainments, though the performance be ever so mean and contemptible. Whereupon the Board unanimously requested the magistrates to take the most effectual measures for suppressing this disorder, by sending for the actors and binding them to their good behaviour, or by such other means as they should think proper."

And so the players moved on to New York, where they played for over a year, and Philadelphia saw no more plays until Lewis Hallam's English Company came in 1754, giving their first performance in the large brick warehouse of William Plumstead, situated in King or Water Street between Pine and Lombard, where the first company is thought to have played. The house extended through to Front Street on which there was an entrance by means of stairs placed on the outside of the building. The visit of these players was not arranged without opposition and much printed argument on both sides appeared. Governor Hamilton at last granted the license upon the recommendation of a number of gentlemen of influence and the company began after distributing in the streets a pamphlet setting forth the harmlessness of their occupation and intending to stem the tide of popular disapprobation. Its imposing title was as follows:

> "Extracts of Several Treatises,
> Wrote by the Prince of Conti,
> With the Sentiments of the Fathers,
> And some of the decrees of the Councils,
> Concerning of Stage Plays,
> Recommended to the Perusal, and Serious
> Consideration of the Professors, of Christianity, in the city of Philadelphia."

A better argument on behalf of the players was the alacrity with which they gave the proceeds of one night's performance to the Charity School of the newly founded Academy, now the University of Pennsylvania. General interest, however, was not awakened, as few people cared anything about the actor's art. Science was the fashion and young men of education were interested in Franklin and his discoveries and in the lectures of Professor Kinnersley on electricity. Indeed, it was not until the English Army of occupation brought gay and graceless days to the City that science and lectures played a scantier part.

The opening of Hallam's Company was "The Fair Penitent," followed by a farce, "Miss in her Teens," played before a full house. The temporary theatre was neatly fitted up with the glittering motto, "Totius mundus agit histrionem" over the stage. The only unpleasant occurrence was the summary ejection of an unfriendly opponent from the pit. Thirty performances were given and the theatre closed on the 24th of June, after a brilliant and profitable season. Hallam's Company came back to Philadelphia in 1759 and a theatre was built for them at Cedar or South and Vernon Streets, on Society Hill, just outside the town limits. Religious organizations protested and the Assembly passed a bill prohibiting plays, but the King repealed it and the theatre was opened June 25, 1759. The Company was careful to avoid announcements that would displease and generally promised a harmless "Concert of Music," a moral "Dialogue on the Vice of Gambling," or any other suitable for the occasion. The word "play" was always avoided and "Hamlet" and "Jane Shore" are described as "moral and instructive Tales."

Electricity and rectitude triumphed, however, and the Company only played one season in the little house.

An insidious germ was working in the College and in 1757 Provost William Smith tells us that "Ever since the Foundation of the College and Academy in this City the improvement of the youth in Oratory and correct Speaking, has always been considered as an essential Branch of their Education." He tells us of the success that has attended the oratorical exercises, the youth having "delivered proper Speeches" and acted parts before large audiences. The development was rapid and soon a whole dramatic piece was demanded. This laudable ambition was encouraged by the Professors as an easier method of teaching pronunciation. They had some difficulty, we find, in choosing an "English Performance" which would include a large number of speakers, exalt the sentiments, engage the passions and better the hearts of the youth. The "Masque of Alfred," by Mr. Thompson and Mr. Mallet was chosen, representing the redemption of England from the cruelties of the Danish invasion and was adapted by Dr. Smith so as to eliminate the female parts and put their words into other mouths. Hymns, "Pieces of Music" and A Prologue and Epilogue were added and the whole presented several times during the Christmas Holidays of 1756 in one of the apartments of the College "as an Oratorical Exercise, by a Sett of young Gentlemen." Dr. Smith says the town was entertained, there were crowded, discerning and applauding audiences and each speaker, young and old, "acquired Honor in his Part." It was repeated in January, 1757, before Lord Loudon and the Governors of several of the Colonies who were in Philadelphia consulting upon plans for the common resistance the Indians who were then ravaging the western frontiers.

It was this performance which inspired Thomas Godfrey, Jr., to write the first American play ever publicly acted in the Colonies. It was a strictly moral drama entitled the "Prince of Parthia," and was produced on the 24th of April, 1767, by Hallam's Company, who returned in 1766 to occupy a new theatre built for them at South and Apollo Streets and opened on the 12th of November in that year. This theatre was called the Southwark Theatre and Hallam was as much the soul of it as ever Garrick was of Drury Lane. His "American Company" performed in the Southwark Theatre during the winters of 1768, '69, '70, '72 and '73. During the last season the second original American drama ever performed on the stage—"the Conquest of

Canada; or the Siege of Quebec"—was produced. Soldiers from the barracks and sailors from the King's ships in port gave great effect to the play.

Now came on the troublous times and Congress by resolution in 1774 discouraged all extravagance, dissipation, shows, plays and expensive diversions, as well they might for the little country needed all its treasure and its energy in the tremendous crisis confronting it.

While the British Army occupied the City during 1777–78 the English officers gave all sorts of theatricals in the theatre and Philadelphians found out how delightful it was to be amused. The officers of General Howe's staff did the acting and gave the proceeds to the widows and orphans of the soldiers. Major André and Captain DeLancey were the comedians, scene-painters, costumers and property men. The famous drop-curtain painted by André, representing a waterfall in a forest glade, is always mentioned in contemporary accounts and was used for years until lost in the burning of the Theatre in 1821. The Continental Army, not to be outdone, on its return in 1778, produced a company of actors whose names are now unknown but who gave performances in the Southwark Theatre in September and October.

Congress soon renewed its restrictions and was backed up by Pennsylvania Legislature so that we find no activity until 1785, when Hallam opened the Theatre for miscellaneous entertainments and singing, which soon included parts of plays. The industrious and indefatigable Hallam persisted in finding subterfuges by which he and his players could evade the laws and amuse the Philadelphians. Returning in June, 1789, he opened the "Opera-House, Southwark," with a "concert, vocal and instrumental," in which he boldly introduced "The Grateful ward; or the Pupil in

Love," and "The Poor Soldier," all for the relief of the American captives in Algiers!

Hallam's persistence and evasion of the law brought a crisis in 1789 when a petition signed by 1900 persons was presented to the Legislature asking for the repeal of the law. A remonstrance came at once headed by all the Protestant Ministers in the City and several elders of the Society of Friends. The friends of the theatre were none the less active and a committee consisting of Dr. Robert Bass, General Walter Stewart, Dr. John Redman, Major Moore, John Barclay, William Temple Franklin, Jacob Barge and William West acted for "The Dramatic Association." Every means was used to ascertain public opinion and it was finally determined that 6000 citizens had signed the petition for the theatre and 4000 against it. The restrictions were accordingly repealed and licenses for three years authorized. Hallam and Henry immediately opened the Southwark Theatre with "The Rivals" and "The Critic" followed, during the season, by four American plays. The Theatre was fashionable and the return of Congress insured a good attendance. Its populatity was greatly enhanced by the patronage of the President which is thus described:

"The last stage-box in the South Street Theatre was fitted up expressly for the reception of General Washington. Over the front of the box was the United States coat of arms. Red drapery was gracefully festooned in the interior and about the exterior. The seats and front were cushioned. Mr. Wignell, in a full dress of black, hair powdered and adjusted to the formal fashion of the day, with two silver candlesticks and wax candles, would thus await the General's arrival at the box-door entrance, and, with great refinement of address and courtly manners, conduct this best of public men and suite to his box. A guard of military attended. A soldier was generally posted at each stage-door, and four were posted in the gallery, assisted by the high Constable of the City and other police officers, to preserve something like decorum among the sons of social liberty. . . ."

This was surely not too much dignity or care to take of so great a man and so exalted a position and we may hope that the "Sons of Social Liberty" did not insist upon sharing the box.

The year 1794 was the last season for the old theatre as a place of fashion, as the building was outdone in accommodations by the new Chestnut Street Theatre. A forbidding appearance within and without, oil lamps without glasses and pillars were obstacles which could not compete with the improvements of the new house, which had two rows of boxes and a gallery above, supported by fluted Corinthian columns highly gilt with a crimson ribbon twisted from base to capital. The tops of the boxes were decorated with crimson drapery and the panels were of rose color, adorned with gilding. The old theatre struggled along until the last performance there on the 7th of June, 1817, when Higgins and Barnard opened it for a few nights in the tragedy of "Manuel." It was destroyed by fire on the 9th of May, 1821, but its walls remained to house a distillery a few years ago.

The Chestnut Street Theatre opened on the 17th of February, 1794, although thought to have been started in 1791. It was situated above Sixth Street and held about 2000 People. Thomas Wignell of the old American Company was at the head of the strong company. It was here that Joseph Jefferson, the elder, made his first appearance in Philadelphia in 1803. The company contained many able singers and the operas gave as much satisfaction as the comedies. The first interruption came on Easter Sunday night, April 2, 1820, when fire destroyed the building and its contents. The stockholders, however, immediately set to work to rebuild, and Willim Strickland, an able architect, had the new theatre ready for the opening on the 2d of December, 1822, with "The School of Scandal." The two figures *Tragedy* and *Comedy* by Rush were saved from the old building and placed in the niches of the wings in the new structure. Here Booth made his appearance on the 17th of February, 1823, unknown and it appears with little success.

There was a theatre on Prune Street, now Locust, between Fifth and Sixth, in 1820, which ran for two seasons with success. It was called the Winter Tivoli Theatre and was owned by Stanislaus Surin, manager of the Tivoli Garden. Charles S. Porter took it in 1822 and called it the City Theatre, but it only ran one year. The Walnut Street Theatre, oldest in America at the present time, was fitted up in 1811 by Pepin and Breschard, who combined stage and ring performances in what they built for a circus. This theatre had only a moderate success for a while but its first season is memorable on account of the appearance on the 27th of November of "a young gentleman of this city" as Young Norval. This was no other than Master Edwin Forrest, who was born at Number 51 George Street and was then fourteen years of age. It was here also in 1871 that he made his last appearance in Philadelphia. Two days after Forrest's appearance, Edmund Kean played Richard III at the Walnut Street Theatre.

We cannot recount here all of the plays and players that amused Philadelphia during the early days nor even present a list of all the Theatres. From 1799 to 1871, nineteen theatres, circuses and museums were destroyed by fire, being over one-third of the total number of such places burned during that period, and it is a remarkable fact that there was no loss of life among the audiences.

X: Commons and Parks

HOLMES' map of 1683 shows Penn's design for the five squares which have already been referred to. They were larger than those we know to-day and the two western ones have been pushed a little westward toward the Schuylkill River. It was originally intended that the centre square should be ten acres and the others eight, "to be for like uses as the moorfields in London." The Centre Square was planned by Penn to be for public uses, for a Meeting House, a State House, a Market House and a School House.

In 1684 Philadelphia Quarterly Meeting of Friends decided to build a meeting house of brick in the Centre Square, but as it proved inconvenient on account of being so far out of town, it was abandoned not long after its occupation. The square was without any enclosure for more than a hundred years and seems to have been used pretty generally for any important public use of the moment. As early as 1760 it was leased as a common and a race course was constructed with a half mile track where gentlemen of the Jockey Club tried their horses against each other up to the time of the Revolution. This was quite a jump from a Quaker Meeting House to a race course but perhaps was one of the incidents of the "Toleration," for which the Quakers were famous. The Common was used as a public hanging ground for the city and county and the gallows was a permanent fixture for many years until the Centre House for the water works was constructed in 1799. During the Revolution the Common was used for a drill ground and in 1783 Count Rochambeau and his army of 6000 Frenchmen encamped there. Thousands of visitors flocked to see the foreigners in their white and pink uniforms. After the war General Wayne encamped there upon his return from the western expedition among the Indians by which he opened the middle west for civilization. The militia companies of the city took delight in drilling in the Centre Square and many a parade was held there by the McPherson Blues, Shee's Legion, the First Troop, Captain Morrell's Volunteer Green Cavalry, the Second Troop and others. These parades which attracted crowds of people, fairs and the celebration of national holidays at last became a nuisance on account of gambling and carousals and a determined crusade was started in Zachariah Poulson's Advertiser against them so that Mayor Robert Wharton put a stop to them in 1823.

The first pumping works to supply the City with water were at Chestnut Street on the Schuylkill River, but another one was finished at the Centre Square in January, 1801, after a design by Benjamin Henry Latrobe. The house had a pillared portico with a dome and was long a conspicuous object. The grounds were laid out in circular form and picketed with a white fence. Grass was planted and a fountain erected so that the whole made a very pleasing appearance. The fountain was Rush's statue of "Leda and the Swan," for which Miss Vanuxem, a famous beauty and toast, was the model. The original statue was carved in wood and then cast in bronze. It is now in Fairmount Park. This house remained after the water works at Fairmount were built and was used as a storage place for the oil used in the street lamps. In 1829 the name was changed to Penn Square and Market and Broad Streets run through it.

At Broad and Filbert Streets the Jockey Club flourished in 1767 in a tavern called the Centre House surrounded by the "Lombardy Garden." It was also known as Evan's Garden and was a popular resort in the summer. In 1881 the Pennsylvania Railroad built its station on the corner. The United States Mint opened in 1833 where the Widener Building now stands at the corner of Juniper Street. On the site of the present Wanamaker Store was the Philadelphia High School and the State Arsenal.

In 1837 a new City Hall was projected at the Centre or Penn Square. Interest rose and fell and it was not until 1872 that work was begun. It was finished in 1901 at a cost of $26,000,000. Similarly interest in the Parkway waxed and waned but in 1907 under Mayor John E. Reyburn the beautiful Avenue was started and the roadway of a mile and a half was opened for travel the next year. It is perhaps the most ambitious civic improvement ever undertaken in the United States and will not be completely finished for many years. The Art Gallery on Fairmount at its head is its crowning feature.

The Northeast Square was an open common for many years and in 1721 was leased to Ralph Assheton for 21 years at forty shillings per annum. He must have quit the lease, for in 1741 Thomas Penn, the Proprietor, leased the square to the German Reformed Church, John Philip Boehm, pastor. They used it for a burial ground until 1801, when the congregation yielded it to the city. During the Revolution a powder storage house was built there and John M. Irwin, auctioneer, had a horse and cattle market on the western part. This square also was used for a drill ground and had an important place for this purpose during the War of 1812. In 1815 it was improved, levelled and planted with grass. The name was changed to Franklin Square in 1825 and is now the approach to the Delaware River Bridge.

The Northwest Square was first used for a burying

ground and for some executions. In 1825 it was improved and called Logan Square after James Logan. The great Sanitary Fair was held in 1861 and attracted much attention on account of the relief it brought to the wounded soldiers. It is now called Logan Circle and is a feature of the Parkway.

The Southwest Square escaped the fate of the others as a burying place and was named after David Rittenhouse in 1825, when the State House Yard was named Independence Square.

Independence Square was really the first approach to a little square or park the city had. A wall of brick seven or eight feet high was built around it with a central gate on Walnut Street south of the State House door. This was fifteen or eighteen feet high, decorated with a pediment, cornice, entablature and pilasters. Walks were laid out and grass and trees planted. In 1811 the wall was removed with the large gateway and a low brick wall, such as has been recently placed there, was built three feet high, coped with marble. An iron railing surmounted the whole. It was in early times a favourite place for town meetings and during the Revolution served as a recruiting place.

Southeast Square was a perfect square and extended about three-fourths of the distance to Spruce Street and somewhat beyond Seventh Street, so that the latter was shut off entirely. From 1705 to 1795 the square served as a burying place for strangers. Hundreds of soldiers of the Revolutionary War and victims of the yellow fever epidemic of 1793 were interred there. The soldiers were buried in unmarked trenches and the sexton told John Adams in 1777 that already two thousand had found their last resting place in the ground under his care. Its surface was uneven and a stream from Tenth and Arch Streets ran through the northeast corner to Dock Creek. Timothy Matlack records that as late as 1745 there was a pond where the First Presbyterian Church stands and he used to go there to shoot wild ducks. Luxuriant grass grew about this well watered ground and it was much esteemed for pasturage from the earliest times. The Carpenter and Story family had an enclosure of brick in the middle where they buried their dead and a huge apple tree grew in the centre of it.

Across the street, at the southeast corner, stood the Walnut Street prison of stone, one hundred and eighty-four feet on Walnut Street and the ground extending south to Prune, now Locust Street. It was used as a prison for prisoners of war by both armies during the Revolution and was the main city jail until Moyamensing prison was erected. After people stopped burying there in 1795 nothing much was done with the square, although it was proposed to establish a market there and also the Medical School of the University. The coloured people of the City found it a favourite place for gathering to sing their native songs and give their wild African dances over the graves of the stranger and the soldier.

The name was changed to Washington Square in 1825 and George Bridport, artist and engineer, planned the park for public use. Trees were planted and the Square enclosed with a white paling fence. The attempt to improve it seems to have succeeded, for a committee of the Horticulture Society said of it after an inspection in 1831 that "The whole is beautifully kept and well illuminated at night with reflecting lamps until ten o'clock, all showing the correct and liberal spirit of our city." It became the object of controversy when the location of the new City Hall was planned, but the vote of 1870 was against the location.

Friends' Meeting House
Fourth and Arch Streets
• Built 1804 •

The show place of Philadelphia is Fairmount Park. It may well be so and here once more we see the wise discernment of Penn, who wrote to James Logan in 1701: "My eye, though not my heart, is upon Fairmount." This great area of more than three thousand four hundred acres, so easy of access to the city, has been kept in nearly its natural state. Its wooded hills and vales on each side of the Schuylkill River are traversed by well kept roads and bridle paths which lead out into the country surrounding the city so famous for its beauty as a residential section. In the early days many important people had their country houses on the bluffs overlooking a lovely expanse of river and there retired from the city during the summer months. These fine old Colonial mansions have fortunately been preserved through their acquisition by the City for Fairmount Park. A visit to one of them will make one understand the lure of the place for the old worthies. The two finest, perhaps, are Mount Pleasant, built by Captain John Macpherson in 1761, and Woodford, built by Judge William Coleman about 1756. Mount Pleasant is a country seat of baronial aspect and its occupancy by General Benedict Arnold and his bride, Peggy Shippen, gives it a romantic interest beyond others. Woodford had for its guests important people also and never so many as when Rebecca Franks, a famous belle, lived there. There are, of course, Ormiston, Laurel Hill, Belmont and Glen Fern. Belmont is hardly recognizable as the residence of the celebrated wit and jurist, Judge Richard Peters, first Secretary of War in the young republic. Glen Fern, away up the Wissahickon Valley, was the home of Thomas Livezey and nestled in a romantic glen by the banks of the stream. It is now used as the home of the Valley Green Canoe Club.

Indeed at one time elegant countryseats crowned nearly every hill along the river in what is now Fairmount Park and the well recorded James in Virginia could not have surpassed the loveliness and charm of the Schuylkill winding among rolling highlands on whose summits spacious homes of comely dignity sheltered some of the most distinguished citizens of the metropolis of the Colonies. The upper Wissahickon is still a sylvan wilderness and its romantic scenery beyond the description of the printed word. Automobiles are still refused entrance to its sacred precincts and one may walk or ride along the creek between its wooded slopes and imagine the city and its turmoil far away.

Fairmount Park grew out of purchases for the enlargement of the water works which were suggested by Frederick Graff, the engineer of the City Water Works, and John Davis in 1810. The plan grew in popularity and was achieved by successive gifts and purchases. In 1812 Councils passed an ordinance selecting Morris Hill for the new reservoir and water works. The committee to carry out the project was fortunately composed of men of taste and William Rush, the sculptor, contributed figures to beautify the Fairmount Gardens which were opened in 1825 and became the show place of the city. All strangers were taken to Fairmount Water Works, which were then only five acres in extent but which presented much the same appearance as they do to-day. The ordinance of Councils creating the Fairmount Park Commission to take over the various tracts secured by gifts or purchase was passed in 1867. The great Centennial Exhibition of 1876 was held in Fairmount Park and did much to encourage good taste in this country. Nothing of the kind had ever been held on the Continent before and many people came from all over the country and from abroad to see it.

Many newer parks and squares have been added to the

City's riches in later years and form now a total of more than six thousand acres. Many more acres are on the City Plan and the spirit of the people is fortunately toward this development of health and joy and light.

XI: The Carpenters' Company

WILLIAM PENN'S care and forethought in laying out the City of Philadelphia between two splendid rivers, his plan for the streets and the reservation of four large squares or parks, his hope that each house would have its little garden or orchard and that there should be a promenade along the Front Street with an open prospect to the river and gardens sloping down to it were entirely unique in this country. No other man or settlement had such comprehensive plans. Penn carried his ideas further, as has been described, in choosing men of worth and industry for his colonists, so that the early success of his experiment was assured. Credit must also be given the Founder on this account for the excellence of the houses in durability and taste as he brought over an architect, one James Portius, as well as skilled artisans. By the year 1724 the Master Carpenters were numerous and important enough to compose a guild patterned after "The Worshipful Company of Carpenters of London," founded in 1477. James Portius was one of the most active of this little band to which Philadelphia owes so much in the beauty of its Colonial architecture. At his death in 1736 he left his choice collection of architectural works to his fellow-members, thus laying the foundation of their present valuable library. These men brought tools, ideas, plans and models from the mother country and stuck to them so that in the houses for which they were the architects as well as the builders we have examples of the best in England at that period. Judging from some of the original ideas perpetuated by our own more modern architects within a stone's throw of the hall of the Carpenters' Company we could wish that the guild had assumed complete control. They were, however, a modest and unassuming set of men and the object of their association was not a monopoly but instruction in the science of architecture and assistance to members of their families. They established a "Book of Prices," for the valuation of their work "on the most equitable principles" so "that the workmen should have a fair recompense for their labour, and the owner receive the worth of his money." The last will at once dispel any idea that this was the original labour union. No one but a Master Carpenter was or is eligible to membership and he must have been a master for six years. In 1745 was published a book of directions for joinery which shows that both the art of proportion and technical proficiency were to be expected from the local craftsmen.

The officers consisted of a Master, Assistants and Wardens and the meetings were generally held at the Master's house. It was not until 1770 that a permanent home for the Company was erected upon what was then open ground from Chestnut to Walnut Streets. It was to be expected that this hall would be the dignified and beautiful building we know so well and the pity of it is that encroaching trade has hemmed it in on every side, so that with its distance back from Chestnut Street below Fourth it is unknown to many.

The State House being used by the existing government, the Hall of the Carpenters' Company became the centre of many of the gatherings of patriotic citizens so numerous in the days leading up to the War for Independence when English George in America was to fight against German George in England. Almost all the "town meetings" of that eventful period were held on the lawn in front or within its walls. The Governor, fearing the effect of the patriotic movements upon his interests in the Province, opposed his influence and authority against them and so the State House was not available. The Carpenters' Company well knew the responsibility they were under and the danger of the confiscation of their property but keeping the names of the members voting off the minutes agreed that they "Shall be allowed to meet here."

The members of the First Continental Congress gathered at the Merchants Coffee House on Second Street above Walnut, and on the morning of the 5th of September, 1774, walked in a body to Carpenters' Hall. What a stately procession this must have been! How conscious, and yet unknowing, they must have been of the great epoch in the world's history which they were about to institute. Samuel and John Adams were among them and Joseph Galloway, John Dickinson, Thomas Mifflin, Cæsar Rodney, Thomas McKean, Peyton Randolph, Richard Henry Lee, George Washington, Patrick Henry—all well known names. It is not here the place to recount the deliberations of these solemn men, how on the second day after a first spent in wrangling over a plan of voting, the eloquent Patrick Henry broke a long silence in that splendid plea for the obliteration of all lines, ending with the words, "I am not a Virginian, but an American." This was the sentiment that actuated the body and they began by asking Mr. Duché, an Episcopal minister, to unite them in prayer. Patrick Henry's speech and Jacob Duché's prayer have been brought down to us in the printed word and the painted canvas and John Adams tells us that he saw "the tears gush into the eyes of the old grave pacific Quakers of Philadelphia."

The paintings have not quite revealed to us the real setting, as at that time the large room on the first floor where the Congress met was divided into two rooms, with a spacious hallway running through the centre between the

 Carpenters' Hall : Built 1770
Here met the first Continental Congress

two doorways. This will give us an idea of what a small and intimate gathering was this first assemblage of the representatives of the people.

On the 18th of June, 1776, a Provincial Conference of the State met and on the 23rd declared the Independence of the Colony of Pennsylvania from Great Britain. On the 15th of July this Conference ratified the Declaration of Independence passed by Congress on July 4th and adopted a Constitution which served as the law of the land until after the Constitution of the United States was agreed to. The use of Carpenters' Hall for the patriots' cause was almost continuous and is a splendid tribute to the generosity and courage of its owners who are generally lost sight of in the brilliance of the events that took place within their hall.

There was another struggle for liberty which ought not to be forgotten and whose cradle was the Carpenters' Hall. It was particularly appropriate that this united association for religious liberty should be set on foot in Philadelphia. On the 14th of October, 1774, the Baptist Association was in session in the Hall and had before it the persecution of its members in New England. All friends of religious liberty, in or out of Congress, were invited. The Catholics of Maryland and the cavaliers of Episcopal Virginia were there, while the Philadelphia Quakers seized the opportunity of presenting the grievances of their brethren in New England. John Adams tells us much of the proceedings in his diary and how he rebuked the principal speaker, Israel Pemberton, with great heat, telling the meeting "that in Massachusetts was and ever had been the purest political liberty known." Then up rose Israel with the quiet remonstrance—"John, John, dost thou not know of the time when Friends were hung in thy Colony because they would not subscribe to the belief of thee and thy fathers? Pray don't urge liberty of conscience in favour of such laws."

This was the beginning of the effort which embodies the principles of religious liberty in the Federal Compact and in the Constitution of the States.

The British Army of occupation in 1777 quartered their men in the Hall and used the second story for a hospital. Now begins a long list of important events in the old Hall. A meeting for the Encouragement of American Manufacturers, the United States Commissary General, the Philadelphia Library, the first Bank of the United States, the Bank of Pennsylvania, the United States Land Office, the Apprentices' Library, the Musical Fund Society, the Franklin Institute and the school of John Willitts were all tenants. The separation in the Society of Friends in 1827 was largely between the country and city Friends, the latter being the most wealthy and influential of the "Orthodox" body. The city meeting places therefore being controlled by them, Friends who formed to the "Hicksite" branch were dispossessed as well as disfranchised. They accordingly met for divine worship in Carpenters' Hall, that appropriate shrine of all liberties. This was until they could erect a meeting house of their own at Fifth and Cherry Streets.

In 1828 C. J. Wolbert had a place of auction there where horses were sold. They were shown off up and down the passage-way in front of the building, and the cries of the auctioneer, bidders and hostlers must have been in striking contrast to the eloquence of the patriots and supplications of the Friends. Upon the occasion of the Centennial anniversary of the meeting of the Continental Congress a notable assemblage in the old Hall listened to an oration by Henry Armitt Brown and this was the last distinguished gathering to enter the portal hallowed by memories unforgettable in City, State and Nation.

XII: The Dancing Assembly

IN every community people of similar interests and of blood relationship are drawn together for pleasant intercourse and as these natural conditions are emphasized by refinement, their association becomes more rigid and exclusive. Perhaps there is no community where this has been more continuously the practice than in Philadelphia and the most widely known and principal indication is the Assembly Ball or City Dancing Assembly as it was first called.

In 1738 there existed a dancing class conducted by Theobald Hackett, who taught "all sorts of fashionable English and French dances, after the newest and politest manner practised in London, Dublin and Paris, and to give young ladies, gentlemen and children the most graceful carriage in dancing and genteel behaviour in company that can possibly be given by any dancing master whatever." Later, Kennet taught dancing and fencing, also John Ormsby from London "in the newest taste now practised in Europe, at Mr. Foster's house in Market Street opposite the Horse & Dray."

Naturally the Quakers looked askance at this frivolity and Samuel Foulke published an indignant article about Kennet's notice, saying, "I am surprised at his audacity and brazen impudence in giving those detestable vices those high encomiums. They be proved so far from accomplishments that they are diabolical." This was commendable vigour at any rate and in the first assembly lists we find no Pembertons, Logans, Fishers, Lloyds, Whartons, Coxes, Rawles, Morrises, Peningtons, Emlens, or Biddles.

The clergy approved, however, and surely religion should direct its youthful spirits in their happiness. So the dancing assembly began in 1748 and was held once a fortnight at Andrew Hamilton's house and store, tenanted by Mr. Inglis, who conducted the balls. This was the only place capable of accommodating so many persons and was at Hamilton's Wharf on Water Street near the Drawbridge between Walnut and Dock Streets, where ladies repaired in full dress on horseback. The first managers were John Swift, John Wallace, John Inglis and Lynford Lardner. The subscription was forty shillings, levied upon the gentleman, and included the lady who accompanied him. Tickets for strangers on the same conditions were to be had upon application to the managers at seven shillings, sixpence. These included all the expenses for the entertainment, which soon was held every Thursday evening from January until May, commencing at six o'clock in the evening and not exceeding midnight. Notices were published in the newspapers of which this, from the "Pennsylvania Journal," in 1771, is an example:

"The Assembly will be opened this evening, and as the receiving of money at the door has been found extremely inconvenient the Managers think it necessary to give the public notice that no person will be admitted without a ticket from the directors which (through the application of a subscriber) may be had of either of the Managers."

In 1772 the meeting place was the Freemasons' Lodge and later the City Tavern, Oeller's Hotel, on Chestnut above Sixth Street, the Mansion House on Third Street, at Washington Hall on the same street and at a hall on Library Street. In 1802 Francis' Hotel on Market Street was chosen. Rooms were provided for cards, with fire, candles, tables and cards. Square dances were in vogue and the ladies arriving first were given places in the first set, the rest being arranged in the order of arrival, the ladies drawing for places. Mothers watched with care the movements of their daughters from an enclosure at one end of the room, says a writer in 1817, but no such assemblage of matrons is mentioned in earlier times.

Rev. Andrew Burnaby, who visited Philadelphia between 1759 and 1760, was very favourably impressed with our belles. Here is his comment:

"The women are exceedingly handsome and polite. They are naturally sprightly and fond of pleasure, and upon the whole, are much more agreeable and accomplished than the men. Since their intercourse with the English officers they are greatly improved and without flattery many of them would not make bad figures even in the first assemblies in Europe. Their amusements are principally dancing in the winter, and in the summer forming parties of pleasure upon the Schuylkill and in the country. There is a society of sixteen ladies and as many gentlemen, called the Fishing Company, who meet once a fortnight upon the Schuylkill. They have a very pleasant room erected in a romantic situation on the bank of that river, where they generally dine and drink tea. There are several pretty walks around it, and some wild and rugged rocks, which, together with the water and fine groves that adorn the banks, form a most beautiful and picturesque scene. There are boats and fishing-tackle of all sorts, and the company divert themselves with walking, fishing, going upon the water, dancing, singing, or conversing, just as they please. The ladies wear a uniform, and they appear with great ease and advantage from the neatness and simplicity of it. The first and most distinguished people of the colony are of this society and it is very advantageous to a stranger to be introduced to it, as he thereby gets acquainted with the best and most respectable company in Philadelphia. In winter, when there is snow on the ground, it is usual to make what they call sleighing-parties, or to go upon it in sledges."

The rules were quite strict and one at least of the spirited belles revolted in 1782 by "standing up in a set not her own" and drawing the others of the set into rebellion, thus bringing on a rupture between the gentlemen and and the managers. The sprightly William Black (of the Virginia Commission to treat with the Indians in 1744) praises the beauty and accomplishments of Miss Hetty Levy and Miss Mollie Stamper, afterwards Mrs. William Bingham. Miss Rebecca Franks was the reigning belle during the British occupation particularly, sharing the honours with fair Willings, Shippens and Chews. Joseph Shippen's "Lines written in an Assembly Room" was one of the frequent graceful poetical outbursts of the time. He speaks of "Fair charming Swift," referring to the eldest daughter of John Swift, afterwards Mrs. Livingston, "lovely White," the sister of Bisby White and afterwards Mrs. Robern Morris, and "Sweet, Smiling, fair M'Call"; Polly Franks and Sally Coxe also came in for their share of admiration and Mrs. Jekyll, granddaughter of Edward Shippen.

By 1765 some Quaker names appear, such as Mifflin, Fishbourne, Dickinson, Galloway, Nixon, Powell and Cadwalader, and soon some arrivals from distant parts, such as Ingersolls, Montgomerys, Sergeants, Tilghmans, Wisters and Markoes. Then more familiar families of Clymer, Hazlehurst, Evans, Burd, Lewis, McMurtrie, McPherson, Sims, Ross, Watmough, Biddle, Wharton and Meade. Dancing masters became numerous and the youth of the town with affluent merchant fathers took with avidity to the increase in polite amusements so different from the scanty entertainment of the early days.

The Assemblies were discontinued during the Revolution, although there was an increase in gayety, especially in Tory

circles, during the British occupation. The patriots, however, were engaged in a serious business and their resources
as well as their lives were risked in the great adventure of
their country. After the war aristocratic feelings were
somewhat rudely jarred, although intensified in some quarters. When Squire Hillegas' daughter was married to a
jeweler she was deprived of her place in the old Assembly
and indeed another Assembly, not so fastidious, was formed,
which sent an invitation to President Washington. When
both balls came on the same night the President went to the
newer and danced with a mechanic's pretty daughter. Mrs.
John Adams writes frequently of the Assemblies during
President Washington's administration and says "the company is of the best kind," and the ladies more beautiful
than she had seen at foreign courts. Mrs. Bingham is
mentioned, her aunt, Mrs. Samuel Powell, born Elizabeth
Willing, a younger set of Chews, the Redmans, Bonds,
Miss Wilhelmina Smith, Miss Sally McKean, Mrs. Walter
Stewart, and Mrs. Henry Clymer. Mrs. Adams speaks of
the gayety and prodigality of Philadelphia living in the
same vein as General Greene who called the luxury of Boston "an infant babe" to that of the Quaker City.

In 1803 the first ball was held in Mr. Haines' room in the
new Shakespeare Building, at Sixth and Chestnut Streets,
and afterwards at Francis' Hotel, occupying the Morris and
Washington mansions on Market between Fifth and Sixth
Streets. Lack of harmony prevailed in this year and a new
Assembly was organized and balls held over Barry's furniture store in Second Street. Subsequently balls were held
at the Exchange Coffee House, formerly Mr. Bingham's
house, on South Third Street, and in the City Hotel at Mr.
McCall's old house, Second and Union Streets. Squabbling
and loss of social prestige continued to such an extent that

in 1815 the balls were discontinued. There is little wonder if the following effusion, which appeared in the "Fashionable Trifler," is correct:

"The principal supporters of our City practicing balls are a strange medley of capering youths, who, the moment they are released from the finger drudgery of pen, ink, and paper, repair to the Assembly, where they contrive to kill an evening in the pleasing avocations of dancing and quarreling, occasionally interspersed with the delightful auxiliaries of smoking and drinking. When the promiscuous variety are met, they employ a portion of their time in quarreling for places in a set for a cotillon or country dance, and are famous for a peculiar dialect, for spitfire aggravations, provoking phrases, quaint oaths, and thundering mouth grenades. Should the heat of the weather require more air than exercise they retire to a witt drawing-room, where they stupefy their senses by the narcotic fumes of the cigar, dry their skins to parchment, bake their entrails to cinders, and exhaust all their radical moisture; so that when they return to their partners the room is perfumed like the interior of a warehouse on James River. Some exercise other extravagances— qualify their lemonade with the tincture of pure cognac, of which their fair partners sip a drop or two to prevent danger from the excessive heat, and which these foplings drench in quantities, so that in the conclusion they become as noisy and quarrelsome as apes."

Only two years elapsed, however, before some gentlemen met at Renshaw's Hotel, and resolved "that in the City of Philadelphia, the residence of much elegance, and the resort of much gayety, there ought to be Dancing Assemblies." Accordingly, subscriptions books were ordered to be opened, but in the meantime a notice was published that a Cotillion Party had been formed which postponed the revival of the City Dancing Assembly until 1819.

As early as 1792 money was subscribed for a permanent home and the trustees of the fund actually bought a lot of land. No building was erected, although the project seems to have been kept alive as late as 1824. In 1839 a handsome Bachelor's Ball was given in the hall of the Franklin Institute, on Chestnut Street, and in 1849 we find the first record of the Assembly Balls at Musical Fund Hall, on Locust Street at Eighth, where they continued to be given with some interruptions until 1865, when the Academy of Music became their home. In 1904 the size of the ball demanded enlarged quarters and it was moved to the Bellevue-Stratford Hotel, in Broad Street at Walnut. The Balls are managed by a group of gentlemen who have sometimes been chosen by the subscribers and sometimes by other managers.

XIII: The City Troop

OF Philadelphia's many ancient institutions perhaps none is more widely known than the organization popularly called "The City Troop," that long sustained gleam of brilliancy which came into our peaceful Quaker drab so long ago as 1774. The call which these spirited young gentlemen heeded, have always heeded, was that of their country but they have never traded upon patriotism or record for public favour nor forsaken the old Philadelphia characteristic of modesty and reserve.

At the outbreak of trouble with England there were a number of important organizations for sport and social intercourse among Philadelphians of quality. The oldest was the "Colony in Schuylkill" and there were also the "Schuylkill Company of Fort St. David's," "The St. Andrew's Society of Philadelphia," "The Society of the Friendly Sons of St. Patrick," "The Society of the Sons of St. George," and the "Gloucester Fox Hunting Club." It was from these happy groups that the troop of light horse was almost entirely recruited, especially from the first and second named. On the evening of Thursday, November 17, 1774, while the Continental Congress was sitting in the Hall of the Carpenters' Company, twenty-eight gentlemen met there and associated themselves as the Light Horse of the City of Philadelphia, the first organization of volunteers formed to maintain the rights of the people against the oppression of the British Government.

The officers chosen were:

Abraham Markoe   Henry Hill
Andrew Allen   John Boyle

Samuel Morris

James Mease

Thomas Leiper

William Hall

Samuel Penrose

Samuel Howell, Jr.

James Hunter

James Budden

John Dunlap

John Mease

Robert Hare

William Pollard

William Tod

John Mitchell

George Campbell

Samuel Caldwell

Andrew Caldwell

Levi Hollingsworth

Blair McClenachan

George Groff

Benjamin Randolph

Thomas Peters

George Fullerton

William West, Jr.

The officers chosen were:

Abraham Markoe . . Captain

Andrew Allen . . First Lieutenant

Samuel Morris . . Second Lieutenant and Adjutant

James Mease. . . Cornet

Thomas Leiper . . First Sergeant

William Hall. . . Second Sergeant

Samuel Penrose . . Quartermaster

William Pollard . . First Corporal

James Hunter . . Second Corporal

The members agreed to equip and support themselves at their own expense and to offer their services to the Continental Congress. The uniform adopted was a dark brown coat, faced and lined with white, white vest and breeches, high-topped boots, round black hat, bound with silver cord, a buck's tail; housings brown, edged with white and the letters L. H. worked on them. Arms, a carbine, a pair of pistols and holsters, with flounces of brown cloth trimmed with white, a horseman's sword, with belt for the sword and carbine. Several times a week during winter and spring they met in earnest preparation for active duty, under the instruction of Mr. Moffit as sword-master and horse trainer. Captain Markoe presented the cherished standard to the Troop in the spring and it is remarkable as being the first flag to bear the thirteen stripes, symbolizing the thirteen colonies now joined in a common need. This flag is of yellow with the thirteen stripes in the upper left-hand corner alternately blue and silver.

By this time the Troop was drilling every day, to say nothing of an occasional dinner. One of these at the Buck Tavern on May 20, 1775, offered to some twenty gentlemen a "dressed turtle, 7½ bot. Madeira, 16 bot. Claret, 10 bot. Porter, 6 bot. Beer and 16 bowls Punch." The Troop was assigned to the "Associators" commanded by Colonel John Cadwalader and paraded on June 8, 1775, on the Commons before the Continental Congress and again on June 20th, when it was reviewed by General Washington, Commander-in-Chief of all the North American forces. When the General set out on June 23rd to take command of the Army at Cambridge he was escorted by the Troop as far as Kingsbridge, New York, two of his equipment of five horses being furnished by Cornet James Mease. The last was the beginning of a long list of individual services rendered by members of the Troop which distinguish its records down to modern times. Not satisfied with active service in a small unit, the members have given widely of their capacity as opportunity offered. When in November "Lady" Washington was on her way to join her distinguished husband the Troop escorted her into and out of the City.

In the early part of 1776 Samuel Morris became Captain and led the Troop in the review of May 27th, before Generals Washington, Gates and Mifflin, the Congress, members of the Assembly and "a vast concourse of people." Details of the Troop now began to perform important duties such as bearing despatches, escorting prisoners and conveying money to the several camps of the army, always returning with letters of appreciation and commendation from the General in command. These expeditions were fraught with more danger than appears in their recital, both from natural and military difficulties, very long journeys being made in a wild country. The whole Troop reported to Washington at Trenton on December 2, 1776, and under his immediate direction covered the rear of the retreating army and established headquarters at Newtown. On the eventful Christmas night when Colonel Rahl's Hessians were surprised and taken, the Troop had an active part and acted as Washington's escort. The character and ability of the men seem to have impressed the American Commanders for they were constantly using small details on important duties rather than fighting the Troop as a whole. At Princeton Captain Morris' men performed valiant service and after the army had encamped at Morristown for the winter was relieved from duty as a unit, the Commander-in-Chief tendering the individual members Commissions in the Army as a reward for their gallantry and sending Captain Morris the prized letter complimenting the command "composed of Gentlemen of Fortune" for their "noble Example of discipline and subordination" which he says "will ever do Honour to them and will ever be gratefully remembered by me."

In the late summer of 1777 "an Officer and Six Gentlemen of Philadelphia Light Horse" were directed by the Board of War to escort Benjamin Chew and John Penn, Esq'rs, as prisoners to Fredericksburg, Virginia. This was no doubt a pleasant outing but must have been rather an unpleasant duty. When Washington led his forlorn army through the City to destroy Howe's prospect of a winter in Philadelphia, the Troop, as usual, escorted him, and Captain Morris, with a few others, kept the field to the end of October, serving with General Armstrong at the Battle of Germantown. The men of the Troop "who enjoy in a peculiar degree the gifts of fortune and of a cultivated understanding" being of "Property and Spirit" were on the alert for service and were constantly employed during the following winter and spring as aides and express riders. One is struck with the independence with which the command and its individual members acted. All through the early records this feature is prominent. The Troop would serve for a particular campaign or emergency or for escort to some distinguished personage and then disband until the next occasion arose. One of the most notable civil duties which called the Troop into service was the defense of James Wilson, signer of the Declaration of Independence, who was beseiged in his house by a mob on the night of October 4, 1779, on account of his acting as legal adviser for some Tories who had been indicted for treason. After some violence the Troop came on the scene and amid cries of "The Horse, the Horse," the mob dispersed not, however, without injury. A similar attack the next night upon Private David Lenox at "Grumblethorpe," Main Street and Indian Queen Lane, Germantown, was forestalled by his niece walking to the City and bringing the Troop to the rescue.

In the attempt of Robert Morris to save the national credit by establishing the Pennsylvania Bank in 1780 twenty-eight of the Troop joined and subscribed more than one-fourth of the total capital of the bank. After the surrender of Yorktown the captured British and German colours were brought to Philadelphia and paraded through the streets, escorted by the Troop and a full band of music. On this occasion 72 active members and 11 of the original members turned out. At the close of the war there were eight-eight names upon the roll.

It would be but continued repetition to recite the many

important occasions when the Troop has acted as escort for the President of the United States, Foreign Ambassadors and distinguished persons from at home and abroad. Samuel Morris resigned as Captain in 1786 and Samuel Miles was chosen in his place to be followed in 1790 by Christian Febiger, and by John Dunlap in 1793. Under the last three the Troop was frequently near Washington while he was President, acting as his escort on all public occasions.

The year 1794 marked an important event in the Troop's history. Their uniform was changed. The brown coat became blue faced with red and with white edging. The horse was to have a white saddle cloth with blue edging and a blue and white headpiece. An undress uniform was added consisting of a blue short jacket, red collar and cuffs, and mixed gray overalls. The change was just in time to be shown in the Whiskey Insurrection, which, it should very briefly be explained, was an uprising of certain of the inhabitants of the counties lying west of the Allegheny Mountains in Pennsylvania, in opposition to the recently enacted Excise Law of the United States, imposing duties on domestic distilled liquors. The Troop by resolution at the City Tavern volunteered their services and were sent to the upper end of Washington County where they took Colonel Crawford and his son, Mr. Sedgwick, a justice of the peace, and Mr. Corby, a clergyman of the Baptist persuasion, "with the greatest dexterity." This was the beginning of service in many civil outbreaks in which the Troop was ever prompt to render what service it could to the State and Nation. The Troop unselfishly donated their entire pay for services in the Revolution to the Pennsylvania Hospital, for the foundation of a maternity ward.

Robert Wharton was elected Captain in 1808 and in 1809 another change was made in the uniform.

"Instead of a Coatee, a round Jacket of dark blue Cloth with a small skirt, ornamented with silver Cord. The Facings, Cuffs and Collars to be of scarlet Cloth or Cassimere, each facing at the bottom to be about 4 inches broad and increase gradually to the Chest. Two rows of Buttons on the Breast facing, twelve on each side, with silver Cord to meet in the middle of the breast, and to reach from Button to Button across the Chest, the Jacket to reach the Hip bones. Two Buttons with Silver Cord on each side of the Collar, and three Buttons with silver cord on each sleeve. The Jacket to be lined with White and edged with it."

In this year also the long room at the Shakespeare Hotel was hired at $3.00 per evening for dismounted drill during the winter, no refreshments, "other than Beer, Spirits, Brandy and Segars" to be charged to the fund for defraying expenses of drill.

The trouble with Great Britain caused the formation of a cavalry regiment of which the Troop was a part and Captain Wharton the Colonel. Charles Ross was elected Captain and the Troop exercised several times a month, being also "present at all inspections, reviews and parades," until the taking of the City of Washington in 1814, when it was called into the field and sent toward Baltimore on vidette duty. Former Captain Wharton, who had become a Brigadier General in 1812, was serving again as a private in the Troop and while taking his turn as a company cook on this expedition was called to be Mayor of Philadelphia. The Troop returned in December and celebrated their discharge with a dinner at the Washington Hotel which cost $300 for "Dinner, Dessert, Madeira, Claret, Punch, Segars, Ale, Porter, Cyder, Brandy, etc., and a further sum for some broken Decanters, Wines and Tumblers."

Captain Ross died in 1817 and First Lieutnant John

 Independence Hall
Philadelphia • Built 1732
From the Philadelphia Art Alliance Post Card Series

R. C. Smith became Commander. He led the Troop in the welcome accorded General Lafayette on his second visit to the United States in 1824. The next year Captain Smith was deprived of his command by Court Martial for disobedience of orders and First Lieutenant Lynford Lardner was elected in his place, to be followed in 1827 by William H. Hart. John Butler was made Captain in 1842 and died in service as Captain of the Third United States Dragoons at Mier, Mexico, in 1847. Thomas C. James succeeded him and led the Troop on May 30, 1861, when it entered the conflict between the States as a part of the Second United States Cavalry, George H. Thomas commanding. After active service it was mustered out in August but many of the members returned to the Army and and served with distinction as officers of the Northern side. The remainder went out when Lee's army marched into Pennsylvania and with some recruits saw active service until July 31, 1863, under the command of Cornet Samuel J. Randall. Cornet Randall was chosen temporary Captain in July, 1864, and so served while the Troop attended the body of President Lincoln during its stay in Philadelphia.

After the war there was no immediate election of officers, since so many members had held commissions in the active service of the Nation as to make a choice embarrassing, but in 1866 Fairman Rogers was made Captain, to be followed in 1869 by Mr. Edward Rogers. In 1877 A. Loudon Snowden was elected Captain and commanded in the Pittsburgh railway riots of that year. The next year Private Edward Burd Grubb, a Brigadier General of the Civil War, was chosen and served until 1889, when Joseph Lapsley Wilson took his place, only to return his commission to General Grubb in 1894.

John C. Groome was elected Captain in 1896 and led the Troop to Porto Rico in the War with Spain, during 1898, when it was the first volunteer cavalry organization to land on foreign shores, and brought back the ninety-nine men who went out. Captain J. Franklin McFadden was elected in 1910 and commanded on the Mexican border in 1916. Following came George C. Thayer in 1917, Thomas Cadwalader in 1920 and the present Captain Clement B. Wood in 1921.

The meeting places of the Troop form a long list. The early ones were at various public and private houses, such as the City Tavern on South Second Street, William Ogden's at the Middle Ferry on the Schuylkill River, the old fish house of the "State in Schuylkill" and others. The first fixed home of its own seems to have been in 1828 at Sixth and Carpenter Streets and after more meetings at hotels intervening the members gathered at Eighth and Chestnut Streets and then at Twelfth and Chestnut. In 1864 the Armory at Twenty-first and Ash Streets was opened and the first mounted drills held indoors. Several extensions were made and in 1900 the present armory on Twenty-first Street was built.

On Anniversary Day, November 17th, the Troop has a great celebration each year, when it "parades and dines." This is repeated each Washington's Birthday and begins with a parade from the Armory on Twenty-first Street down to Thirteenth and Walnut Streets, and back. This curious route is caused by an old tradition that on this distinguished occasion the Troopers should parade past "the Club" where their friends were assembled to admire them. Of course "the Club" was the Philadelphia Club which for many years has been housed at Thirteenth and Walnut Streets.

The origin of this occasion is interesting. In the old days, when they held their meetings in the small rooms of inns, their numbers so crowded the room that the waiters could not spread the banquet that followed the meeting, consequently the Troopers were politely asked to take a walk while the dinner was being laid. Where should they go but to "the Club" and how should they go but in military formation.

Philadelphia is justly proud of its old Troop of "Light Horse" and they are trotted out upon every important occasion as of old. Nor are they met with quip or jest by the populace as are many similar organizations of "gentlemen" elsewhere, because most people know what they have done and what they are always ready to do.

XIV: The Wistar Parties

THE letters of John Adams to his wife are enthusiastic in describing the luxurious living prevalent among the "Nobles of Pennsylvania" but among his gossipy references to the people he meets and their bounteous entertainments no better observation is recorded than that he has found "high thinking" here which is better than high living. The best example of this feature of Philadelphia life is found in the notable gatherings at Fourth and Prune Streets, now Locust, under the hospitable roof of Dr. Caspar Wistar. These represented the genial and social side of learning. The house, which has been restored within and without to much of its original beauty, was built about 1750 and lived in for a time by Dr. William Shippen, perhaps the most talented member of his family. His marriage to Alice Lee, daughter of Thomas Lee of Virginia, was one of the many connections between the Colonial families of Philadelphia and the county families of Virginia and Maryland, and made his house the centre for the Virginia aristocrats visiting Philadelphia.

In 1799 Dr. Caspar Wistar moved from High Street near Fourth to Fourth and Prune Streets and continued to live there until his death in 1818. Dr. Wistar was a very busy man, having an extensive practice and a chair at the University. His unusual traits of character and his genius for intellectual leadership made him an object of affectionate homage by his friends who loved to enjoy the hospitable moments of his leisure time. As these were necessarily limited, the custom was formed of dropping in on him on Sunday evenings when they were pretty sure of finding him at home. As the years passed these weekly gatherings became one of Philadelphia's most cherished institutions, the same group of friends meeting week after week. They included most Philadelphians of distinction, and as all strangers of note were introduced into this circle of choice spirits, it became the centre of the literary and scientific society of the City. Dr. Wistar's close association with the American Philosophical Society made his house the rally point of the learned world, and, in time, there came to be an approximate identity between the smaller body for social intercourse and that of the larger and world-famous scientific body.

The entertainment was simple, consisting of wine and cake, tea and coffee, as Dr. Wistar's idea was an intellectual rather than a convivial gathering. The table was seldom spread. In 1811 the night of the meeting was changed from Sunday to Saturday evening and ice cream, raisins and almonds were added to the refreshments. Terrapin, oysters and other delicacies were introduced later. The guests usually ranged from ten to fifty in number and the regular habitues had the privilege of bringing whom they would. Invitations began in October or November and continued to be sent out until April, gathering the best the new world civilization could produce of talent, learning, courtly grace and good breeding. Some of the most notable visitors were Baron von Humboldt, the naturalist; Bonplaud, the botanist; the witty Abbe Correa de Serra, Mr. Samuel Breck, of Boston; Dr. John W. Francis, of New York; Robert Walsh, Joseph Hopkinson, Nicholas Biddle, Dr. Nathaniel Chapman and the older physicians, Dr. Benjamin Rush, the many-sided, who "belonged to humanity"; Dr. Adam Kuhn, both the William Shippens, father and son, eminent physicians practicing at the same time, and the peaceful Dr. Griffitts, William Rawle, lawyer and theologian; Chief Justice William Tilghman, whose biographical sketch of Dr. Wistar survives; George Clymer, statesman and patriot; Peter Du Ponceau, the Moravian missionary; John Heckwelder and the Unitarian philanthropist John Vaughan at the extremes of doctrine, and a host of other celebrites, whose names are a sufficient guarantee of the brilliance of these gatherings.

Dr. Wistar's fame does not, however, rest upon the Wistar Parties. He had studied medicine at Edinburgh and was a professor in the University, a teacher, physician, man of science and the author of the first American treatise on Anatomy. His demeanour was dignified, modest and courteous and he was ardent in inciting the members of the Philosophical Society, while he was its president, to collect the materials of American history before it was too late. He made the work of its committee so interesting by his own anecdotes that they sat long into the night listening to him.

When Dr. Wistar died in 1818 a few of his more intimate friends determined to continue their pleasant association and formed an organization which they called the "Wistar Parties" with membership in the Philosophical Society and a unanimous vote requisites for joining. Three parties a year were held until the Civil War broke up for a time the wholesome conviviality. Members were selected for their attainments and twenty Philadelphians were permitted as guests with no limit to strangers. Attendance was punctual at eight o'clock and the entertainment remained simple and unostentatious.

In 1835 Job R. Tyson bought Dr. Wistar's old house and once more it opened to the learned and jovial brotherhood, the meetings being held in rotation at the houses of the members.

In the early part of the eighteenth century Philadelphia was better known abroad than any other American city and all travellers of consequence came to it. These were entertained, if fortunately nearby, at the Wistar Parties and we find such names as General Moreau, the younger Murat, the Marquis de Grouchy, the poet Moore, Prince de-Canino, son-in-law of Joseph Bonaparte, President Madison, the diplomat William Short, representative of the United States to France, Spain and the Netherlands, the Duke of Saxe-Weimar, President John Quincy Adams, Thackeray, Mr. Pedersen, minister from Denmark, Colonel Beckwith and several French Chevaliers.

Upon one occasion the whole company of about one hundred were regaled with chicken salad, oysters, ices, wine, punch and the like at an expense of $24.87, including the whiskey for the punch, spermaceti candles, oil for the lamps and extra fire in one room.

Written invitations were used until 1835 when Mr. Vaughan speaks of the engraved card similar to the one used to-day with the quaint, queued head of Dr. Wistar upon it. The gatherings continued in brilliancy with such citizens present as Robert Vaux, Mathew Carey, and his son, Henry C., political economists, Joseph Hopkinson, the elder Peale, Dr. Frederick Beasley, Provost of the University, Dr. Robert M. Patterson, Robert Walsh, Horace Binney, William M. Meredith, John Sergeant, Joshua Francis Fisher, Judge Kane, Langdon Cheves, Thomas Wharton, Dr. Robert Hare, Dr. Thomas C. James, Dr. John K. Mitchell, Dr. Isaac Hays, Dr. Franklin Bache, Dr. George B. Wood, Dr. Charles Meigs, Moncure Robinson and Dr. Isaac Lea.

It was not until 1886 that the scattered members resumed the Wistar Parties, loyally adhering to ancient traditions, except perhaps in the simplicity of the repast. The same kind of men are still pleasantly mingling together in intellectual fellowship at the fireside of some good old Philadelphian of attainment.

XV: A Medical Centre

ALTHOUGH Gabriel Thomas tells us in 1698 that there is no need for Lawyers or Physicians because the country is "very Peaceable and Healthy," yet there were some of each in Philadelphia at a very early date to begin her continued reputation for both professions. Two trained Welsh physicians, Thomas Wynne and Griffith Owen, came with Penn in the *Welcome* and found constant occupation in fighting small-pox, measles and yellow fever. Following these two came Dr. John Kearsley and Dr. Thomas Graeme and then that brilliant group—Lloyd Zachary, Thomas Cadwalader, William Shippen, Sr., Thomas and Phineas Bond, John Redman and John Bard, all trained abroad in London, Edinburgh or Leyden. We will learn how John Morgan saw the necessity for better means of study at home and founded the first medical school on the Continent at his Alma Mater, the University of Pennsylvania.

Twenty years after this notable beginning there were enough successful practitioners in Philadelphia to feel a desire for a union through which, by discussion and research, they could mutually assist each other in the progress of their profession. The earliest record of their meeting is January 2, 1787, when Dr. John Redman was chosen President and the first Tuesday of each month chosen for regular meetings. Nine senior and four junior fellows were present and the senior fellows were limited to twelve, with no limits to the juniors. Dr. Benjamin Rush read the first scientific paper "On the Means of Promoting Medical Knowledge." The membership for the first year was 29 and the meetings were held in the building of the University in Fourth Street near Arch. The College moved in 1791 to the hall of the American Philosophical Society, where a room was fitted up for their use.

The College was diligent in addresses to the City and State Governments on the public health, and as early as 1793 advocated the cleanliness of the streets as a preventive of disease. It also took a very active part in dealing with the regulation of the practice of physic within the State, the establishment of a quarantine and a hospital for contagious diseases.

Thomas Wynne and Griffith Owen were "concerned Friends," the former taking an active part in politics and the latter in preaching. Thomas Graeme and John Kearsley were also active in politics and Kearsley has left us a masterpiece in Christ Church of which he was the architect. He was an able speaker and his eloquent addresses in the Colonial Assembly on the rights of Americans often caused him to be carried home on the shoulders of the people. John Redman, John Bard and Lloyd Zachary studied under Kearsley. The last was a gifted and devoted physician, teacher of students and faithful in his service to the hospital. Associated with him were the Bonds, the younger, Phineas, having studied in London, Paris, Edinburgh and Leyden. Dr. Thomas Cadwalader studied abroad and became physician, philanthropist and man of affairs. He was a founder of the Library and Hospital, a Provincial Councillor and Trustee of the University. His descendants form a long line of patriots, jurists and distinguished citizens.

Dr. William Shippen was for a long time one of the leading physicians and is thought to have received his early training under one of the Welsh "chirurgeons" brought over by William Penn. He was a modest man and once on being congratulated upon his success, remarked, "Nature

does a great deal, and the grave covers up our mistakes."
Dr. Shippen's son, William, studied abroad and attained
much distinction. During the Revolution he was director-
general of the Medical Department of the Continental
Army from 1777 to 1781.

John Morgan studied abroad after graduation from the
College, now the University, and on his return urged upon
the Trustees the foundation of a Medical Department.
There were several physicians on the Board and the ardent
proposal of the young student backed by indorsement from
many and exalted sources prevailed and he was elected the
first professor of the Theory and Practice of Physic in 1765.
His address at the ensuing Commencement acquired much
notoriety and his prediction that the example thus set would
be copied by other institutions and thus "spread the light
of knowledge throughout the whole American continent"
has been amply fulfilled. An early associate in the University was Dr. Adam Kuhn, who studied abroad and became
Professor of Botany and Materia Medica.

Perhaps the most distinguished of Dr. John Redman's
pupils was Benjamin Rush, who also studied under Dr.
Shippen and abroad. He brought home a chemical apparatus presented to the University by Thomas Penn and a
recommendation from him and was unanimously elected to
the Chair of Chemistry in 1769. Dr. Rush was an author
of prominence and had a talent for public discussion. His
oration before the Philosophical Society on the history of
medicine among the Indians, with comparison of their diseases and remedies with those of civilized nations made
him famous. The feature of this address was his discussion of the evils of the intemperate use of intoxicating
liquors which was the first instance of such a discussion in
Philadelphia. Dr. Rush was a member of the Continental
Congress and a signer of the Declaration of Independence.

Shortly afterward he became Surgeon-General of the Army for the Middle Department, but his participation in the Conway Cabal for the removal of General Washington soon led to his resignation. Dr. Rush's part in the yellow fever outbreak of 1793 was notable. He adopted a heroic practice which he boldly asserted was of domestic and not foreign origin and it raised loud outcries against him. He kept going day and night during this terrible year, sometimes fainting in the street from exhaustion, yet attending more than a hundred patients in twenty-four hours. His never-forgotten note-book was always at hand and from it he wrote the history of the plague. His death caused universal sorrow, only exceeded, it was thought, by that at the death of Washington. The College of Physicians was established mainly through his influence.

Its first President, Dr. John Redman, has been frequently referred to as a teacher of medicine. He began practice in Bermuda after studying with Dr. John Kearsley and then completed his studies in Edinburgh, Paris, and Leyden. For more than half a century he lived in Second Street near Arch, retiring from active practice many years before his death. In his later years he used to visit his old friends on a fat pony which he hitched to the turn-buckle of the mansion shutter, so that she always stood on the foot-pavement. Greatly respected for his learning and good sense he was also notable for his antiquated appearance. He usually wore a broad-skirted dark coat, with long pocket-flaps, buttoned across his under dress, and wearing, in strict conformity to the cut of the coat, a pair of Baron Steuben's military-shaped boots, coming above the knees. "His hat flapped before and cocked up smartly behind, covering a full-buttoned powdered wig, in the front of which might be seen an eagle-pointed nose, separating a pair of piercing black eyes, his lips exhibiting, but only

SAINT PETER'S CHURCH
Third and Pine Streets, Philadelphia
Built 1761 · Attended by Washington 1781-82

From the Philadelphia Art Alliance Post Card Series

now and then, a quick motion, as though at the moment he was endeavouring to extract the essence of a small quid." Thus almost daily he was to be seen on his short, fat, black, switch-tailed mare riding in a brisk rocking canter about the streets.

Dr. Samuel Bard, educated abroad, was selected as Washington's physician in Philadelphia and served faithfully in the yellow fever outbreak, almost perishing of it himself. Dr. John Jones also attended Washington in Philadelphia, and Franklin, too. He was the first Vice-President of the College of Physicians. Dr. Caspar Wistar and Dr. James Hutchinson were men of influence and note. Both studied abroad and both served the University well. Dr. Wistar was President of the American Philosophical Society and a gentleman of wide influence and learning. More of him is told in another place. These are some of the early physicians who were interested in the College. William Shippen, Jr., followed Dr. Redman as President, and Dr. Adam Kuhn succeeded him. Like every institution, it had its ups and downs. In 1818 there were but 18 Fellows. In 1820, in answering a request of the municipal authorities for guidance in dealing with an epidemic of a "pestilential disease" a committee composed of Doctors Hewson, Griffitts and Emlen recommended "the prosecution of the plan now in contemplation for removing the whole of the buildings from the east side of Front Street, inclusive, to the river, beginning at Vine and ending at South Street, according to the original plan of William Penn, the wise and intelligent founder of our City." Here was the great plan again, but it was not carried out.

In 1827 each Fellow was compelled to read an original paper at each stated meeting and the hour of meeting was changed from the afternoon to the evening at seven from October to March and at eight from April to September.

In 1845 the College moved into the building of the Mercantile Library Company at the southeast corner of Fifth and Library Streets, where the third floor was occupied. In 1854 another move was made when the "picture house" of the Pennsylvania Hospital was leased. Two years afterward Dr. Mutter made an offer of his valuable collection of pathological specimens and a sum of $30,000 for a lecturer and additions provided the collection was placed in a fireproof building. By diligent effort the College was able to avail itself of the generous offer and in 1863 the building at Thirteenth and Locust Streets was ready for occupation, being then, however, of only two stories. The third story was added in 1883 and the College remained here until 1908, when a handsome new building was erected at Twenty-second and Ludlow Streets.

Philadelphia's reputation as a medical centre is thus long established. Beside the University's Medical School, Jefferson, Hahnemann, and the Medico-Chirurgical (now a part of the Graduate School of Medicine at the University of Pennsylvania) Colleges have kept up the standard. The names of Agnew, Wood, White, Tyson, Pepper, and Deaver are well known everywhere.

XVI: The Pennsylvania Academy of the Fine Arts

AFTER the Revolution portrait-painting was exceedingly fashionable in all American cities and Washington set an example by being painted over and over again. Charles Wilson Peale and his fellow-artists were kept busy painting Philadelphia's great men, and, above all, her handsome daughters, as noted apparently for their charms as were their English great-grandmothers in the gay days of the second Charles. Peale was a man of extraordinary resource and indefatigable genius. He was a Captain of Volunteers in the Battle of Trenton, a portrait painter of merit, a soldier, clock-maker, silversmith, glass-moulder, taxidermist, dentist, modeller and engraver. He expressed his reverence for art by naming his six children Raphael, Rembrandt, Vandyke, Titian, Rubens and Angelica Kauffman.

In 1791 he began a collection of paintings and sculpture which he later called a Columbianum, and founded a school of art. His associates were William Rush, the woodcarver, the Guiseppe Ceracchi, a Roman sculptor, all of such different and positive natures that they soon disbanded. Peale then began a collection of rarities in the Philosophical Hall of the State House with a plaster cast of Venus de Medici brought to Philadelphia by Robert Edgar Pine, as a nucleus about which was built a class in drawing. Pine was not permitted to keep this statue in his studio where it could be generally seen and the nymph carved by Rush, which is now in Fairmount Park, caused a storm of protest when placed in Centre Square, although amply draped. So we may see the obstacles placed in the path of art by the inconsistent public, whose conceptions of propriety were nevertheless not shocked by the portraits of Philadelphia belles with bosoms unveiled to the careless eyes of men.

Peale finding no one willing to act as a model for the life-class in his school, stood himself and bared his handsome torso to instruct his ambitious pupils. As an advertiser he seems to have adopted modern methods, for he gave a supper party of thirteen within the ribs of a mammoth skeleton which he had in his museum. All failed together, however, sculpture hall, gallery of paintings and life-class, but the tireless worker and enthusiast, nothing daunted, kept at it and the day after Christmas, 1805, collected the men who were the founders of the oldest institution dedicated to fine arts in the United States. Their charter was granted in 1806 and Peale lived to contribute to seventeen annual exhibitions of the new institution.

Of the 71 signers of the horny brown sheepskin of the compact in the Declaration room of the State House, Joseph Hopkinson, the author of "Hail Columbia," seems to have been the greatest influence for executive and cementing strength. George Clymer was chosen president and William Tilghman, William Rawle, Moses Levy, Joseph Hopkinson, Joseph B. McKean, William Meredith, William Rush, John R. Cox, M.D., and Charles Wilson Peale, Directors. As President, Mr. Clymer has been succeeded by the following line: Joseph Hopkinson, Joseph Dugan, Edward L. Carey, Joseph R. Ingersoll, Henry D. Gilpin, Caleb Cope, James S. Claghorn, George S. Pepper, Edward H. Coates, Henry Whelen, and John Frederick Lewis.

The early meetings were held at Judge Hopkinson's house and the first building was at Tenth and Chestnut Streets, designed by Benjamin Henry Latrobe, a lover of classic architecture, and the designer of the old water works in Centre Square. The appearance of the building was of a simple, impressive Greek style with broad marble steps leading up to a portico whose pediment was supported by a pair of Ionic columns.

Under the direction of Nicholas Biddle, then secretary of legation at Paris, a number of copies of statuary were made and purchased, representing gems collected by Napoleon in his conquests. With these the Academy was formally opened to the public by President Clymer in March, 1806. The collection grew and it became the custom to give or bequeath works of art to it. The casts which Nicholas Biddle sent over from the Louvre models stood the town on end and the managers were obliged to set apart one day in each week for female visitors, when the nude figures were swathed from head to feet in muslin sheets!

In 1812 twenty-one paintings and fifty-two engravings were collected by Joseph Allen Smith, who despatched them from Italy for the Academy in *The Marquis de Somernclos,* an American ship. She was captured by a British cruiser and taken to Halifax, where a creditable bit of magnanimity was displayed, especially in view of the fact that swarms of American privateers were at that time driving English merchantmen from the sea. The Academy's application to recover its consignment was decided favourably by the Honourable Alexander Croke, LL.D., in a court of Vice-Admiralty at Halifax. It was a handsome piece of justice liberally interpreted and out of all harmony with some of the customs of modern warfare. "Heaven forbid," said Mr. Croke, "that such an application to the generosity of Great Britian should ever be ineffectual!" He mentions the innumerable cases of the mutual exercise of this courtesy between nations in former wars and "if such cases were unheard of every Briton would be anxious that his country should set the honourable example." He finished with a compliment to the "very eminent American President of the Royal Academy" in London and confidently foresees a time when England and America "shall know no other enmity than a liberal rivalry in every elegant and manly accomplishment," and then decrees restitution.

West, Peale, Sully and Stuart were represented in the collection when the fire of 1845, attributed to a maniac relative to the janitress, destroyed the Academy's building. The edifice was much injured and although there were many brave acts the more ponderous contents were lost. The volunteer fire companies, as was often the case, damaged more than they saved in their unintelligent zeal. The structure was rebuilt on the old site and after the old design and it served well until the removal to the present site in 1876. After this the building became Fox's Theatre and later was entirely transformed.

In 1886 Fairman Rogers, Professor Schussele and Thomas Eakins established the new school which has become so justly famous. In 1890 President Edward H. Coates inaugurated the annual private views and receptions, and many of the present generation remember the concerts on Thursday afternoons by the Germania Orchestra under William Stoll which were so popular.

The Academy was the recipient of several notable collections of historical American portraits. It contains a a noble group of portraits by Gilbert Stuart and an ancestral picture gallery of Philadelphia displaying persons of wit, beauty and genius by Sully, Neagle, Juman, Peale and others.

BENJAMIN FRANKLIN 1706-1790

Venerated for Benevolence
Admired for Talents ~
Esteemed for Patriotism ~
Beloved for Philanthropy ~

From The Autobiography of Benjamin Franklin, published by Ginn and Company

XVII: The Academy of Natural Sciences

TWO young men, a chemist and a dentist, called together a few friends in their own walk of life, rented a little room over a little shop, placed in it, with infinite pride, a dozen stuffed birds and a jar or two of reptiles, and met there at night to discuss "the operations of nature," pledging themselves wisely to leave politics and religion entirely out of their debates. From this modest beginning sprang the Philadelphia Academy of Natural Sciences, the oldest institution of its kind in America, which has diffused knowledge over the eastern states and counted among its members the scholars and scientists of the land. These two young men were John Speakman and Jacob Gilliams, who thought that if their friends could come together at stated times where they would be free from interruption and could discuss what they knew of the natural sciences it would be more pleasant and profitable than desultory talk.

Accordingly, such a meeting was held at Speakman's house at the northwest corner of Second and High Streets on Saturday evening, January 25, 1812, and there were present besides the host, Doctors Gerard Troost and Camillies Macmahon Mann, with Jacob Gilliams, John Shinn, Jr., and Nicholas S. Parmentier. The meeting is described as "a meeting of gentlemen, friends of science and of rational disposure of leisure moments" and it was agreed that the exclusive object of the society should be the cultivation of the natural sciences.

There were not many in the city who cared for this subject and there were no displays to awaken curiosity or libraries to satisfy it had it existed. There were two or three collections of minerals belonging to gentlemen who had brought them from Europe, but they were not accessible to the public. Those interested in the subject were all busy in making a living during the day and occasional gossip at inns did not help them much in the search for exact knowledge.

In order not to be a burden on Mr. Speakman's hospitality the early meetings were held at Mercer's Cake Shop on High Street, near the corner of Franklin Place, and the title Academy of Natural Sciences was first used on March 21, 1812. It was suggested by Dr. Samuel Jackson of the University, and at this meeting Thomas Say was included as a founder.

John Speakman was a Friend and his apothecary shop was one of the centres of literary and scientific gossip. Jacob Gilliams was a leading dentist, John Shinn, Jr., a manufacturing chemist, Nicholas S. Parmentier, a distiller of spermaceti oil, Gerard Troost, a manufacturing chemist and the first President of the Academy, and Dr. Camillies Macmahon Mann the first Recording Secretary. Thomas Say was associated in business with Speakman and a born naturalist. It was due to his devotion that the Academy was kept alive.

In April a small second-story room in a house on the east side of Second Street, near Race, was rented and the nucleus of the present library and museum formed. Each member gave something and in September the collections were removed to larger quarters on Second Street, north of Arch, then number 78. The year closed with fourteen members and thirty-three correspondents. The next two years were more prosperous and lectures were given by Mr. Say and Doctors Waterhouse and Barnes.

At the beginning of 1815 the need of increased accommodations again necessitated a removal and Mr. Gilliams built a hall in the rear of his father's house on the north side of Arch Street east of Second, to which the collections were moved in July. At the instance of Mr. Maclure, the Academy decided to publish a Journal and the first number appeared May 20, 1817.

By 1820 there were one hundred members and one hundred and ninety correspondents on the roll. In 1823 new quarters seemed necessary and in 1826 a building at the southeast corner of Twelfth and Sansom Streets was purchased for $4300. This had been used as a place of worship for Swedenborgians and $1700 was expended to rent it. Prosperity now attended the Academy and it was served by such zealous officers as William Maclure, George Ord, John Price Wetherill, William Hembel, William H. Keating and Dr. Samuel George Morton.

The popularity of the institution again caused a need for more room in 1839 and a lot at the northwest corner of Broad and Sansom was bought and the first meeting held in the new building February 18, 1840. The transfer of the library and collections was accomplished at a cost of $34, the members giving their time and strength to the service so as to save time and expense. The spectacle of the dignified scientific citizens of the City ambling through the streets with the birds and beasts must have been an edifying one!

Soon after this Dr. Joseph Leidy was elected to membership and for 46 years he exerted a potent influence upon the well-being of the institution in all its endeavours.

The next move was to the present location at Nineteenth and Race Streets in 1868 and the change was completed in 1875. Recent appropriations by the State Legislature have provided a modern fire-proof building for the large and valuable collection and library and the publication and lecture departments have now become an equally important part of the Academy's work.

XVIII: The Library Company

ALL the world knows that one cannot go far in the history of Philadelphia without encountering Benjamin Franklin. He seems to be at one's elbow ever afterward or gazing steadfastly, calmly, and half humorously into one's eyes at every turn. So much has been written about every side of his character and endeavour, and indeed much would have to be written to cover them, that this book cannot enlarge upon these most interesting and instructive subjects but only make the suggestions which are necessary.

A club which Franklin formed in 1728 for the mutual improvement of its members marked the birth of learning in the Province for out of it, directly and indirectly, came most of its useful institutions. This was the Junto, sometimes called the "Leather-Apron Club." Into it he "formed most of his ingenious acquaintance" of no elevated origin, who met on Friday evenings first at a tavern but afterward at the house of Robert Grace, near Second and Hight Streets in Jones' Alley. Every member in his turn was required to "produce one or more queries on any point of morals, politics, or natural philosophy, to be discussed by the company," with an essay from each once in three weeks. No better idea of their doings can be written than that to be gained from their rules, which were not dogmatic like a constitution and by-laws. They were queries which were read at the opening of the meetings:

"Have you read over these queries this morning in order to consider what you might have to offer the Junto touching any one of them? Viz:—

1. Have you met with anything in the author you last read, remarkable or suitable to be communicated to the Junto, particularly in history, morality, poetry, physic, travels, mechanic arts, or other parts of knowledge?

2. What new story have you lately heard agreeable for telling in conversation?

3. Hath any citizen in your knowledge, failed in his business lately, and what have you heard of the cause?

4. Have you lately heard of any citizens thriving well, and by what means?

5. Have you lately heard how any present rich man, here or elsewhere, got his estate?

6. Do you know of a fellow-citizen who has lately done a worthy action deserving praise and imitation, or who has lately committed an error proper for us to be warned against and avoid?

7. What unhappy effects of intemperance have you lately observed or heard, of imprudence, of passion, or of any other vice or folly?

8. What happy effects of temperance, of prudence, of moderation, or any other virtue?

9. Have you, or any of your acquaintance, been lately sick or wounded? If so, what remedies were used, and what were their effects?

10. Whom do you know that are shortly going on voyages or journeys, if one should have occasion to send by them?

11. Do you think of any thing at present in which the Junto may be serviceable to mankind, to their country, to their friends, or to themselves?

12. Hath any deserving stranger arrived in town since last meeting, that you have heard of? And what have you heard or observed of his character or merits? And

whether, think you, it lies in the power of the Junto to oblige him, or encourage him as he deserves?

13. Do you know of any young beginner lately set up, whom it lies in the power of the Junto any way to encourage?

14. Have you lately observed any defect in the laws of your country, of which it would be proper to move the Legislature for an amendment? Or do you know of any beneficial law that is wanting?

15. Have you lately observed any encroachment on the just liberties of the people?

16. Hath any body attacked your reputation lately? And what can the Junto do towards securing it?

17. Is there any man whose friendship you want, and which the Junto, or any part of them, can procure for you?

18. Have you lately heard any member's character attacked, and how have you defended it?

19. Hath any man injured you, from whom it is in the power of the Junto to procure redress?

20. In what manner can the Junto, or any of them, assist you in any of your honourable designs?

21. Have you any weighty affair on hand in which you think the advice of the Junto may be of service?

22. What benefits have you lately received from any man not present?

23. Is there any difficulty in matters of opinion, of justice and injustice, which you would gladly have discussed at this time?

24. Do you see anything amiss in the present customs or proceedings of the Junto which might be amended?"

A pretty wide range were these of intelligence office, star chamber, gossip club and business protective union. The members were required to declare that they respected each member, loved mankind in general, believed in freedom of opinion and loved truth for truth's sake. The original members were Benjamin Franklin, Hugh Meredith, Joseph Brientnall, Thomas Godfrey, Nicholas Scull, William Parsons, William Maugridge, Stephen Potts, George Webb, Robert Grace and William Coleman.

It was hard to join and not very solemn at first, had a song or two, an anniversary banquet, and many picnic meetings in rural places "for bodily exercise." During its forty years of existence it was never very large. Franklin mentions only eleven persons and Roberts Vaux has added about a dozen more names to the list—all respectable but few of any special prominence. It was influential, prosperous, popular and profitable from the start.

About 1730 Franklin proposed, since their books were often needed in their meetings, that they should bring them all together, so that they might be consulted and used as a library by the members. So three little bookcases were fitted up in the small room in Jones' Alley and a few books put into them. Constant handling and little care soon caused dissatisfaction and each member took his books home. Nothing daunted, however, Franklin went on and proposed that the Junto procure fifty subscribers of forty shillings each to begin with, and ten shillings a year for fifty years, to start a subscription library. As the subscriptions came slowly twenty-five were held to be enough and when forty-five pounds was in hand the Library Company determined to send to England for books, commissioning James Logan to select them.

The instrument of association was dated July 1, 1731, and the first directors were Benjamin Franklin, Thomas Hopkinson, William Parsons, Philip Syng, Jr., Thomas Godfrey, Anthony Nicholas, Thomas Cadwalader, John Jones, Jr., Robert Grace and Isaac Penington. William Coleman was elected Treasurer and Joseph Brientnall, secretary, and thus originated the "Library Company of Philadelphia," the mother of all North American subscription libraries.

The books were first kept in Robert Grace's house from which those who had signed the articles of association were allowed to take them home "into the bosom of private families." Grace's house was on the north side of High Street below Second, nearly opposite the town hall. It was one of the oldest brick houses in the city and had an arched carriage-way in the rear upon Jones' Alley, or Pewter Platter Alley, as it was later called on account of the popular inn of that name situated upon it. It was through this rear archway that the members of the Junto and the Library Company entered so as not to disturb the inmates of the house.

The collection remained here for ten years and was in 1740 removed, by permission of the Assembly, to the upper room of the western-most office of the State House. The Proprietaries granted the Company a charter in 1740 and also contributed a lot on Chestnut between Eight and Ninth Streets, but it was too far out of town to build upon. The books increased by gift and purchase. James Logan, widely respected as a man of learning and the best judge of books in the Province, took an active interest in the Library and as we have seen made the selection of those to be bought in England with the first funds of the association, amounting to £45.

The first Librarian was Lewis Timothee, who attended on Wednesday afternoons and on Saturday from ten to four. In 1737 Franklin succeeded him, then William Parsons, Francis Hopkinson, Zachariah Poulson, George Campbell, J. J. Smith, and Lloyd P. Smith.

Books were allowed to be used in the library-room by "any civil gentleman," only subscribers and James Logan being allowed to take them home. These little restrictions were made by the directors who met at the house of Nicholas Scull and seem to have felt no need for supplying the feminine mind. Or may we not think that the gallant gentlemen knew that their present stock would be neither useful nor interesting to the ladies of the City?

The library had numerous donations of articles usually accepted by Museums but particularly undesirable in a library which lacked space for books. Other libraries sprang up but all merged with the parent in 1771 and two years later removed to the second floor of Carpenters' Hall, where the officers of both Armies found an occasional solace in perusing them, especially when the the library-room was used as a hospital. Not a book was lost or mutilated and all fees were scrupulously paid during this period of usurpation. In August, 1774, it was ordered "that the librarian furnish the gentlemen who are to meet in Congress in this city with such books as they may have occasion for during their sittings, taking a receipt from them" and so we have the first Congressional Library.

The corner-stone of the library's first real home was laid in 1789 in Fifth Street, corner of Library. Franklin wrote the inscription, excepting that part which refers to himself as founder, and his statue, executed in Italy and presented by William Bingham, was placed in a niche over the doorway. The early morning aspect of the figure draped in a toga was suggested by the illustrious scholar himself and it is said to have cost five hundred guineas. It still stands over the portal of the library building at Juniper and Locust Streets, erected in 1880 to accommodate the vast accumulation of books. One can easily believe that the queer recipe for the statue was a curious distortion of some simple remark of the sage.

At the close of the Revolution the library contained 5000

books and a home of its own became imperative. The modest building was the first in the United States devoted to the use of a public library. In 1792 James Logan's library was added to the collection and in 1869 the bequest of Dr. James Rush placed at the disposal of the Company the beautiful building known as the Ridgway Branch of the Philadelphia Library, where a hundred thousand volumes repose in a dignified seclusion. It is situated at Broad Street between Christian and Carpenter Streets and is a granite mausoleum of Doric Architecture, finished in 1877.

XIX: The American Philosophical Society

WE have already observed enough of Franklin's plans to note the catholicity of his mind. As the population increased and the colonies became more densely settled he saw the need for a society of wider scope than the Junto of 1727 and in 1743 issued his well-known circular entitled "A Proposal for Promoting Useful Knowledge Among the British Plantaytions in America." The proposal was well received and the next year he says they have "had several meetings to mutual satisfaction." He names the members: "Dr. Thomas Bond as Physician, Mr. John Bartram as Botanist, Mr. Thomas Godfrey as Mathematician, Mr. William Parsons as Geographer, Dr. Phineas Bond as General Natural Philosopher, Mr. Thomas Hopkinson, President, Mr. William Coleman, Treasurer, Benjamin Franklin, Secretary" and to these he adds Mr. Alexander of New York, Mr. Morris Chief Justice of the Jerseys, Mr. Howe Secretary, Mr. John Coxe of Trenton and Mr. Martyn of the same place. He expects, he says, that several other gentlemen of the City will join, as well as some from Virginia, Maryland, Carolina, and the New England Colonies. Thus was launched the first scientific society in the new world. It flourished side by side with the Junto, which in 1766 broadened out as the "American Society held at Philadelphia for promoting and propagating Useful Knowledge" and in 1769 the two were united with Franklin as President, an office which he held until his death.

By this time the Society had members in the different colonies, in the Barbadoes, Antigua, Heidelberg, Stock-

{ 167 }

holm, Edinburgh, London and Paris. Franklin advised a correspondence between the central organization and those distant members and with the Royal Society in London and in Dublin. Thus persons residing in remote districts of America were put in direct communication with the Old World Scientists in all their lines of work and to men of intelligence living far from the centres of education and enlightenment in the days of few books and periodicals, this was very important.

Governor John Penn refused to be the Patron of the Society because Franklin was the "greatest enemy" to his family, but his successor, Richard Penn, was more gracious and courteously considered the appointment an honour. The Quaker Assembly looked with favour upon the philosophers and voted a thousand pounds to assist them in planting mulberry trees for the benefit of silkworms. A care of smoky chimneys and an interest in manures, among other subjects, occupied their attention and the pressure of erudition was relieved by very good dinners. To increase the comfort and prosperity, as well as the scholarship of the province, was the laudable ambition of the Philosophical Society, and its members were drawn from every creed and walk of life.

There was Ebenezer Kinnersley, a professor in the College to whom Franklin owed much of his success in important electrical discoveries. Kinnersley contrived an amusing "magical" picture of King George II, so arranged that anyone attempting to remove his crown would receive a shock.

David Rittenhouse, the greatest American astronomer, who succeeded Franklin as President, was Vice-Provost of the University and first Director of the Mint, contributed the first purely scientific paper in the series of Transactions of the Society. In June, 1769, he made observations on the transit of Venus, only seen twice before, from the observatory erected in the State House yard. It was from this balcony that John Nixon first read the Declaration of Independence to the people. He constructed an orrery representing the revolutions of the heavenly bodies, which appeared upon the seal of the University for a time. David was not above a little practical work and Washington depended upon him to grind the glasses for his spectacles made famous by that remark of the first President as he adjusted them to his nose, "I have grown gray and blind in your service."

Brother Jabetz, Prior of the Ephrata Cloister, was wont to walk eighty miles, it is said, to attend the meetings, and his tall spare figure in flowing robe, girt by a hempen cord, added a charming element of picturesqueness; as well as a flavour of asceticism which seemed just what the philosophers wanted.

Jefferson was the third President and was an early member, combining with Franklin the ideal and the practical. While abroad he disputed the arguments of the learned Count de Buffon, another member, on the degeneracy of American animals and finally sent him the bones, skins and horns of an enormous New Hampshire moose. Franklin answered a similar argument on the degeneracy of American men by making all the Americans at the table and all the Frenchmen stand up. The Americans happened to be fine physical specimens and they towered above the little Gauls. Jefferson got a gold medal from France for designing a plow almost as good in its way as Franklin's model stove. He calculated the number of bushels per acre at Monticello. He was also the architect of his beautiful home and the stately buildings of the University of Virginia nearby. During the bitter factional strife of Jefferson's administration he was always ready to neglect politics for science, the one, as he said, being his duty, the other his passion. Indeed he filled one of the rooms of the White House with bones and fossils and frequently consulted Dr. Caspar Wistar about his scientific investigations and discoveries. Proud of his interest in these things Jefferson was not careful to conceal his joy in them. Indeed his propensity became a feature of the criticism heaped upon him as can be imagined from Bryant's lines in the Embargo:

"Go, wretch, resign the Presidential chair;
Disclose thy secret measures, foul or fair;
Go, search with curious eyes for horned frogs,
'Mid the wild wastes of Louisiannian bogs,
Or where the Ohio rolls its turbid stream
Dig for huge bones, thy glory and thy theme."

The gala days of the philosophers were the annual dinners and the entertainments to distinguished visitors where many lively raconteurs and bon vivants were gathered about the board. Here were the Abbe Correa de Serra, Judge Richard Peters, Peter Stephen Duponceau, Dr. Caspar Wistar, John Vaughan, Robert Walsh, George Ord, William Strickland, Dr. Nathaniel Chapman and Nicholas Biddle.

Perhaps the most unusual of Richard Peter's many attainments was his keen wit and brilliant conversation. He used to follow the assizes or circuits of the courts in all the surrounding counties and always relieved the tedium of the legal atmosphere by his humorous sallies. When the Pennsylvania delegation went to the conference with the Indians at Fort Stanwix, in New York State, Peters accompanied them, and, during the negotiations, so insinuated himself into the good graces of the Indian chiefs that they proposed to adopt him into their tribe. Their offer was accepted and Peters was introduced to his adopted relatives

Grave of Benjamin Franklin
Christ Church Burial Ground
❖ Fifth and Arch Streets ❖

From The Autobiography of Benjamin Franklin, published by Ginn and Company

by the name "Tegohtias," bestowed in allusion to his amusing talkativeness.

In 1771 he became Register of the Admiralty, retaining this post until the Revolution broke out. Although this association might have been expected to attach him to the King's interests, he did not hesitate to espouse the cause of American rights and organized a company in the neighborhood of his home, filling the post of captain. His administrative and executive abilities were so well known, however, that he was soon summoned to act as Secretary of the Board of War and thus became on June 13, 1776, the first Secretary of War of the new republic. Everyone who has read the record of that memorable time can imagine the difficult and trying position in which he was placed and it was undoubtedly due to his indomitable energy and unceasing labours that Washington's Army had what provisions and ammunition they got. Some notion of the army's frequent grievous state and of the tremendous burden Peters bore on his shoulders during all the anxious years of strife may be gained from one of his letters:

"I was Commissioner of War in 1779. General Washington wrote to me that all his powder was wet and that he was entirely without lead or balls, so that, should the enemy approach, he must retreat. When I received this letter I was going to a grand gala at the Spanish Ambassador's, who lived in Mr. Chew's fine house in South Third Street. The spacious gardens were superbly decorated with variegated lamps, the edifice itself was a blaze of lights, the show was splendid, but my feelings were far from being in harmony with all this brilliancy. I met at this party my friend, Robert Morris, who soon discovered the state of my mind. 'You are not yourself tonight, Peters, what is the matter?' asked Morris. Notwithstanding my unlimited confidence in that great patriot, it was some time before I could prevail upon myself to disclose the cause of my depression, but at length I ventured to give him a hint of my inability to answer the pressing calls of the Commander-in-Chief. 'The army is without lead and I know not where to get an ounce to supply it; the General must retreat for want of ammunition.' 'Well, let him retreat,' replied the high and liberal-minded Morris; 'but cheer up; there are in the Holker Privateer, just arrived, ninety tons of lead, one-half of which is mine and at your service, the residue you can get by applying to Blair McClenachan and Holker, both of whom are in the house with us.' I accepted the offer of Mr. Morris."

Peters then goes on to relate how he approached Mc-Clenachan and Holker, both of whom, however, demurred because of the large sums already owing them. Thereupon Morris came forward, assumed the whole responsibility, the lead was delivered and so the army for the nonce had a supply of bullets.

After the surrender of Cornwallis, Mr. Peters resigned his post and received the thanks of Congress for his "long and faithful services." He was thereupon elected to Congress and had his share in the business of ending the war and aranging the longed-for peace. He was a member of the Assembly in 1787 and its Speaker from 1788 to 1790. One day during this time a member tripped on the carpet and fell flat. This was followed by laughter on the part of the House but Judge Peters with great gravity called, "Order, order, gentlemen! Do you not see that a member is on the floor!"

When Washington was on his way to New York for his first inauguration as President of the Uinted States, Peters and General Thomas Mifflin, the Speaker of the State Senate, were the representatives of Pennsylvania who met him as he entered the state.

The University made him a trustee in 1789 and in 1791 he became the Speaker of the State Senate. Declining the Comptrollership of the United States Treasury he was commissioned Judge of the Federal Court of Pennsylvania in 1792 and held the office until his death.

Judge Peters was one of the founders of the Philadelphia Society for Promoting Agriculture, the first of its kind in America, and held the presidency of it until his death. From the farm at Belmont came many model things. His specialty was dairying and the Belmont butter went to market put up in one-pound packages.

Unfortunately for the judge, his one-pound weight, according to the new assize of weights and measures, was too light, and the whole consignment was seized by the inspector and confiscated for the benefit of the poor. The judge then sent his old weight to be examined and corrected by the standard and when it was returned the letters "C. P." (for Commonwealth of Pennsylvania) were stamped upon it. The servant who brought it back carried it at once to the Judge, who was at dinner with a party of friends. Taking it, he carefully inspected it and looking gravely at his wife, said, as he held it up for her to see, "My dear, they have at last found us out. Here is the old weight come back with C. P. stamped in it which can stand for nothing in the world but Cheating Peters."

Although the surroundings of Belmont were unusually beautiful the fields often presented a shabby appearance, for the judge was so occupied with public affairs and with agricultural experiments that he had little time to devote to the practical management of his farm. One day a German, who had often read the judge's agricultural reports, made a pilgrimage to Belmont. He found the gate without hinges, fences dilapidated, and the crops not equal to his own. When the judge came out to speak to him, the rustic bluntly expressed his disappointment at the appearance of the place. "How can you expect me," said the judge, "to attend to all these things when my time is so taken up in telling others how to farm?" The old German was disgusted and drove away without asking any more questions.

As may be imagined, Belmont was the scene of lavish and constant hospitality and while Philadelphia was the seat of the Federal government the chief statesmen, diplomats and foreign notables were frequent guests there.

The judge dearly loved to surround himself with his friends, and his political prominence, his intellectual brilliance, and his genial personality drew a large coterie about him. Washington and Lafayette were on terms of great intimacy with him, and the former, "whenever a morning of leisure permitted," was in the habit of driving to Belmont and there, free for a time from the cares of state, would enjoy his host's vivacious flow of conversation, walking for hours with him in the beautiful gardens between "clipped hedges of pyramids, obelisks and balls" of evergreen and spruce, or beneath the shade of ancient trees.

Judge Peters's many stories and bon mots were wholesome and without the least trace of ill-humour or sharpness. On one occasion while attending a dinner of the Schuylkill Fishing Company he was seated beside the president, Governor Wharton. Toward the end of the dinner more wine was required and the Governor called a serving-man named John to fetch it. Said the judge, "If you want more wine you should call for the demi-John," adding that he himself "drank like a fish" from his goblet of water.

To advertise one of his suburban tracts of lands he posted a plan of the locality on a signboard and carefully covered it with glass, saying that if he left it exposed "every hunter who comes along will riddle it with shot and then everybody will see through my plan." The project was not successful and one of his friends advised him to have it officially laid out. "All right," said Peters, "it's time to lay it out. It's been dead long enough." Once when going to court, a very fat and a very thin man stood at the entrance of a door into which his honor wished to pass. He stopped for a moment for them to make way, but perceiving they were not inclined to move, he pushed on between them, exclaiming, "Here I go then, through thick and thin."

As he grew older his nose and chin approached each other and a friend observed that they would soon be at logger-heads. "Very likely," the judge replied, "for hard words often pass between them."

Judge Peters was one of the courtliest of men and retained the ancient mode of dress long after others had abandoned it. To his dying day he wore knee-breeches and silver buckles on his shoes, always powdered his hair and dressed it in a queue. He died August 22, 1828.

A famous story of Ord's was of a fellow member, Dr. Abercrombie, rector of Christ Church and St. Peter's, who went to Shrewsbury, New Jersey, dined on good old Madeira and then preached from the text, "And the barbarous people showed us no little kindness."

Delightful memories there are of John Vaughan's celebrated breakfasts, Dr. Wistar's Sunday evening parties, and Henry C. Carey's Sunday afternoon vespers participated in by Dr. Benjamin Rush, Chief Justice Tilghman, Jared Ingersoll, Dr. Robert Patterson, Jonathan Williams, John Fitch, Rev. William Smith, Dr. Barton, Charles Wilson Peale, Charles Lucien Bonaparte, Noah Webster, Josiah Quincy, Washington Irving, Elisha Kent Kane,

Count de Lesseps, Mr. Gladstone, Oliver Wendell Holmes, George Bancroft, James Russell Lowell, Louis Agassiz and Joseph Leidy.

Interrupted by the Revolutionary War, the members reassembled on the 5th of March, 1779, and a year later were granted their first charter, and a lot of ground adjoining the State House on which to build a hall. In 1789 this Hall was completed and stands to-day filled with priceless relics. One of the most curious of these is a strange instrument, called a Horologium or Planescope, which Dr. Christopher Witt gave to the society in 1767. Dr. Witt was the last surviving member of the Majestic Brotherhood of the Wissahickon and the instrument came to him in 1708 from Kelpius, the hermit who lived in a cave on the banks of that stream near the present Rittenhouse Street. It is supposed to have belonged to Magister Zimmerman, who formed in Germany the Order of the Wissahickon and cast the horoscope of the new undertaking before the brothers sailed. It was used generally for social and business affairs in early Philadelphia and the pastor of Old Swedes' Church, previous to the laying of the corner-stone, requested a noted mystic named Seelig, residing on the Wissahickon, to cast a horoscope and find a propitious day for the commencement of the building. The occult brotherhood were present in a body at the laying of the foundation stone in the fall of 1698 and took part in the ceremony by furnishing the instrumental music and intoning the Psalms and responses. Ancient volumes handled by men whose names are household words, paintings, and manuscripts comprising the greater part of the Franklin papers, and funds for various useful purposes are in the Society's care. Its general meetings held annually in the spring bring together important persons from at home and abroad, while its regular fortnightly meetings add papers and discussions of great value.   They are held on Friday evenings as in the old Junto days.

The American Philosophical Society has given the impulse to historical societies, scientific schools, academies of natural science and kindred institutions in other cities and is still inspired by the broad spirit and diligent industry of its founders.

XX: The Pennsylvania Hospital

BENJAMIN FRANKLIN in his "Brief Account of the Pennsylvania Hospital," published in 1754, tells us of the concern that was felt in the City about the end of the year 1750 on account of the want of shelter and care for sick and distempered strangers too poor to pay for expensive lodging, nurses and physicians. In his autobiography he tells how his friend, Dr. Thomas Bond, conceived the idea of establishing a hospital and started out to obtain subscriptions for it. Dr. Bond found it slow work and those solicited wanted to know if it had Franklin's approval before they would give. Always willing to aid any good public enterprise, Franklin accordingly entered heartily into the project, and as was his custom, prepared the people's minds for it by writing in the newspapers. Subscriptions began to come in faster and the Assembly was appealed to with success. The old fellow says he does not remember any of his political manoeuvers the success of which gave him more pleasure or for which he "more easily excused myself for having made use of some cunning." To obviate the criticism of physicians' fees dissipating the funds, Doctors Thomas Bond, Lloyd Zachary and Phineas Bond offered their services without pay and the charter was granted May 11, 1751.

The managers first chosen were Joshua Crosby, Benjamin Franklin, Thomas Bond, Samuel Hazard, Richard Peters, Israel Pemberton, Jr., Samuel Rhodes, Hugh Roberts, Joseph Morris, John Smith, Even Morgan, Charles Morris and the treasurer, John Reynell.

Joshua Crosby was the first President of the Board of Managers, and Benjamin Franklin was its first clerk. The

house of the lately deceased John Kinsey, on the south side
of High Street below Seventh, was rented and on February
6, 1752, an advertisement inserted in the *Pennsylvania
Gazette* stating that the hospital was prepared to receive
patients. Almost all of the money came from the Quakers,
who kept the hospital under their control, it being a party
stronghold, as the College was to the Episcopal and Proprietary party. The managers were fined for absence and
lateness, the Towne Clock or the watch of the oldest person
present being the standard to determine the time. Doctors Graeme, Cadwalader, Moore and Redman were appointed to consult with the original three in extraordinary
cases. Several spining wheels, two pairs of cards, wool and
flax were secured to furnish light labour for the patients.

The eloquent Whitefield sent the receipts of a persuasive
sermon, England sent much material aid and Parliament
gave all the unclaimed funds of the Pennsylvania Land Company, amounting to £13,000. So after some controversy
the square between Spruce and Pine and Eighth and Ninth
Streets was obtained and the dignified building we all know
was erected after the plans of Samuel Rhodes. On its
ancient corner-stone is deeply cut this inscription:

> "In the year of Christ, MDCCLV,
>   George the second happily reigning,
>   (For he sought the happiness of his people)
>   Philadelphia flourishing,
>   (For its inhabitants were public-spirited)
>   This Building
>   By the bounty of the Government,
>   And of many private persons,
>   was piously founded
>   For the relief of the sick and the miserable
>   May the God of Mercies
>   bless the undertaking."

Franklin succeeded Crosby as president in 1756 and drew up the very sensible rules for the direction of the hospital.

Hugh Roberts planted the ample lawn with two rows of beautiful buttonwood trees, and with a scion of the famous Treaty Elm, and Franklin characteristically had tin boxes, lettered in gold "Charity for the Hospital," placed to receive the donations of friends and visitors. Gifts from prominent citizens evidenced the popularity and usefulness of the institution which was uninterrupted until the Revolution and its attendant confusion of the public service well-nigh ruined it. The diligent and resolute Quaker managers, however, averted the catastrophe, although it was years before it regained its old degree of usefulness.

The First Troop of Philadelphia City Cavalry gave to the Hospital the entire sum received for its services during the Revolutionary War and the Maternity Ward for poor married women was built and endowed with this money. John Penn, grandson of the Founder, in 1804 presented the leaden statue of his illustrious ancestor, which had originally stood in Wycombe Park, Bucks, England, where it was greatly admired by Franklin. In 1817 Benjamin West, then president of the Royal Academy in London, sent a replica of his famous painting of "Christ Healing the Sick," from which the adroit managers of the Hospital realized $20,000 from the eager crowds who thronged to see it.

The minutes of the managers are interesting records of patients and methods. Indian fighters and many soldiers wounded in the struggle of England and France for supremacy in America were among the early patients in this first hospital of the Colonies. During the British occupation of the City the military authorities took possession and filled it with their sick and wounded. When they left in June, 1778, they carried off the bedding, instruments and medicines without giving the least compensation.

The Pennsylvania Hospital·
· · Founded, 1751, by Benjamin Franklin

A curious source of income in the days when insane persons were thought incurable was derived from a charge of fourpence made for the permission of visitors to walk through the hospital and "see the crazy people." As these unfortunates increased it was found necessary to move them to a separate and much larger accommodation, so in 1841 the department for the insane known as "Kirkbride's" was built in West Philadelphia. This popular name was derived from the personality of the first superintendent, Dr. Thomas Kirkbride, who filled the position with marked success until his death in 1883. Dr. Benjamin Rush was especially active in studying the insane cases and caring for them.

In 1762, Dr. John Fothergill, the Quaker physician of London, presented the hospital with a splendid collection of anatomical casts and drawings and these were made the basis of lectures by Dr. William Shippen, Jr., once a fortnight at a dollar apiece. In 1766 Dr. Thomas Bond began clinical lectures. The anatomist of those days pursued his investigations at the risk of his life and his abode was looked upon as the haunts of body-snatchers and the favourite abiding place of ghosts. The dead bodies were brought there, it was said, and "their flesh was boiled and their bones burned down for the use of the faculty." Boys would advance as far as they dared and retreat suddenly, singing:

"The body-snatchers! They have come,
     And made a snatch at me;
It's very hard them kind of men
     Won't let a body be!

Don't go to weep upon my grave,
     And think that there I'll be;
They haven't left an atom there
     Of my anatomy!"

-⟨181⟩-

The Hospital was, as has been said, the rallying point of the Quaker or Assembly party. Most of the distinguished and able members of the Society of Friends have been interested in it down to the present time and its service is eagerly sought by every graduating medical student of note at the University. The beautiful old buildings in the midst of their verdure are next to the State House group one of the most charming in the United States.

XXI: Fire Protection

ABOUT 1735 Franklin wrote a letter, which was published and attracted considerable attention. He says:

"In the first place, as an ounce of prevention is worth a pound of cure, I would advise how they suffer living brandsends or coals in a full shovel to be carried out of one room into another or up or down stairs, unless in a warming-pan and shut; for scraps of fire may fall into chinks and make no appearance until midnight; when your stairs being in flames, you may be forced (as I once was) to leap out of your windows and hazard your necks to avoid being over-roasted."

He then goes on to advise the passage of a law, forbidding "too shallow hearths" and the detestable Practice of "Putting Wooden Mouldings on each side of the Fire Place," and says:

"If chimneys were more frequently and more carefully clean'd, some fires might thereby be prevented. I have known foul chimneys to burn most furiously a few days after they are swept; people, in confidence that they are clean, making large fires. Everybody among us is allow'd to sweep chimneys that please to undertake that business; and if a chimney fires thro' fault of the sweeper, the owner pays the fine and the sweeper goes free. This thing is not right. Those who undertake the sweepings of chimneys and employ servants for that purpose, ought to be licensed by the Mayor; and if any chimney fires and flames out 15 days after sweeping, the fine should be paid by the sweeper; for it is his fault. We have at present got engines enough in the town, but I question whether, in many parts of the

-{ 183 }-

town, water enough can be had to keep them going for half an hour together. It seems to me some publick pumps are wanting; but that I submit to better judgments."

Subsequently Franklin refers to this paper as being "spoken of as a useful piece" and one result of it seems to have been the founding of the Union Fire Company, in 1736, by Franklin and four of his friends. The Union Fire Company was an association for mutual assistance. Each member agreed to furnish, at his own expense, six leather buckets and two stout linen bags, each marked with his name and the name of the Company, which he was to bring to every fire. The buckets were for carrying water to extinguish the flames, and the bags were to receive and hold property which was in danger, to save it from risk of theft. The members pledged themselves to repair to any place in danger upon an alarm of fire, with their apparatus. Some were to superintend the use of the water, others were to stand at the doors of houses in danger, and to protect the property from theft. On an alarm of fire at night, it was agreed that lights should be placed in the windows of members near the fire "in order to prevent confusion, and to enable their friends to give them more speedy and effectual assistance." The number of members was limited to thirty. Eight meetings were held annually. At each meeting there was a supper costing three shillings. Members who came late were fined one shilling. Upon this plan, with slight variations, all the fire companies in Philadelphia were conducted until long after the Revolutionary War.

Franklin's Company, the Union, had a long and useful career. It was the pioneer and existed for over eighty-four years.

Franklin in his Autobiography tells of soliciting contributions from the peace-loving Quakers ostensibly for "a fire engine" when a "great gun" was to be purchased for the protection of the City from the enemy, as "a great gun is certainly a fire engine," said he.

At the beginning of the 18th Century, the problem of fires had become of some moment. There were about seven hundred dwelling houses in Philadelphia; fires were not numerous but they were unnecessarily destructive, and the only appliances for extinguishing them were the bucket, the ladder, and the hook, the latter being used for pulling down buildings. As early as 1719 an English fire engine was purchased for £50. The cost of the fire apparatus was provided for by a series of fines, levied for various offenses, and among them was one for 12d. for presuming to smoke tobacco in the streets of Philadelphia, either by day or night.

It was quite natural, therefore, that the thoughts of Franklin and other prominent men should have turned to the subject of Fire Insurance, but it was not until February 18, 1752, that the following notice appeared in the *Pennsylvania Gazette:*

"All persons inclined to subscribe to the articles of insurance of houses from fire, in or near this City, are desired to appear at the Court-house, where attendance will be given, to take in their subscriptions, every seventh day of the week, in the afternoon, until the 13th of April next, being the day appointed by the said articles for electing twelve directors and a treasurer."

Accordingly, on April 13, 1752, the subscribers convened at the Court House and organized The Philadelphia Contributionship for the Insurance of Houses from Loss by Fire.

The Lieutenant Governor of the Province, James Hamilton, was the first who subscribed, and the first private name was that of Benjamin Franklin. Twelve Directors were elected: Benjamin Franklin, William Coleman, Philip Syng (who was also an original member with Franklin, of the Union Fire Company), Samuel Rhodes, Hugh Roberts, Israel Pemberton, Jr., John Mifflin, Joseph Norris, Joseph Fox, Jonathan Zane, William Griffitts and Amos Strettell.

John Smith was made Treasurer and Joseph Saunders Clerk.

The first advertisement after the company had begun business appeared in the *Pennsylvania Gazette* of June 11, 1752, as follows:

"Notice is hereby given, That the Insurance Office, for shipping and houses, is kept by Joseph Saunders, at his house, where Israel Pemberton, Senior, lately lived, near the Queen's Head, in Water Street."

The offices of the Contributionship was for many years afterwards at No. 99 High Street (now No. 239 Market Street) where Caleb Carmalt, the Clerk for forty-two years, lived.

In 1818 the office was No. 25 (now No. 109) Dock Street, and in 1835 No. 96 (now No. 212) South Fourth Street was purchased, and the present office building erected thereon, where until the advent of safe deposit companies the Secretary and Treasurer was required to live as custodian of the securities.

The plan of the company was that of mutual assurance and the members were called contributors. Policies were issued for a term of seven years, upon payment of a deposit, the interest of which, during the continuance of the policy, belonged to the company. At the first meeting of the Directors held May 11, 1752, "a seal for the company was ordered, being four hands united," the badge of mark of which was placed on every property which was insured.

The minutes of May 23, 1752, show that "Benjamin

Franklin is desired to get a sufficient number of policies printed," and those of December 24, 1753, that Benjamin Franklin attended to the engrossing of the insurance articles and also that he "do publish an advertisement in the *Gazette*" relative to the risk of storing gunpowder and breaming of ships, which was cleaning their bottoms by burning off the barnacles.

Owing probably to his numerous absences from this City on public matters, Franklin did not serve as a Director after 1754, but he retained his active interest in the company, and in 1763 he insured another house, in addition to those insured by Policies Nos. 19 and 20, taken out in 1752. In 1767 he insured his new house "where his family dwells" for £500, by Policy No. 1148. Later he wrote from abroad several letters relative to fireproof construction, to Samuel Rhodes, who for eleven years had continued as Director.

As has before been said, at first every policy in The Philadelphia Contributionship was for a term of seven years. A certain deposit was made at the beginning of the term, a policy issued and an account opened with each contributor. His deposit was charged its proportion of the expenses and losses, and credited with any interest which might have been earned. If during the seven years the deposit, owing to losses, was used up, another deposit was made. At the expiration of the seven years, the contributor might withdraw so much of his deposit as remained, or renew his insurance.

In 1763 a change was unanimously voted by the contributors, and it was agreed that thereafter the interest on the deposits should be carried to a common account and out of it the losses should be paid, and the deposit money should not be drawn upon until the interest was exhausted; the contributor, however, not to be liable beyond his deposit money.

This method has been continued to this day and with such marked success, that the contributors in 1894–95 agreed that the funds had accumulated sufficiently to warrant paying dividends out of the yearly net income therefrom. The company was incorporated in 1768; its policies continued to be seven-year policies until 1810, when they were made and have ever since continued to be perpetual.

The "Hand-in-Hand," as "The Philadelphia Contributionship" is familiary known, is a purely mutual company, although its members are not liable for assessment. It has no stockholders, consequently the only interest to be considered is that of the policyholders. After one hundred and fifty-four years this company, of which Franklin was the first Director, is still in business for the public good, and for all these years it has never ceased to fulfill its mission of giving indemnity against loss by fire, and has ever continued to spread its usefulness, and stands to-day not only the oldest Fire Insurance Company in America, but also one of the strongest active Fire Insurance Companies in the World.

The prevention of fires in the early days was not easy and many conceived that there was a grave jeopardy in the overhanging branches of shade trees which might catch fire from a blazing chimney and spread it farther in winter, and in both summer and winter must interfere with the application of water in the endeavour to extinguish the fire. The apprehensive directors of the Contributionship called a meeting of the subscribers of that organization in April, 1781, to consider the propriety of "Ensuring or Re-insuring Houses having Trees planted before them in the Street." The owners of shade trees being in a minority at this meeting, it was resolved that "no Houses having a Tree or Trees planted before them shall be Insured or Re-insured," and, "that if any Person in future having a House Insured shall plant a Tree or Trees before it in the street, if not removed in three months from the time of planting, he shall forfeit the benefit of Insurance." Legislation followed against the objectionable use of trees, in 1782 only to be repealed a few months later, upon the urgent solicitation of tree lovers. Indignant owners of the debarred properties immediately set about organizing a rival insurance company so that they might have the trees which were "agreeable and convenient to them." The new company sprang into existence in 1784 and the badge or house mark was naturally a leaden tree on a shield shaped board. Thus was born The Mutual Assurance Company for Insuring Houses from Loss by Fire, more frequently called the "Green Tree." The subscription papers were lodged with William Craig in Second Street and John Philips at the corner of Front and Pine. The office was opened by John Jennings, Clerk, at his house in Quarry Street between Moravian Alley and Third Street and notice was given that Matthew Clarkson, in Front between Market and Arch Streets, "will also receive applications" for insurance.

When the original deed of settlement was drawn up at the meeting in September, 1784, trees were allowed by the policy, under a charge of 17 to 20 shillings, with a proviso that they should be kept trimmed down to the eaves of the house, and if any tree was planted and not reported within a year, the policy should be declared void.

The charter was obtained February 27, 1786. The incorporators named were Matthew Clarkson, William Craig, Benjamin Wynkoop, John Phillips, John Clement Stocker, Thomas Franklin, Isaac Jones, John Harrison, Joseph Sims, Philip Wager, James Cooper, Presley Blackiston and John Wharton. These were also named as trustees of the company until the annual meeting in the following October.

The act of incorporation also created the office of treasurer, and named George Emlen as the incumbent of that office, directing, at the same time, that he should remain in office until the annual meeting of the insurers on the first Monday of the October following.

The office of president does not appear for many years after the commencement of business by the company. Those who were occasionally called president received this title only by virtue of being the presiding officer at the meetings of the board of trustees. The title of president was not recognized in the by-laws. The senior member of the Board usually presided.

In the old records of the company the following references to the president are mentioned: "January 13, 1810, the death was announced of the late President, Thomas Ewing, May 13, 1811, William Puyntell, president. October 14, 1812, James Read, president, and occasionally chairman. November 10, 1813, letter from James Read, Esq., resigning his seat as president of the board." October 5, 1814, Robert Wharton, president to October 7, 1829; 1830, Daniel Smith; 1834, James C. Fisher; 1841, Richard Willing; 1855, Thomas Biddle; 1857, George Cadwalader; 1879, Samuel Welsh; 1890, John Lambert; 1901, S. Weir Mitchell; 1906, J. Dickinson Sergeant; 1909, Henry W. Biddle.

The list of the company's treasurers is as follows: 1786–96, George Emlen; 1796–1801, Joseph Sims; 1801–02, William Poyntell; 1802–03, Paul Beck; 1803–05, William Poyntell; 1805–29, John B. Palmer; 1829–33, John Clement Stocker; 1833–56, Lawrence Lewis; 1856–81, David Lewis; and 1881 up until the present time, Clifford Lewis.

In the old days meetings were held in the Court House, City Hall, Indian King, and the house of Henry Knorr, on the Schuylkill, until the purchase of an office, in 1812, at

No. 54 Walnut Street. The company continued to meet here until 1856, when it purchased the building No. 526 Walnut Street, where it retained its offices till the occupancy of its present buildings, Nos. 238–240 South Fourth Street, on November 1, 1912.

It is related that at the time of the death of President Washington, the news reached the board of trustees while at their monthly dinner. Since that period the memory of the first President of the United States has always been revered by a standing toast upon these occasions.

The method of effecting insurance in the company has always been quite simple. A deposit is paid at the time the policy is issued, the property continuing to be insured as long as the deposit remains with the company. In the event of a policyholder wishing to discontinue his insurance, the amount of the deposit is returned to him on demand, less 5 per cent., and the policy cancelled.

There have never been any stockholders in the concern, and the interest received from deposits invested created a fund out of which to pay the losses and expenses.

Nearly every Philadelphian is familiar with the metal badges of the Fire Insurance Companies which appear high up on the front walls of the older houses, but few realize the significance which these fire-plates—or, more properly, fire-marks—bore in the early days of fire insurance.

With the modern fire department trained to respond quickly to all fires, without question as to whether the building menaced is insured or not, it is difficult for us to conceive of a fire company answering the alarm and, discovering that the building did not bear the mark of their own insurance company, quietly going home and to bed, leaving the fire to be put out by the owner with what assistance he might get from his neighbors. Yet such was the practice of the Fire Brigades of the early days. Each insurance company maintained its own corps of men trained to extinguish fires, and their activities were strictly confined to buildings insured in their own company. Indeed, one English company made it a rigid rule that its firemen were not to render assistance at any burning building which did not bear its own distinctive mark. The mark therefore was very useful. Many insurance policies were not complete until it had been affixed to the house.

With the advent of the paid Fire Department—or even, before, when the various volunteer fire companies agreed to overlook selfishly material considerations and in accordance with truly humane principles offer their assistance at every fire—the fire-mark lost its former usefulness and became merely a decorative emblem of the company. Hence, the distinction between the fire-mark and the fire-plate, the former being useful and the latter decorative.

The use of the fire-mark seems to have originated in London, and was almost coincident with the founding of the system of fire indemnity. It was in 1667, immediately after the great fire which devastated that metropolis, that Dr. Nicholas Barbon established the first office for the transaction of fire insurance. In 1680 his business was taken over by a company called the Fire Office. This company maintained a fire brigade, the first of the organized and trained volunteer companies. It is at this time that the use of fire-marks began. They were made principally of lead, though later they seem to have been of tin, copper and cast-iron. The numbers of the policies for which they were issued were either stamped, cut-out or painted on the bottom. The marks were then painted, often in red and gold, making a very brilliant appearance. Most companies would not issue a policy for over £1500 sterling; hence it frequently happened that a building having several of these gay marks affixed, would present to the world a decorative effect truly Oriental and bizarre. A rhyme published in 1816, referring to a certain English lord, aptly says:

"For not e'en the Regent himself has endured
(Though I've seen him with badges and orders all shine
Till he looks like a house that was over insured)—"

On this side of the water the use of fire-marks began with the establishment of fire indemnity. The Philadelphia Contributionship for the Insurance of Houses from Loss by Fire was fashioned after the Amicable Contributionship of London. Its mark of four leaden hands, clasped and crossed, and mounted on a wooden shield, was a modification of the two clasped hands of the London Company, and hence was known as the "Hand-in-Hand" Insurance Society. That they early turned their thoughts to the matter of a proper fire-mark is shown by the fact that at the meeting of May 20, 1752, Hugh Roberts, one of the directors, was directed "to treat with John Stow about making the marks for Houses Insured," and on July 22, 1752, "An Order was drawn on the Treasurer to pay John Stow for One Hundred Marks, the Sum of Twelve pounds, ten Shillings." It would appear, therefore, that the use of fire-marks began in this country in 1752.

The assured was charged seven shillings, sixpence—or about a dollar and eighty-seven cents—for policy, survey and marks. Lest it be thought that the Contributionship derived an extraordinary profit from this charge, it must be said that the marks cost two shillings, sixpence apiece; the same sum was paid the surveyor for each survey, leaving only about sixty-two cents to cover the cost of the policy, affixing the mark, and each policy's proportionate share of office expenses.

The usefulness of the fire-mark in those early days is clearly shown by a significant extract from the minutes of the meeting of October 3, 1755, wherein it is related that the directors "proceeded to View the House of Edward Shippen in Walnut Street No. 103, that was damaged by means of a Fire which happen'd at the House of William Hodge, situate in that Neighbourhood; Which House of E. Shippen having no badge put up. The Directors observing that much of the damage was done thro' Indiscretion, which they think might have been prevented had it appear'd by the Badge being placed up to Notify that the House was so immediately under their Care; to prevent the like Mischief for the Future; It is now Ordered that the Clerk shall go round and Examine who have not yet put up their Badges; and inform those that they are requested to fix them immediately, as the Major part of the Contributors have done, or pay Nathaniel Goforth & William Rakestraw, who is appointed for that service."

Upon the cancellation of the insurance on a building an allowance of two shillings, sixpence was made for the return of the mark, thereby reducing the original cost of the policy. This original cost remained seven shillings, sixpence until the Revolution, when because of the great demand for bullets, the clerk was "ordered to receive seventeen shillings Earnest for each policy after this date, the Price of Lead being so much increased as to make this necessary."

Franklin refers in his Autobiography to the origin of the first volunteer fire company, which has already been mentioned, and says:

"The utility of this institution soon appeared; and many more desiring to be admitted than we thought convenient for one company, they were asked to form another, which was accordingly done, and this went on, one new Company after another being formed, till they became so numerous as to include most of the inhabitants who were men of property."

Among the early companies was the Queen Charlotte, all of whose members were from the German Lutheran Church; the Northern Liberty Fire Company, the Diligence and the Hand-in-Hand, organized in 1741. Among the incorporators of the last were Benjamin Franklin, Benjamin Rush, Robert Morris and John Clymer.

The Hand-in-Hand claimed to have a continuous existence from 1741 to 1870, but there has been some dispute as to whether its existence was continuous, and an important law case grew out of this controversy, with much taking of testimony, in 1858, the issue being whether the Hand-in-Hand or the Hibernia was entitled to march first in the Firemen's Parade.

The Hibernia, the nationality of whose founders cannot be in doubt, was formed in 1852. Upon its coat-of-arms was appropriately placed the motto, "To assist the suffering and protect the weak."

From the By-Laws and Minutes of the Hibernia, one learns something of the methods of fire fighting in those days. Each member had to provide two leather buckets, two bags and one large wicker basket with two handles. The bags and baskets were used to save articles of property, and the use of the buckets is obvious. This personal fire apparatus was to be kept by the member in his hall, immediately by the front door. At an alarm of fire, given on a great gong by the State House, each member was to put candles in the windows of his own home, so that his fellow-firemen would know which house should first receive attention, for under the constitution of the Hibernia it was only "when none of our own houses, goods and effects are in danger." If an alarm sounded at night, a member would hurry to his front door, put his buckets, bags and baskets into the street where others on the way to the fire might pick them up and take them along promptly. He would then hastily dress and rush to the scene.

Even prior to the formation of the Union Fire Company, there was in Philadelphia a sort of fire-engine which had been imported from England by a public-spirited citizen. The Hibernia imported another engine in 1758. A bucket line would form from a pump neighbouring to the fire, or from the Delaware River, and the buckets would be filled, passed from hand to hand along the line, and poured into the little hand engine. Water was precious, so the gutters would be dammed up to catch any that ran back from the fire, and this would again be bailed into the engine. In 1791, the Union procured 80 feet of hemp hose, which was kept in salt pickle to preserve it. This kind of hose did not work well, but constantly leaked. In 1803 someone invented a leather hose of spiral strips of leather riveted together, sold at 80 cents a foot; and 300 feet were purchased by the Hibernia.

In 1781 Franklin had cause to write in the Autobiography:

"so that I question whether there is a city in the world better provided with the means of putting a stop to beginning conflagrations; and in fact, since these institutions, the city has never lost by fire more than one or two houses at a time, and the flames have often been extinguished before the house in which they began has been half consumed."

In 1821 there were 35 fire companies in active service in Philadelphia. By 1838 there were 44, and these 44 companies incorporated the Fire Association of Philadelphia. This Association was authorized by its charter to issue policies of fire insurance and the profits and dividends of the business were distributed among the fire companies. Thus did Quaker thrift make out of virtue more than its own reward. In 1856, the volunteer companies, then numbering 78, with an active membership of 2100, and a total membership of 7500, were confederated to form the Fire Department of Philadelphia. In the same year the first steam fire engine was bought, but of it the Chief of the Department said: "So far as regards extinguishment, it is an utterly worthless article." Two years later the Hibernia bought an improved steam engine; it cost $4500 and was such a novelty that it was exhibited and received a great ovation in New York, Brooklyn, Boston, Newark and Charleston. When Fortress Monroe was being attacked in 1862, President Lincoln called upon the Hibernia for eight volunteers and the use of their steam engine to protect that important fortress. In 1870 a paid Fire Department superseded the volunteer system, for reasons obvious from the following records:

> 1814, Jan. 29—Gin at the fire, 65 cents.
> 1814, May 1—Gin at the fire, $1.00
> 1814, Oct. 25—Quart of gin at the fire, 34 cents.
> 1815, Dec. 13—One-half gallon of gin at the fire, 62½ cents.

The American Hose Company, as did all the companies, had a schedule of fines for offenses. "For being visibly intoxicated while wearing the equipment or badge of the company—for the first offense, $5.00; for the second offense, $10.00; for the third offense, expulsion." The constitution of that company provided "Spirituous liquors shall not be admitted into the house on any occasion." There was a fine of $2.00 imposed upon any member who "aids or encourages the carriage in a trial of speed with that of any other company returning from a fire or false alarm." In the rules established by the Fire Department in 1855, there is record evidence of another prevalent fault: "Any company who shall be guilty of rioting or fighting in the public streets, shall pay a fine for the first offense, $25.00; for the second offense, $35.00; and for the third offense, $50.00." Evidently firemen were favoured, if not in the eyes of the law, at least in its administration, for the report of the Chief Engineer of the Department in 1856 recommends a strict enforcement of the criminal law against members who participated in fighting, then so common at fires, and he regrets that "at present, every one arrested in case of an outbreak, can, if he has a friend or two outside to interest themselves in his behalf, escape from punishment, and finding that with the influence of his friends to sustain him, he can violate the law with impunity, he becomes more turbulent than ever." As so often is the case some few members brought the whole into disrepute, and the old order of the volunteer system changed and gave place to the new paid department because these few were, to use the language of the Police Court, "drunk and disorderly."

On the Old York Road near Noble Street there was a tall flag pole with the figure of an Indian upon the top. It was the custom of the fire companies to take their engine there to test it by seeing if they could throw a stream of water to the top of the "Indian Pole," as it was called. These exhibitions attracted crowds of people and are remembered by persons now living.

The rows between rival fire companies at a fire became characteristics of the time and many of these fights for priority took precedence over the fire in the attentions of the companies.

Some of the fire companies, notably the United States, were composed chiefly of Quakers, and it was a curious sight to see these enthusiastic Friends rushing to a fire in their brightly coloured tin hats and plain coats.

XXII: America's First University

THE Province of Pennsylvania was founded and settled because of religious persecution, and the movement which developed into the University of Pennsylvania, begun in Philadelphia in 1740, had a like origin.

It was a time of intense religious feeling and very appropriate for a visit from the most celebrated evangelist of his day, Rev. George Whitefield, who arrived in 1739 on his way to his parish at Savannah, Georgia. Whitefield was but twenty-four years old, but as a preacher had already outstripped his brethren of the Episcopal Church. When he was ordained and preached his first sermon in Gloucester Cathedral complaint was made to the Bishop that fifteen people had been driven mad by it. The bishop was, however, a loyal and vigourous soul and merely replied that he hoped the madness might not be forgotten before another Sunday.

Whitefield's ministry lasted four and thirty years and during this time he preached eighteen thousand times. His eloquence and the power of his voice were notable, and Franklin wrote of him to a friend, "I knew him intimately for upwards of thirty years. His integrity, disinteredness, and indefatigable zeal in prosecuting every good work, I have never seen equalled, and shall never see excelled." He adds that Whitefield used sometimes to pray for his conversion, "but never had the satisfaction of believing that his prayers were heard."

Whitefield's vigour, directness and the way he denounced ecclesiasticism and frivolity soon caused the doors of Christ

Church and St. Peter's to be closed to him, and the crowds assembled to hear him were too great for any house in the city, and a movement to provide a non-sectarian charity school was stimulated by a number of plain persons of various denominations to provide a building which would accommodate the people and protect them from the weather. Franklin was foremost in the work and tells us that sufficient sums were soon received to procure the ground on Fourth Street below Arch and to erect the building, which was 100 feet long and 70 broad, "about the size of Westminster Hall." The work was carried on with such spirit that Whitefield preached in it in November, 1740. The oldest record in the possession of the University is the bill for the work on this building from Robert Smith, the builder, and now thought to have been the designer of Independence Hall and Christ Church. The bill is for work on "The Charity School House," mentions no other purpose and is dated "June 14th 1740." This was the lasting purpose which the trustees of this building had in mind and which appears in their advertisement in July of 1740 where they say it is "for a charity school for the instruction of poor children, gratis, in useful literature and the knowledge of the Christian religion." The proposal ran thus:

"Proposed Advertisement of the Charity School of Philadelphia, 1740":—Advertisement,

It has pleased Almighty God of his infinite Goodness and Mercy in these latter Days to visit with his Holy Spirit the Hearts and Minds of many professing Christianity in this as well as diverse other Parts of the World however divided or distinguished in denomination or Interest, so as to make them lay aside Bigottry and party Zeal and unite their endeavours to promote the truly Noble Interest of the Kingdom of the Blessed Jesus.

With this View it hath been thought proper to erect a large building for a Charity School for the Instruction of Poor Children

Gratis in useful Literature and the Knowledge of the Christian religion and also for a House of Publick Worship in this Place being insufficient to contain the Impracticable to meet in the open Air at all Times of the Year because of the inclemency of the Weather.

"It is agreed that the use of the aforesaid School and House of Religious Worship be under the direction of certain Trustees Viz. and other persons to be appointed by them who in Case of the Decease of one of their Number to succeed to his Place and so from Time to Time as often as any of the before named Trustees or others so as to be chosen shall dye the Place of such deced Trustees shall be supplyed by the Votes of a Majority of the Surviving Trustees.

"Which Trustees before named and hereafter to be chosen are from time to Time to appoint fit and able School Masters and School Mistresses and introduce such Protestant Ministers as they judge to be Sound in principle acquainted with experimental Religion in their Hearts and faithful in their Practice without regard to those distinctions or different sentiments in lesser matters which have unhappily divided real Christians.

"These are therefore to give Notice to all Charitable Persons who are inclined to encourage the undertaking that the Building is actually begun under the direction of and the foundation laid on a Lot of ground (late of Jonathan Price and Mary his Wife, who have generously contributed) Situate near Mulberry Street in the City of Philada where Materials for the Building will be received as also Subscriptions for Money and Work taken in by the underwritten persons.

"Philada July 1740"

The undertaking was naturally in the hands of persons with no strong sectarian feelings and they thought it a good opportunity to supply the lack in educational facilities for the poor. The advertisement of July indicates a previous association, but the deed for the ground and building was not executed until September 15, 1740, when Edmund

Woolley, carpenter, and John Coats, brickmaker, John Howell, mariner, and William Price, carpenter, were named as the legal representatives of the subscribers, whose names are unknown. These made a deed of trust November 14, 1740, engaging to hold the property subject to the direction of certain "Trustees for the Uses" who were also to have the power to direct a transfer of the property to others. The Trustees for the Uses were George Whitefield, of Georgia, William Seward of London, Thomas Noble, Merchant, New York, John Stephen Benezet, Merchant, Samuel Hazard, Merchant, Robert Eastburn, Blacksmith, James Read, Gent., Edward Evans, Cordwainer, and Charles Brockden, Gent., of Philadelphia. The indenture defines the object of the trust in the very words of the advertisement of July 1740.

As one of the Trustees, Whitefield was commissioned to select a master and a mistress for the Charity School. What measure of success was attained for this school has never been positively determined, but it is these clauses incorporated word for word in the deed to the Trustees of the Academy in 1749 that connects the University with the origin of 1740.

Franklin's first proposal for a "complete education of youth" was mentioned in 1743, but it was not until his publication of "Proposals relating to the Education of Youth in Pennsylvania" 1749, that the idea took the form of a definite prospectus, which he distributed freely among the principal inhabitants. It is well to note his departure from the common practice of the time of emphasizing the usual classical education, in his particular mention of the importance of keeping our mother tongue foremost in the aims of the institution. He was ahead of his time also in urging that as "art is long," and their time is short, they "learn those things that are likely to be the *most useful* and *most ornamental;* regard being had to the several professions for which they are intended." Also "that to keep them in Health, and to strengthen and render active their Bodies, they be frequently exercised in Running, Leaping, Wrestling, and Swimming, etc."

Franklin was ably seconded by Dr. Richard Peters, afterward rector of Christ Church and St. Peter's. Franklin wanted him to organize and head the Academy in 1743, but he declined. He became President of the Board of Trustees in 1756 and was the leading spirit during Franklin's long absences abroad.

The 24 gentlemen who associated themselves to carry this project into being were:

James Logan, Esquire
John Inglis, Merchant
Thomas Lawrence, Esquire
Tench Francis, Esquire
William Allen, Esquire
William Masters, Esquire
Lloyd Zachary, Practitioner in Physic
Samuel McCall, Jr., Merchant
Joseph Turner, Esquire
Benjamin Franklin, Printer
Thomas Leech, Merchant
William Shippen, Practitioner in Physic
Robert Strettel, Esquire
Philip Syng, Silversmith
Charles Willing, Esquire
Phineas Bond, Practitioner in Physic
Thomas Hopkinson, Esquire
William Plumsted, Esquire
Joshua Maddox, Esquire
Thomas White, Esquire
William Coleman, Merchant

Abram Taylor, Esquire

Richard Peters, Esquire

Thomas Bond, Practitioner in Physic

Thus they are named and described in the deed of conveyance of the property on Fourth Street and in their first Minutes. They were the most talented, richest and influential men in the Province.

In taking over the "New Building," as it was called when erected for Whitefield, the conveyors dictated a continuance of their original purpose of the Charity School and in each of the Charters granted to the institution this has been continued, forming an unbroken connection back to 1740. The original Trustees, besides, contributed a considerable amount of the money for the Academy of 1749 at the time of the transfer of their property.

The first meeting of the new subscribers was held at Robert's Coffee House, February 1, 1750, when Messrs. Benezet, Hazard, Eastburn, Read, and Evans directed their associates, Edmund Woolley and John Coates, to make the deed conveying the property on Fourth Street near Arch to the new Trustees.

Franklin wanted the Rev. Samuel Johnson, of Stratford, Connecticut, to head the Academy and journeyed thence to persuade him, but in vain, and David Martin, M.A., was chosen Rector to start the undertaking. He died in 1751 and Francis Alison was chosen in his place "upon Trial."

In the Academy there were then "schools" after the example of some foreign Universities—one for Latin—one for English—one for Mathematics. Dr. Francis Alison, who afterward became a Presbyterian Minister of eminence and Vice-Provost of the College for nearly 25 years, was Rector of the Academy, and Master of the Latin School; David James Dove was Master of the English School;

and Theophilus Grew was Master of the Mathematical School. These masters were aided by Ushers or Tutors, one of whom, Charles Thompson, afterward became the distinguished Secretary of the Continental Congress. There were also the Charity School and, when Dr. Smith came, the Philosophy School under his care.

In 1753 Governor Penn gave the institution a Charter under the name of "The Trustees of the Academy and Charitable School in the Province of Pennsylvania" and there was much rejoicing among both Trustees and Pupils, the latter delivering several declamations in Latin to celebrate the event.

The Academy was growing and soon the necessity of enlarging its sphere was apparent. The publication of a scheme for an ideal "College of Mirania" by William Smith, who had been educated at the University of Aberdeen, attracted much attention in 1752, and in enclosing a copy to Franklin the author inquired about the placing of his pupils in the Philadelphia Academy. The correspondence led to a visit and finally to the choice of William Smith as Provost of the College in 1755. The career of this remarkable man was long and distinguished. It is to his skillful management that the rise and success of the University must be attributed. The plan of his ideal "College of Mirania," which he endeavoured to put into practice was a step in advance in education and the courses of study which he first inculcated have formed the basis of nearly all the American Colleges. These advanced ideas were in harmony with those of Franklin and his associates, so that the modern theory of American education had its beginnings at Philadelphia nearly a hundred years before it was established in any other community in the country. Dr. Smith was eloquent, forcible and courageous. He drew up the new

Charter in 1755 incorporating the College, which name was added to its title, still including the "Charity School" of 1740.

The beginning of American drama was working in the College, as we have already been told.

The beginning of American Fine Art was also fostered in the College in the person of Benjamin West, of the Class of 1757. The God-given talent of painting possessed by this Chester County Quaker had already been recognized by Friends and while at College he was encouraged and inspired by Francis Hopkinson and "Billy" White, afterward Bishop, who used to stroll along the sylvan banks of the Schuylkill reading the classics to the young artist. With Benjamin Franklin they helped his sweetheart to escape by night from her stern brother and sent her to her marriage with him in England, where he became a founder and President of the Royal Academy.

John Morgan of the Class of 1757 shed great glory upon his Alma Mater. Beginning his medical studies under Dr. Redman, who served as a surgeon of the Provincial Troops against the French and Indians until 1760 when he went to Europe to complete his medical education at Edinburgh, London and Paris. Returning to Philadelphia 1765 he laid before the Trustees of the College at a special meeting on the 3rd of May, a recommendation of his plans for a Medical Department from Governor Thomas Penn and similar letters from James Hamilton and the Rev. Mr. Richard Peters, two trustees then in England.

The Trustees immediately entered into the project with enthusiasm and appointed Dr. Morgan Professor of the Theory and Practice of Physick. Thus was begun the first Medical School in America, which as Thomas Penn said, gave "Reputation and Strength to the Institution" and made it the first University on the Continent, a fact which was strengthened by the first Law Department in 1790. It is this great achievement of the old College which has maintained Philadelphia as the centre of Medicine in this country, an achievement redered permanent by the recent merger of other medical schools with the pioneer, and the establishment of the Graduate School of Medicine.

At the Commencement 1783 Washington v. as given the degree of Doctor of Laws, although he did not receive it in person until he was in Philadelphia in December, on his way to Annapolis to resign his commission. Washington had a high regard for James Wilson of the College Faculty. In 1790 when he was President and James Wilson was made Professor of Law at the University, he attended, on December 15th, the introductory lecture in College Hall which was the beginning of the first law school in America. Mrs. Washington accompanied the President on this important occasion, as did also the Vice-President, John Adams, both houses of Congress, President Thomas Mifflin of Pennsylvania, and both houses of the Legislature "together with a great number of ladies and gentlemen, the whole composing a most brilliant and respectable audience." Washington placed his nephew Bushrod under James Wilson for the study of law. He became a Justice of the Supreme Court of the United States. Two other nephews, George Steptoe and Augustine Washington, were entered in the College by their uncle and were of the class of 1792. Thomas Jefferson sent his nephew, John Randolph, to the University to study Medicine.

In 1779 the men who had once ruled the Colony, driven from office and power and almost even from social influence, were gathered together in the College. These were men like Robert Morris and James Wilson, signers of the Declaration of Independence and framers of the Constitution of the United States. It seemed to be the object of President

Reed of the Supreme Executive Council of the state to drive such men out of prominence and the destruction of the College seemed to be the final blow in this design. Reed's party, called the Constitutionalists, had already handled the College as roughly as they could. They had quartered soldiers in it, suspended the functions of its Trustees and called it a nest of Tories and Traitors, although there was nothing to justify the accusation, and its officers had been among the most distinguished patriots. All but three of the twenty-four Trustees had taken the oath of allegiance. The attack indeed was not on account of the so-called Tories in the Board, but on account of the Patriots in it, who differed politically from the Constitutionalists. The spoiling of the College was consummated in 1779, the charter declared void, the Board of Trustees and Faculty dissolved and the property given to new Trustees of the Constitutionalists' Party, who were to be called the University of the State of Pennsylvania. Provost Smith was banished to Maryland where he founded Washington College. They seemed to have supposed that great Universities could be created on paper. They destroyed a true College, a growth of years, containing the first and greatest medical school in America and put in its place a sham. For the next eleven years there were two colleges in Philadelphia, both of them worthless.

The old Trustees of the College kept up a struggle for the restoration of their property, which was successful in 1789. The old buildings at Fourth and Arch Streets became too contracted and too badly situated for further usefulness, and the minds of the Trustees were turned toward the securing of a new location. On Ninth Street between Market and Chestnut, there was a large and handsome building erected at the expense of the State as a dwelling place for the President of the United States when it was expected that Philadelphia would remain the National Capital. But destiny chose a far different spot for the White House, and the Philadelphia presidential mansion remained untenanted. In 1802 this building was secured for the College, which immediately emigrated thither from its old Fourth Street home. Alterations and additions were made from time to time, till in 1829 it was torn down and two buildings were put up on the same site, one for the Department of Arts, and one for the Medical School. In 1825 the College course was raised from three to four years, entrance requirements were made more rigorous, and then, or not long previously, a rule was made that students should not be admitted under fourteen years of age.

The middle of the last century found a distinguished group of teachers in the College. Henry Reed, Charles J. Stille, Samuel Wylie, George Allen and Ezra Otis Kendall were among these and a little later came Francis Aristide Jackson, William A. Lamberton and John Bach McMaster. In the Law School there were Mitchell, Sharswood, Hare and Parsons, and in Medicine, Long, Leidy, Agnew, Wood, Pepper, Tyson, White and Deaver, with many others whose names are widely known in their professions.

In 1872 the great break with the past was made by the removal from the City to the West Bank of the Schuylkill River. Beginning with 1880 during the administrations of Provosts Pepper and Harrison the physical development of the University of to-day was begun.

The move to West Philadelphia proved to be the beginning of a new life, especially as it coincided with the administration of a new Provost, Dr. Stille. What the Fourth Street location had become by 1802, the Ninth Street site had become by 1872. It was surrounded and hemmed in by the world of business. In West Philadelphia the University had elbow-room, and it began promptly to take advantage of its opportunity for expansion. In the years immediately succeeding was erected the original group of four buildings, consisting of College Hall, Medical Hall, the Medical Laboratory, and the University Hospital. All these buildings were of green serpentine stone and were designed by Professor Richards.

Between 1880 and 1890, during Dr. Pepper's provostship, several more buildings were erected, among these the Library, the present Botanical Building, and the old Veterinary buildings, which have since given way to the new Medical laboratories, erected in 1904. Between 1890 and 1900 the additions to the University group of buildings included the Observatory, the beginning of the Dormitory system, the Harrison Laboratory of Chemistry, the Randall Morgan Laboratory of Physics, the Museum, Wistar Institute, Houston Hall, Dental Hall, and the Law School. During this period the direction of the University passed from Dr. Pepper to Charles Custis Harrison, LL.D., whose term of office as Provost dated from 1894 to 1910, Vice-Provost Edgar F. Smith, Sc.D., LL.D., succeeding him in office.

Since 1900 the physical equipment of the University has been materially augmented, the erection of the following buildings attesting a period of remarkable development and extension: the new Medical laboratories, already referred to; the Engineering Building; the Veterinary Hall and Hospital; the Gymnasium; the Training House and Franklin Field; the remodeling of the University Hospital; enlargement of the Museum of Science and Art; additions to the Dormitories; the School of Dentistry; the Women's Dormitory; the Phipps Institute for the Study, Prevention and Treatment of Tuberculosis; and the University Settlement House. A new heat plant and Bennett Hall for

Women have just been completed and the Irvine Auditorium will soon be started. In addition, the University has acquired, by grant from the city, a neighboring tract of about fifty acres, which extends the Campus to the western edge of the Schuylkill River, and gives it a total acreage of one hundred and ten, exclusive of streets and sidewalks.

But after all, the Campus and buildings are only the shell of the University. It is the history of the life within them which is important. During the period from 1870 to 1913 a number of new departments of study were established, in the Scientific courses, in Biology, in Finance and Economy, in Architecture, in Dentistry, in Music, in Veterinary Medicine, in Education, and in the Graduate School, in addition to corresponding extensions of the old departments, the College, and the Medical and Law Schools; the separation of the Wharton School and the Towne Scientific School from the College in 1912 was an important administrative change. The Moore School of Electrical Engineering was added in 1924. The number of students in all departments had risen from less than a thousand, in 1870, to 16,581 in 1926, and the number of instructors from less than fifty to more than one thousand. Representatives from every state of the Union and forty-one foreign countries are included in the student enrollment.

A parallel movement has been the growth of a series of connections between the University and the community at large. For instance, between 1883 and 1887, a commission of members of the Faculty and of the Board of Trustees carried out a series of investigations in modern spiritualism and published their results. During the same period Mr. Eadweard Muybridge anticipated the invention of the commercialized moving picture by performing, under the supervision of the University, a system of experiments on the photography of animals in motion. The publication of the results of his experiments furnishes a valuable and interesting document in the history of the development of the motion picture. The Babylonian explorations, which have since made valuable contributions to the world's knowledge of ancient history, were begun at about the same time. The Museum of Art and Science, in which the Babylonian collection and other valuable collections are exhibited, is now the mecca of week-end pilgrimages of school childern and others throughout the year. The free clinics in the Medical, Dental, and Veterinary Schools annually provide treatment for thousands of the city's sufferers. The Phipps Institute for the Study, Prevention and Treatment of Tuberculosis is also a splendid instance of the double function of the University. The work of the Psychological Clinic, in studying and treating backward and defective children, is rapidly becoming recognized as an important adjunct to the community. Instances multiply in which the various laboratories of Medicine, Botony, Zoology, Physics and Engineering have been drawn upon by the national, state, or municipal bureaus for expert assistance. Each year one or more commissions, such as the Chestnut Blight Commission, make the University a headquarters for research work. In a similar way, the various departments of the Wharton School of Finance and Commerce have given practical and valuable assistance in the solving of problems affecting national and municipal finances and administration. The solution of many of the perplexing questions of policy, arising out of the construction of the Panama Canal, was achieved by members of the Wharton School faculty. The Department of Architecture also, through its students and faculty, has rendered efficient aid to many municipalities. In many other ways does the University respond to requests for expert assistance.

The free public lectures by distinguished members of the

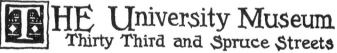

THE University Museum
Thirty Third and Spruce Streets
From the Philadelphia Art Alliance Post Card Series

Faculty on Saturday afternoons have been appreciated by large audiences and have been since 1913 a large factor in bringing the University and the public closer together.

The more purely social side of the University life goes farther back, and has been less changed of recent years than the intellectual or the athletic side. Fraternities, musical and dramatic clubs, college literary societies, and such organizations have their roots well back in the last century. However, the custom of keeping up fraternity houses in which members live while at College has sprung up within the last twenty-five years. Many attractive houses have recently been built by local chapters of national societies.

But of all the changes that have taken place in the life of students of the University since 1872, when the removal to West Philadelphia was made, the most important, if not the most conspicuous, is the greater closeness of connection of the students with the University, the large part of their life which centres in it. This has resulted partly from the erection of the Dormitories, partly from the establishment of Houston Hall, in which so many of the students meet one another and spend much of their time, partly also from the policy of the University authorities, and the growth of a habit among the students of looking upon the University as the centre of all their interests. Twenty-five years ago the greater number of the students had had little more connection than that involved in attendance during lecture or recitation hours. It has since then become more and more general for a student to feel during the three or four years of his course that all his interests, material, intellectual, social, and religious, gather around his University. There he spends almost all his time and there he finds enough to satisfy all his normal instincts and interests.

Ten of the fifty-six men who signed the Declaration of

Independence and seven of the twenty-eight signers of the Constitution of the United States were of this University. The University's record in every national crisis has been splendid, both as to personnel and to numbers. Anthony Wayne of the Class of 1765, Jacob Brown, 1790, and George B. McClellan, 1844, became Commanders of the Army of the United States. In the Civil War the University furnished more men and more distinguished officers than any other University, including six Major-Generals, two Corps Commanders and Quarter-Master General Meigs, who equipped and supplied all the Armies of the North. Some 2000 surgeons alone from the University of Pennsylvania served in the Armies of the North and the South. In the late Great War 10,000 University of Pensylvania men served, many with marked distinction.

The list of United States Senators, Justices of Federal and State Supreme Courts, Attorneys General of States and Nation, Governors and Cabinet Officers from among Pennsylvania graduates is a long one, and of persons of lesser distinction the records are full. To Arts and Letters, to Sciences, particularly Medicine, to the Law, to Religion, and to Education the University has contributed many well known names. Such a record of service to mankind is the real measure of any institution.

The University now comprises the following Departments or Colleges:

1. The College, 1740
   Arts and Science Courses
   Teachers Courses
   Biology Courses
   Preparation for Professional Departments
2. Towne Scientific School, 1875
   Courses in Engineering (Mechanical, Civil & Chemical)

Courses in Chemistry
3. The School of Fine Arts, 1875
   Courses in Architecture
   Courses in Music
   Courses in Painting and Sculpture
4. The Wharton School, 1885
   The School of Finance and Commerce
   Evening and Extension Schools
5. The Moore School of Electrical Engineering, 1923
6. The School of Education, 1912
7. The School of Medicine, 1765
8. The Law School, 1790
9. The Evans Institute, Dental School, 1878
10. The Veterinary School, 1884
11. The Graduate School, 1882
12. The Graduate School of Medicine, 1919
13. The Wistar Institute of Anatomy and Biology, 1892
14. Auxiliaries:
     1. The Library
     2. The Phipps Institute (Tuberculosis)
     3. The School of Hygiene
     4. Military Science and Tactics
     5. The Hospitals
     6. The University Museum
     7. The Flower Astronomical Observatory
     8. The Summer School
     9. Physical Education
     10. The Dormitories
     11. Training School for Nurses

The University occupies more than seventy buildings on one hundred and ten acres of land on the west bank of the Schuylkill River in Philadelphia, ten minutes from the centre of the city by electric car.

As a city university it is unique in having its principal

activities upon one plot of ground. The Hospitals, Courts, great manufacturing and industrial plants of the City, as well as the opportunities in music and the fine arts, afford unusual opportunities for the broad cultural education of the students, as well as special experiences in their chosen courses. The scholar or lover of literature who would seek a step aside from the immediate can readily find seclusion and monastic quiet within the limits of the University. One has but to retire within the bosky limits of the Botanical Gardens, the enclosures of the beautiful Old English Dormitories, or to stroll along Hamilton Walk with its ample shrubbery and poplar sentinels, to find the blessings of solitude.

Pennsylvania's prominence in athletics is well known. Nineteen sports are fostered upon Franklin Field and the three river fields. The Relay Races are the centre for American athletes each spring and physical education is regarded as a part of the preparation for life which every American boy should have. To this end all athletics are under the control and supervision of the University authorities.

Fraternities are attractively housed adjacent to the Campus and form a pleasant and congenial phase of College life. A daily and three monthly publications, the Musical Clubs, Dramatic Societies and the famous Mask and Wig Club are other happy associations to be had at Pennsylvania, while the Christian Association is one of the best supported and sanest influences on the Campus.

The leaders have been:

THE CHARITY SCHOOL

Rev. George Whitefield, M.A.
    Appointed by the Trustees of the "New Building" to

select a Master and a Mistress for the School, 1740. No record of this selection.

THE ACADEMY & CHARITY SCHOOL

David Martin, M.A., Rector 1750–1751
Francis Alison, M.A., D.D., Rector 1752–1755

THE COLLEGE, ACADEMY & CHARITABLE SCHOOL

William Smith, D.D., LL.D., Provost 1755–1791

THE UNIVERSITY OF PENNSYLVANIA

Provosts

John Ewing, D.D., LL.D.	1791–1802
John McDowell, LL.D.	1807–1810
John Andrews, D.D.	1810–1813
Frederick Beasley, D.D.	1813–1828
Rt. Rev. William Heathcote Delancey, D.D., LL.D.	1828–1833
John Ludlow, D.D.	1834–1853
Henry Vethake, LL.D.	1854–1859
Damiel Raynes Goodwin, DD., LL.D.	1860–1868
Charles Janeway Stille, LL.D.	1868–1880
William Pepper, M.D., LL.D.	1881–1894
Charles Custis Harrison, LL.D.	1894–1911
Edgar Fahs Smith, Ph.D., Sc.D., Litt.D., Chem.D., LH.D., M.D., LL.D.	1911–1920
Josiah Harmar Penniman, Ph.D., LL.D.	1921–

XXIII: Ships and Shipping

A WALK along Philadelphia's river-front to-day will not greatly impress one with the extent of its shipping and there is always rather a despairing note, tinged with anger, in its mention by the public press. In the *building* of ships, however, an altogether different note is struck and the Delaware has often been called the "Clyde of America."

From the time of the founding of the City one of the principal industries of Philadelphia has been that of ship-building. In 1685, three years after the arrival of Penn in the Colony, six sea-going ships and many boats had already been built in Philadelphia, and in 1700 there were four shipyards building sea-going vessels, besides smaller concerns which built river boats and fishing craft, together with shops engaged in industries related to shipbuilding, such as ropewalks, block and sailmakers shops. The early shipyards were built along the beach between High and Callowhill Streets. By 1750 all the shipyards had moved either northward or southward to make room for wharves required by the growing commerce of the port. One of the yards was that of Mr. West, at that time the leading shipbuilder in the Colonies. Two of the ships built at this yard were as large as any merchant vessels built in England up to that time, and were bought by the East India Company for their fine East India and China fleet.

Gabriel Thomas tells us in 1697 of the large and commodious wharves and of Robert Turner's ship-yard. Captain Bartholomew Penrose, progenitor of that name hereabouts, had a ship-yard on the river at the foot of High or

Market Street in which William Penn and Robert Trent were partners. Prior to 1725 twenty vessels might be seen on the stocks at one time and the clearances were numerous for that day. The City had by the middle of the century many wealthy merchants engaged in foreign trade and in 1771 the tonnage was 50,000 entered and cleared. At the time of the Revolution Philadelphia was the first city in naval architecture. Among characteristic enterprises were huge rafts built for the shipment of a great quantity of timber. The "Baron Renfrew" of upward of 5000 tons, made a safe passage to England with such a cargo. The adjacent iron works on the Schuylkill aided much in the building of ships and these superior advantages caused many of the naval vessels constructed for the defense of the Colonies to be built here. The flourishing commerce of the port was swept away by the war, but revived after peace was declared. In 1793 the tonnage built in Philadelphia doubled that at any other port in the United States, and the exports exceeded those of New England and New York, and indeed were one-fourth of the whole Union. Thomas Godfrey invented the quadrant and Franklin made many improvements in the models of sailing vessels, among them the water-tight compartments now deemed essential.

Michael Royll had a yard at the Drawbridge over Dock Creek, Charles West owned extensive yards at Vine Street, Parrock at Race Street and so on. The bowsprits of the ships extended across Front Street to the eaves of West's house, indeed many still living can remember a similar scene on Delaware Avenue. Carved figure-heads were very popular in the early days of shipping and the work of William Rush excited wide admiration at home and abroad.

The first ships for the American Navy were built by Joshua Humphreys, the foremost naval Architect of his time, in Southwark below Old Swedes' Church. Later the

United States established a yard at Front and Federal Streets, where Humphreys built the *United States* and the *Philadelphia,* equal to anything afloat at that time. The *Pennsylvania* was launched here in 1837 in the presence of 100,000 people and a multitude of ships in the river. She was entirely of wood and the largest in the world, her masts being 250 feet high. From the jib-boom to the end of the spanker-boom was 375 feet and the main yard was 120 feet in length. She had three gun decks and 140 guns.

During the colonial period it is estimated that 180 square rigged ships and over 700 brigs and schooners, besides smaller vessels, were built at Philadelphia, which led the Colonies in the size and total tonnage of ships constructed.

During the Revolution Philadelphia took a leading part in the construction of vessels for the "State Navy" and continental navy, and a great number of privateers. The first squadron was composed of merchant vessels converted into men-of-war in the Philadelphia yards; these were followed by six frigates, four of which, the *Washington, Randolph, Delaware,* and *Effingham* were built at Philadelphia.

It was on the Delaware that Esek Hopkins, the Navy's first Commander, first hoisted his flag. That event occurred in January, 1776, when, in the presence of a great crowd lining the water front, and amid the booming of cannon and cheers, Hopkin's stepped into a ship's boat at Walnut Street wharf and was rowed to midstream where he boarded the ship *Alfred.*

That ship, a staunch sailing vessel that was later to give a good account of itself, was well known along the water front as the *Black Prince,* which in the merchant service of John Nixon had been under the command of young "Jack" Barry, the first commissioned officer of the Navy, then waiting his chance to go to sea as the captain of the newly converted war ship *Lexington.*

When Hopkins reached the *Alfred* there was at his side another young naval officer, Lieutenant John Paul Jones, who, at his order, raised above the *Alfred* the famous rattlesnake flag with its warning: "Don't Tread on Me," and there is traditional authority, at least, for saying that on this occasion Jones also raised the first "Grand Union Flag," of thirteen stripes with the English union jack in the field, similar to the Cambridge flag Washington had raised over the Army at the first of the year and which was copied after the insignia of the First City Troop.

Vessels belonging to the State Navy and the various sailing craft in the harbor "dressed ship" on this occasion, and the new Continental Navy consisted of the ships *Alfred* and *Columbus*, the brigs *Andrea Doria, Cabot* and *Providence*, the sloop *Hornet* and the schooners *Wasp* and *Fly*, whose combined batteries contained one hundred guns.

At the beginning of the 19th century Stephen Girard was the great shipping merchant of the city and became one of America's richest men. He has sometimes been depicted as a solitary and miserly figure, but his personal courage and work during the yellow fever outbreak, his financing of the War of 1812, and his great benefaction in the founding of Girard College, show him to have been one of the most distinguished of patriots and philantropists.

Thomas P. Cope was one of the city's greatest ship-owners, and most of his ships were built in Philadelphia. He established in 1821 the first regular line of packet-ships between the City and Liverpool. The names of Vaughan and of Eyre are the most prominent among the early ship-builders of Kensington, but of course there is none more widely famous than that of Cramp, who began building ships in 1830 after an apprenticeship with Samuel Grice, the most celebrated shipbuilder of that period.

Cramp's Ship-yard of to-day is the result of the growth

and development of a ship-yard established by William Cramp in 1830. Originally located at the foot of Otis Street (now East Susquehanna Avenue), and later at the foot of Palmer Street (the present site of the Company's dry dock, marine railways and repair shops), the plant of the early days bore little resemblance to that of to-day. But even then, as now, its ships represented the latest and most perfect examples of shipbuilding. In 1872 the business had outgrown the Palmer Street yard and about one-third of the water front of the present establishment was purchased. In March of that year the Company as it now exists was incorporated under its present name "The William Cramp & Sons Ship & Engine Building Company."

It is now generally recognized that John Fitch's claim to the invention of the steamboat is well-founded. As early as 1817 a committee of the New York Legislature decided that Robert Fulton's craft was "in substance the invention patented by John Fitch in 1791." Research in Federal and State archives now proves conclusively that Fitch built and operated a steamboat of his own conception in 1785. John Fitch, a watch and clock-maker in Philadelphia, actually ran the first steamboat on the Delaware in 1788, after this design made in 1785. Paddles, working within a framework, propelled the little boat to Burlington, New Jersey, and afterward to Trenton, returning the same day and moving at the rate of eight miles an hour. His first excursion indeed was on the 1st of May, 1787, but he was ahead of his time and it was left for Fulton to perfect the design and secure the glory. Much help in Fitch's design came, no doubt, from Oliver Evans, a blacksmith of Philadelphia, who proclaimed in 1781 that he could drive wagons and mills by steam. He prophesied that the time would come when people would travel by steam wagons moving at the rate of twenty miles an hour and that railways would be laid on paths of broken stone to travel by night as well as by day, and that boats will be propelled by steam. Friends were too conservative and careful in those days to take up the visionary schemes of these young men, ideas destined to revolutionize travel in the years to come, and so the necessary capital to promote their plans was not to be had in the Quaker City.

A story characteristic of the temperament and training of early Quakers is told of Captain Whitall whose ship lay in foreign waters frequented by pirates. Spying a hardlooking fellow coming up a rope over the side one night the worthy Friend taking a knife remarked, "Friend, if thee wants that rope thee may have it"—and cut the rope.

XXIV: Two Philadelphia Clubs

THE oldest social organization in the English speaking world is what is now known as The Schuylkill Fishing Company. In 1729 some Welshmen formed themselves into the "Society of Ancient Britons" and met on St. David's Day, March 1st, at the Queen's Head Tavern kept by Robert David in King Street, now Water. From thence they walked in solemn procession, with leeks in their hats, to Christ Church, where a sermon was preached to them in the original Cymric by Dr. Weyman. After the sermon the society returned to the tavern and dined with ceremonious form, the chief notables of the province being present. They celebrated St. David's Day in this way for many years and their members formed a fishing company whose "fort" was on a broad, high rock at the Falls of Schuylkill, on the east bank, from which they made war from the rude timber shanty, on the catfish for which the river was famous. This was the forerunner of the "Colony in Schuylkill" formed in 1732, and was afterwards merged with it.

"The Colony in Schuylkill" was a company of sportsmen of jovial and convivial mien. With lordly manner and feudal form they assumed eminent domain and uncontrolled legislation over field and stream within their jurisdiction, choosing governor, assembly, council, sheriff, coroner and citizens who went through all the forms of a real government like an independent North American Colony.

Thomas Stretch was governor; Enoch Flower, Charles Jones, Isaac Snowden, John Howard and Joseph Stiles, members of assembly; James Coultas, Sheriff; Joseph Stiles, Secretary and Treasurer; William Hopkins, Coroner; and William Warner, Baron, "Baron" Warner owned the estate on which the fish-house was erected, and received, as rental, the first perch caught at the opening of the season. This land is now in Fairmount Park and the first castle, or fish-house, was erected in this sylvan wilderness above the west end of the present Girard Avenue bridge. The members were a frolicsome lot of the best social set and this seems to have been the only organization of the olden time which did not include Benjamin Franklin as a member.

The first castle was destroyed by fire and rebuilt on the same spot in 1812, and in 1822 when the dam at Fairmount obstructed the passage of the fish it was removed to the vicinity of Rambo's Rock on the east or left bank of the river near Gray's Ferry. This was quite an undertaking and was accomplished with the help of two specially constructed flat boats. When the oil works were built and the stream became so contaminated as to interfere with fishing the castle was again taken down, in November, of 1887, and moved to its present site on the Delaware River at Eddington near Andalusia.

The annual elections are the great times at the castle. The expenses used to be moderate and consisted chiefly in providing a good repast of beef, pig, steaks and the results of their fishing and fowling, accompanied by flowing bowls of good punch, lemonade and Madeira, followed by pipes and tobacco. An account of 1748 showed a total expense of £6, 18s 8d, for 84 persons. A good turtle and a barbecue were common features at election dinners to which strangers and friends of members were usually invited.

No one without permission ever intruded on their possessions, or invaded the rights said to have been granted them by some Indian chief of the Delaware tribe, and when the Provincial Government of Pennsylvania appointed com-- missioners to survey the river they graciously authorized James Coultas, a fellow-member and one of the Commissioners, to perform his duties.

When independence was declared many of the members enlisted with the First Troop of which their Governor, Samuel Morris, was the Captain. They then changed the name to the State in Schuylkill. The memories of Washington and of Governor Morris are always pledged at every stated meeting. While Philadelphia was the capital President Washington was a frequent visitor at the castle and both he and Lafayette, who visited them later, were honorary members. There are but five of these, and never more than thirty active members. Five "apprentices" have the privilege of the club until the death of a member, when the senior novice is taken into full membership. There are thirteen appointed fishing days in each year, at equal periods between May 1st and October 1st, when the company assembles at the castle and a citizen, designated "Caterer," assisted by the apprentices, prepares the golden perch in the ancient pans and old manner. An important and solemn ceremony is this, for the apprentices must stand a test which has been passed by every dead and living member of the club. He must hold three perch in a long-handled frying pan over the blazing wood fire until one side is done to a turn, then, with a quick twist of his wrist, toss the fish up the old chimney, catching them as they fall on the uncooked side. This is no easy task with three fish and is only accomplished after diligent practice. The perch are served to the company assembled about the ancient table, on one of William Penn's platters presented to the club by his son John who was a member while Governor. "Fish-house Punch" is famous far beyond Philadelphia and was brewed from an old Colonial recipe and served to the members from a bowl brought from China by Captain Ross of the Troop. No servant, save a caretaker, ever enters the "castle" and the building is also barred to women. Matches are also barred, on account of the memory of the destruction of their first home and punk is used for lighting the pipes.

On May 1, 1832, there was a high celebration of the centenary of the club. The feast was more sumptuous than usual and these convivial gentlemen drank fourteen toasts, it may be assumed, in their famous Fish-house punch. They drank to the memory of the founders, who, 100 years before, had united to establish the "Colony in Schuylkill" after which, Johnson's "Centennial March" was sung. They drank to the revered memories of Stretch and of Morris, departed Governors of the State, whose remembrance of their worth would, they declared, be co-extensive with the sovereignty and independence of the State in Schuylkill. They drank to the memory of Washington, when a Centennial dirge was played. They also drank to their angling ancestors, "who had exchanged the troubled waters of this world for the calm Ocean of Eternity." Then came Robert Wharton, their late Governor, now in the autumn of existence, as an honourable, active and efficient Governor of City and State." And this was followed by the "Governor's March." They did not forget General Lafayette, though parted from him "by the great Herring Pond," they remembered with infinite pleasure his visit to "the waters of their State." And in unison they intoned, "Should Auld Acquaintance be Forgot."

The Navy of the State in Schuylkill came next—"it never fishes in troubled waters." And the eighth toast was Good Old Laws and Regulations, revered and strictly adhered to,

the grand secret of the unparalled prosperity and duration
of the Fishing Company of the State in Schuylkill. Of
course, they drank to "The Fair"—"when angling for
hearts may their hooks ever be baited with modesty and
good nature." And the sentimental gentlemen sang, "Oh,
Woman!"

After which they drank to the finny tribe. "We welcome
the scaly fellows in their annual visits to our State," they
said, and then sang, "Haste to the Sports of the Water."
"Our visiting brethren" followed those joining in the celebration of the day: "In the evening of life may its festivities take an elevated rank in their pleasurable reminis-
cences," which suggested to them "The Stranger." Being
still thirsty, apparently, they drank to "Our Country,"
"dear to the immigrant as a home, dearer to us as the
blessed land of our nativity." The obvious song was
"Home, Sweet Home." The First City Troop, "ever foremost in our regard," was not forgotten. "Its earliest members and four of its commanders were citizens of our State."
It is permitted to assume that by this time their voices
were a bit hoarse, when they sang, "The Trooper." But
they had enough strength to drink to the memory of good
old Izaak Walton, the devout man and industrious fisher-
man. Whereupon those who still had enough strength left
to do so, struck out a "solemn dirge." Any one initiated
in the mysteries of the old Fish-house Punch will probably
agree that was the only thing left for them to do.

One doesn't hear much about the "State in Schuylkill"
nowadays, but why should one? The hearty lot of gentlemen who enjoy its privileges make no more pretense than
a healthy mingling after the fashion of their congenial ancestors in a community where blood is distinctly thicker than
water, and then, over the entrance to this hall of conviviality hangs a translation of the verse of Horace:

 WASHINGTON'S HEADQUARTERS
• at Valley Forge •

From the Philadelphia Art Alliance Post Card Series

> Ne fidos inter amicos sit,
> Qui dicta foras eliminet.

which means:

> Let no one bear beyond this threshold hence
> Words uttered in friendly confidence.

Although not a very old institution, as Philadelphia reckons age, the Philadelphia Club is nevertheless an institution of institutions. It was founded in 1833 by Henry Bohlen, James Markoe, Joseph Parker Norris, Henry Beckett, Joseph R. Ingersoll, Commodore James Biddle, George Mifflin Dallas, John M. Scott, and William and Henry Chancellor. These represent some of the oldest and most prominent families of the City and their association is universally known as the oldest and most conservative City club. It first had rooms on Fifth Street below Walnut Street, then on Ninth above Spruce Street and on Walnut above Ninth. In 1850 the club was incorporated as the Philadelphia Association and Reading Room and the present location at Thirteenth and Walnut Streets was secured. In May of the same year the name was changed to the Philadelphia Club. The house had been built by Pierce Butler of South Carolina, that he and his famous old Madeira might pass the winter seasons in the north. It is a spacious building, like so many Philadelphia houses of the olden time and this characteristic is one of the links which seems to connect the City with the South. The sumptuous and lavish design of some of the Philadelphia edifices of Colonial days is in striking contrast to the frugal, chastened beauty of Boston's puritanical exteriors. One can easily imagine the Charlestonian lure for the wealthy Carolinian whose house has become the home of Philadelphia's most exclusive set. In this atmosphere New York is merely acknowledged as the place which one has to pass through in going to New England or Europe for the summer. The typical Philadelphian always plays the game according to the rules and this can best be illustrated by an occurrence at the Philadelphia Club as narrated by the visitor to whom it occurred:

"A stranger recently in Philadelphia on business bethought himself, in his friendless state, of a one-time casual acquaintance who had given as his address a Philadelphia club. From his hotel the visitor telephoned the club and asked if he might speak with Mr. John Doe. The telephone-clerk asked the inquirer's name, and after a decent interval replied that Mr. Doe was not in the club. The inquiry was then made whether Mr. Doe was in town and likely to be reached by a note sent to the club. The clerk politely regretted that he was not allowed to give any such infomation concerning a member of the club. The visitor protested, and was finally allowed to speak to the secretary's office. He gave his name again and, in answer to what seemed an odd query, that of his hotel. He explained that the shortness of his stay in Philadelphia was the reason of his anxiety to know whether he was likely to get hold of Mr. Doe during it or not. The secretary also politely regretted his inability so to violate the privacy of any member's life. The visitor, now vaguely feeling that he was being treated like a dun, or a detective, protested in slight exasperation that his designs upon Mr. Doe were honourable and purely social—that indeed he felt so sure of Mr. Doe's desire to welcome him to Philadelphia as to be inclined to insist upon some disclosures of even a club-member's whereabouts. The secretary now grew the least bit weaker, moved either by an inner kindliness or by some note of social authority in the visitor's voice, and at last grudgingly said that although the rules of the club were perfectly clear upon the point, he would as a courtesy consult one or two members of the board of governors who happened at that moment to be in the smoking-room. There was again a decent if tedious interval, and the secretary's voice was once more heard. He reiterated that it was contrary to the rules of the club to give information as to the whereabouts of any member, but that it had been decided, that, in this special case, an exception might be made. He was pleased to inform the visitor that Mr. John Doe had died in December of the preceding year!"

XXV: Some Old Houses

"WORDS," says Dr. Samuel Johnson in the preface to his dictionary, "are the daughters of earth, but the things they stand for are the sons of heaven." So the quaint and beautiful old houses in and about Philadelphia must be visited to be appreciated and the printed word can but inadequately bring their charm and inspiration to the reader. Hereabout there are more of these ancient structures preserved in good condition than perhaps can be found in any other quarter of America. This is surely true as regards their diversity and quality. Houses, like men, have personality and what characteristic can be more impressive? They reflect the taste and substance of their owners and their stories are ofttimes the history of the community.

Philadelphia's houses of the early time are as substantial as their builders and while many of them, owing to their Quaker owners, lack the ornament of the pretentious homes of the south, yet their very simplicity, comfort and exquisite proportions bring a sense of beauty that is unsurpassed elsewhere. There is always a balance and lack of over-elaboration that comes with these qualities, which is particularly satisfying as a daily experience.

Many of the important public edifices such as churches and State House have been mentioned, as has the Bishop White house, 400 South Front Street, and the Stocker house next door, the Blackwell house, 224 Pine Street, the Wharton house, 336 Spruce Street, the Barclay house, 422 South Front Street, the Morris house, 225 South 8th Street, the Wistar house, 4th & Locust Streets, and the Cadwalader house next door, and the Waln house, 254 South Second Street. There are many others typical of old Philadelphia particularly on Water, Front, Second, Third, and Fourth Streets. A few on Water near South, at Front and Lombard Streets, at Fourth and Spruce Streets, and several small streets from Second to Front for a few squares north of Market, notably Cherry Street.

At 322 DeLancey Street is the old Evans house typical of the "plain Friend's" residence of olden time. The Evans family came to Gwynedd about 20 miles from the City, from Wales in 1698, and the original farm is owned and lived upon to-day by Joseph Evans direct in descent. Jonathan Evans, a grandson of the immigrant, moved to Philadelphia and built the DeLancey Street house. He became a leader among the Quakers and was the most prominent figure in the "Separation" of 1827, which divided the Society into "Orthodox" and "Hicksite" Friends. Many of the conferences of that bitter time were held in the old house.

The Powel house at 244 South Third Street was built by Samuel Powel, who was the grandson of one of like name who came to Philadelphia in 1685 and was a member of the Society of Friends. It is particularly a spacious house and was of elegant construction. One of the rooms has been removed to the Metropolitan Museum in New York City. Mr. Powel was well connected and socially prominent. He became Mayor of the City and a distinguished patriot. During the British occupation the Earl of Carlisle had his quarters in Mr. Powel's house and during Washington's Presidency the house was the scene of many social gatherings attended by the President. John Adams, who could always be trusted to duly chronicle anything that tickled his palate, licks his chops, so to speak, in his diary over Mayor Powel's dinners. Here is one of his entries:

"September 8, Thursday.—Dined at Mr. Powel's with——and many others; a most sinful feast again! everything which could delight the eye or allure the taste; curds and creams, jellies, sweetmeats of various sorts, twenty sorts of tarts, fools, trifles, floating islands, whipped sillibub, etc., etc. Parmesan cheese, punch, wine, porter, beer, etc."

The large house at 321 South Fourth Street always attracts attention by the beauty of the great fan-light over its door. Henry Hill of Madeira wine fame built the house in 1786. General George McCall was born here and in 1817 Dr. Philip Syng Physick, "Father of American Surgery," bought it.

Before we leave the older section of the city in this brief ramble among her outstanding landmarks, it may be well to mention two romantic traditions attached to two Quaker maidens of the Colonial period which most visitors have heard:

Betsy Ross has been heralded as the maker of the first American Flag. That she was an early flag maker is evidenced in the records of the Continental Congress and tradition persists among her descendants to-day that she did originate with one clip of her scissors the five-pointed star which adorns our national emblem. In recent years an enterprising promoter seized upon the tradition and selecting the only old house, at 239 Arch Street, in the neighbourhood in which she lived, organized an association to preserve it and collected a large sum of money for the purpose. These comprise all the known facts.

Lydia Darragh, the other heroine of the time in song and story, lived at 177 South Second Street in what was called "Loxley Hall." Her house was the place of meeting for British Officers on December 2, 1777, and listening at the keyhole of their room she overheard the plan to attack Washington's Army at Whitemarsh on the fourth. Early on the following morning she took her bag for flour and set out on a walk of many miles over snowy roads to a point where she encountered Colonel Craig of the American Army to whom she imparted the news and so saved the patriots from disaster, for Howe's Army found Washington fully prepared and was "compelled to march back like a parcel of fools."

The Schuylkill's banks were once a veritable paradise. This it is easy enough to believe of the part of the river that flows through Fairmount Park, but it takes a good stretch of the imagination to picture oneself that portion of the stream below Callowhill Street bridge as ever possessed of alluring sylvan characteristics. Before factories, wharves, and gas-works blemished its shores, however, heart could not wish a fairer spot than the rolling ground that extended all the way to the borders of the reedy marshes near the mouth. So, at any rate, it seems to the Colonial worthies who built their countryseats over-looking its waters as they wound by, to lose themselves in the distance amid beds of rushes and sedgy flats that well-nigh conceal the entrance and caused the early Dutch explorers to bestow the same "Schuylkill" meaning "Hidden River."

Below the Market Street bridge, the site of the old "Middle Ferry," the nearest Colonial mansion still standing, built on one of the highest points of the west bank, is the Woodlands, the country-seat of the Hamilton family, from whom a part of West Philadelphia, east of Fortieth Street and south of Market, took its name of "Hamilton Village." The grounds of the Woodlands long since became a cemetery, but the old name remained with a new association, far different from that to which the gay society of a century ago was accustomed. The house itself, one of the noblest of a period when they were wont to build nobly, now contains the offices of the cemetery company and shelters the family of the superintendent.

Like so many of the old houses, the Woodlands had no back nor front, or rather, to be more accurate, we should say it has two fronts and no back. Architects in the eighteenth century thought it not necessary to make a great parade of the scullery and kitchen arrangements and, for the most part, kept them well out of sight. Their existence, however, was fully proved by the excellent and bountiful dinners that came thence.

Across the north front at regular intervals are six Ionic pilasters above whose tops runs an elaborately ornamented cornice, the whole surmounted by a pediment. Before the house is a low and broad paved terrace filling the space between the semi-circular bays that project from the ends of the building. Between the two middle pilasters, a round arched doorway with a fan-light opens into the hall. On the south or river front a flight of steps ascends to a lofty white-pillared portico from which a door opens directly into the oval-shaped ball-room, once the scene of many a brilliant social gathering.

The Hamiltons were noted for their entertaining and both at the Woodlands and Bush Hall, the latter their town house of which nothing is left but the memory and the seldom-heard name of the adjacent neighborhood, lavish hospitality was extended to the numerous guests whom it pleased them to honour. The land comprised in the Woodlands estate came into the possession of the family in 1735, being purchased by Andrew Hamilton, the first of his race in America. Not long afterward, a house was built thereon which was occupied by the second Andrew, who in turn was succeeded by his son William.

Before the Revolution this first house made way for the present spacious and elegant structure which was more in keeping with the luxurious tastes and manner of life of its builder, the William Hamilton just mentioned. The walls within were hung with valuable paintings and in the library were shelves well furnished with the choicest books, for the master of the Woodlands was a man of catholic interests and withal something of a connoisseur. . . . Extensive gardens surrounded the house and contained an extraordinary collection of exotic trees and plants as well as an abundant collection of such native North American plants and shrubs as could stand the Philadelphia winters. There was a greenhouse whose front, including the hothouses on each side, measured one hundred and forty feet. When Hamilton was in England after the Revolution, his letters to his secretary show the utmost solicitude about all his plants and sometimes there is evidence of considerable irritation because the secretary does not remember, or, at any rate, does not tell all the minutiæ anent every plant on the place. William Hamilton was a born gardener; his secretary was not. This visit to England proved a great incentive to his gardening activities and on his return he redoubled his efforts to make the grounds of Woodlands second to none and succeeded. He it was who introduced the Ginkgo tree and the Lombardy poplar into America, besides many other plants.

William Hamilton loved display, kept a retinue of servants, and maintained a splendour of style that quite eclipsed the domestic arrangements of most of his neighbours. This he could well afford to do for he was one of the wealthiest men of his day. When he drove abroad he commonly went in a chariot-and-four and postillion boys in livery. He was fond of giving dinner parties and always surrounded his well-laden board with an assemblage of eminent men of various professions in addition to the usual coterie of social celebrities. Sunday was one of his favourite days for dinner giving and many were the notable gatherings that took place on Sunday afternoons in spring, summer and autumn. Thursday was also another day associated with Woodlands parties.

In 1762 when he graduated at the Academy of Philadelphia—that was before the present house was built—he gave a fête for his college friends, among whom were men afterward prominently known in the affairs of the State and Nation as Judge Yeates, Judge Peters, Mr. Dickinson Sergeant, the Reverend Doctor John Andrews and Bishop White. This is probably the first University class dinner of which we have any record.

When the Revolution broke out William Hamilton at first espoused the patriot side and raised a regiment in the neighbourhood of the Woodlands. He was, however, opposed to a complete break with the mother country and upon the Declaration of Independence he resigned his commission. After the British evacuation of Philadelphia he was arrested for high treason, charged with assisting the British troops. Notwithstanding the rancorous zeal of his ancestors, he was acquitted and allowed to remain in possession of his estates.

Descending the Schuylkill, the next Colonial seat of interest on the right bank of the river below the Woodlands is the Bartram House which, with the surrounding gardens, the City now owns. The Lower Ferry or Gray's Ferry, it was known by both names, was originally the means by which all southern and western travel entered the city so that it was an extremely important place. Just south of this spot, in 1728, John Bartram bought a tract of land afterward to become famous as a botanical garden. On this farm was a small house dating from Swedish times but insufficient, presumably, for the needs of Bartram for, in 1730, he began to build what may be considered the main

portion of the house and finished it in 1731, perpetuating
the date of its completion by setting a stone in the gable
bearing the inscription:

MAY GOD SAVE
JOHN AND ANN BARTRAM, 1731

That he actually laboured on the walls with his own
hands is, perhaps, too much to say positively, but at any
rate tradition, and seemingly reliable tradition at that, has
it that he did. Of the many successive alterations and additions the house has undergone and of which it shows more
traces inside than out, it appears that the last must have
been made somewhere near 1770, at which time he placed
a carven stone above his study window bearing the inscription:

It is God alone almyty Lord
The holy One by me ador'd.
John Bartram, 1770.

The Bartram House, like the Woodlands, though by no
means nearly so pretentious, has interesting fronts both
east and west. The east or river front with its great
roughly hewn stones, its rude pillars, its clustering ivy, and
the rose vines by the windows has an air of mingled refinement and rusticity, a strange combination of simplicity and
stateliness. There is nothing quite like it anywhere else.
The usual entrance is on the west side of the house by
a trellis-shaded doorway at each side of which are little
Dutch seats.

Within, the house discloses no particular plan, as indeed
it could scarcely be expected to since it has grown through
so many years by capricious additions, made when divers
occasions and times demanded. In the space it contains,

without appearing spacious, and in the unexpected way that rooms multiply, it is not unlike some of the old Dutch houses of the Hudson.

The story is told of Bartram that one day as he was ploughing he stopped to rest in the shade of a tree. By chance he plucked a daisy as he sat there and musing upon its structure was impelled to learn something concerning its history, habits and uses. From this small beginning came the impulse that spurred him to the studies and investigations that placed him in the foremost ranks of botanists. Ordinarily in autumn, when he could spare the time from his farm labours, Bartram travelled extensively through the Colonies gathering plants for his collection.

In the East Park not far north of the Girard Avenue bridge there stands a house of baronial aspect, flanked by barns and porters' lodges. The grouping is impressive and eloquent of the manorial state maintained by the gentlemen of Colonial days. The seat is called Mount Pleasant and commands from its wooded height a broad view up and down stream and across to the hills of the farther shore.

It was Captain John Macpherson who bought land in this fair place and set to building his great house in 1761. East and west fronts are alike of imposing mien. To the west the land falls rapidly away to the river. The house is set high as the crown jewell of the setting and is approached on both fronts by a broad flight of stone steps with iron balustrades leading to doorways of generous breadths. Stone walls covered with yellow grey rough cast are framed in heavy brick quoins and great quadruple chimneys joined into one at the top by arches, give the structure an air of stolidity. The pillars of the doorway, the Palladian window above and the pediments all contribute to the elegance of the pile, perhaps one of the handsomest in America.

Captain Macpherson commanded the privateer *Britannia* in 1757 and grew rich at this licensed piracy. He called his fine house "Clunie" after the seat of his Scottish Clan. The interior is a thing of beauty. The elaborate carving of the woodwork and the dignified charm of the rooms must be seen to be appreciated. Here he lived handsomely and busied himself inventing various contrivances, lecturing on astronomy, publishing papers on moral philosophy and issuing the first city directory (1785) wherein he took occasion to express his personal pique at those that proved uncommunicative to his canvassing queries.

Financial troubles and a longing for the sea caused the versatile Captain to lease the place to Don Juan de Merailles, the Spanish Ambassador, and finally, in 1779, to sell the estate to General Benedict Arnold, who gave it as a marriage gift to his bride, Peggy Shippen. Arnold was placed in command at Philadelphia after the British occupation and with his charming bride to grace his household, began a series of lavish entertainments that increased the carping of his enemies when his personal fortune became impaired.

He was hectored and badgered in public and private affairs until his hot temper broke in a storm against his tormenters. His repeated requests for the large sums due him by Congress were unavailing and the pestiferous Joseph Reed, who also attacked such staunch patriots as Robert Morris and James Wilson, followed him with vindictive malevolence charging him with crimes which he could not substantiate in the trial before a Committee of Congress. Reed finally forced a court martial after repeated delays, and Arnold was exonerated except upon two very insignificant matters. Washington's letter of reprimand on this account was practically one of recommendation.

The rest is well known. We need not attempt to palliate his unfaithfulness to the Colonial revolt, but many a man with less provocation has proved as faithless.

After Arnold's attainder and the confiscation of his property, Mt. Pleasant was leased to Baron Steuben, then through several hands to General Jonathan Williams of Boston, who remained there and his family after him until the middle of the 19th Century when the property with the surrounding territory was acquired by the City and made a part of Fairmount Park.

Ormiston, on the verge of a deep glen that separates it from Laurel Hill, is a square rough-cast building of two storeys and a hipped roof, substantial and comfortable but without much architectural pretension.

Its principal charm is its site overlooking the river far below. There are broad porches on both the land and river fronts, and in the days when its condition was properly kept up, it must have been a delightful place to pass the summer months.

Towards the end of the Colonial period it was the home of Joseph Galloway, an eminent lawyer and one of the most distinguished Loyalists. He was born at West River in Maryland, in 1731, but came to Philadelphia at an early age. In 1748 he was elected a member of the "Colony in Schuylkill." While still a young man he attained great distinction in the law and was held an authority in all matters touching real estate. He was the intimate friend of Benjamin Franklin and when the latter went to England in 1764 he placed his valuable papers and letter books in Galloway's hands for safekeeping. In 1757 he was elected to the Assembly,and from 1766 to 1774 was speaker of that body, being usually elected by unanimous vote. In 1753 he married Grace Growdon, the daughter of Laurence Growdon, of Trevose.

After serving in the Congress of 1775 he withdrew from politics. Doctor Franklin then sought to induce him to espouse the cause of independence but he could not conscientiously do so, and in December, 1776, joined General Howe and accompanied the British Army. During the British occupation of Philadelphia, at the request of General Howe, he assumed the duties of Superintendent-General of Police and Superintendent of the Port, being assisted by his friend and neighbor, Samuel Shoemaker.

After the British evacuated Philadelphia, Galloway was attainted of high treason and his estate adjudged confiscate. Mrs. Galloway in order to protect her property remained at Ormiston until she was forcibly ejected by the commissioners in charge of confiscated estates. In ·this connexion the great Charles Wilson Peale does not appear in an amiable light. He was one of the commissioners and he it was who ran Mrs. Galloway out by the shoulders, forcing her from her home and into Benedict Arnold's coach—he was then a near neighbour and had not yet fallen into disgrace—which was waiting at the door to convey her away.

Ormiston along with all the neighbouring seats is now a part of the park property, and is used by the family of one of the park employees.

Conspicuous among the seats that line the east bank of the Schuylkill is Laurel Hill. Separated from Ormiston by a deep-wooded combe and standing on a high bluff overlooking the river, it commands an unexcelled view up and down the banks of that stream, which for natural beauty has few peers and for the social distinction of the dwellers along its shores had not its equal in the Colonies. In Colonial times and for long afterwards, until the land was taken for park purposes, within the compass of a few miles, beside its water were to be found more plantations belonging

to folk of quality and substance than in any like neighbourhood. Great distances separated many of the Hudson
manors, and on the James a like state of comparative isola-
tion was not uncommon. The Schuylkill, on the contrary,
combined virgin loveliness of scenery with an unsurpassed
opportunity for easy and frequent intercourse with the most
agreeable of neighbours as well as convenient proximity to
the city.

The house at Laurel Hill—the name, by the way, is derived from the luxuriant growth of laurel for which the
bluffs along the river were once noted—though not as large
as some others nearby, is a striking example of Georgian
architecture, two storeys in height with hipped roof. The
walls are of brick painted yellow and all the woodwork is
white. The main entrance, on the eastern or land front, is
through a spacious classic doorway with flanking pilasters
and a pediment above.

Joseph Shute, who owned large tracts of land close by,
built Laurel Hill about 1748. In 1760 Francis Rawle
bought the estate for his summer residence and it was during the occupancy of the Rawle family that the place began
to figure on the stage of history. In 1828, William Rawle,
as trustee under his mother's will, sold Laurel Hill to Doctor Philip Syng Physick, reference to whom is made elsewhere, and from him the estate passed to his descendants,
the Randolphs, who retained it till the city bought it for a
part of Fairmount Park in 1849. After being let out for
divers uses by the park commissioners the house was at
last put in the care of the Colonial Dames of America, who
now maintain it in good order and there hold stated meetings.

Woodford is situated in the East Park at York and
Thirty-third Streets near the Dauphin Street station of the
Fairmount Park Electric Railway. The fine old doorway

 STENTON · 1728 ·
Residence of James Logan

is reached by six soapstone steps and opens into a large hall with an entrance at once into front rooms on either side. Beyond these doors are square columns against the walls of the hall with crosspiece of detail work, but no stairway appears. This ascends from a large hall in the centre of the house reached by a door in the side. The stairway and halls are spacious and the rooms large, each with a fireplace with ornamental iron back and square bricks for hearth. In the front south room the tiles surrounding the fireplace are blue and represent Elizabethan knights and ladies. The cornices in the rooms are rounding, the boards of the floor an inch and a half thick and dowelled together. The doors have brass hanging loops instead of knobs and the woodwork, including mantels and wainscot, is in fine condition.

The ground upon which it stands was granted by William Penn, February 16, 1693 to Mary Rotchford, who deeded the tract of two hundred acres to Thomas Shute in the same year. At his death in 1754 it was sold to Abel James, a son-in-law of Thomas Chalkley and one of the consignees of the tea in the *Polly* which was sent back to England. He sold it to Joseph Shute, son of Thomas, in 1756, and immediately afterward it was sold at sheriff's sale, twelve acres going to William Coleman, who built the house. He was a friend of Franklin, member of the "Junto," a scholar, and an eminent jurist.

William Coleman was a member of Common Council in 1739, justice of the peace and judge of the County Courts in 1751, and judge of the Supreme Court of Pennsylvania from 1759 until he died, aged sixty-four, in 1769. The mansion on the "East side of the river Schuylkill and west side of Wessahykken Road" shows him fond of study and retirement.

The executors of William Coleman sold the place to

Alexander Barclay, Comptroller of His Majesty's Customs at the Port of Philadelphia. He was the son of David Barclay and the grandson of Robert Barclay of Ury, the famous Quaker theologian and "Apologist."

He died in 1771 and the property then became the home of David Franks, the son of Jacob and Abigail Franks, and an eminent Jewish merchant. He was very prominent socially and a public-spirited man, the signer of the Non-Importation Resolutions of 1765, in which the signers agreed "not to have any goods shipped from Great Britain until after the repeal of the Stamp Act," a member of the Provincial Assembly in 1748, the register of wills, and a subscriber to the City Dancing Assembly. He married Margaret, daughter of Peter Evans, and has been thought to have deserted the faith of his fathers. This, however, is disproved by an affidavit he made before Judge Peters in 1792. The family was descended from Aaron Franks, the companion and friend of King George of Hanover, to whom he loaned the most valuable jewels in the crown at the coronation. The son Jacob came to New York about 1711, and his son David came to Philadelphia soon after 1738, a niece having married Haym Solomon, whose money joined with Robert Morris's in financing the Revolution.

David Franks was the agent of the Crown in Philadelphia during the troublesome times and was made commissary of the British prisoners in the American lines until 1778, when he was detected in endeavouring to transmit a letter inimical to the American cause. His neighbour General Benedict Arnold, in command of Philadelphia and living in the Macpherson mansion nearby, arrested him and threw him into gaol. He was deprived of his commission as commissary and compelled to remove to New York in 1780. His sister, Fila Franks, married Captain Oliver DeLancey, of New York, who, with Major André, painted the decorations for the "Mischianza" and served with credit in the Provincial troops during the Revolution. He was made a brigadier-general and died in England in 1785.

David Franks had four children—Abigail, who married Andrew Hamilton of the Woodlands, afterwards attorney-general of the State; Jacob, Mary or Polly, and Rebecca, who married Lieutenant-Colonel, afterward General, Sir Henry Johnson, defeated and captured by General Anthony Wayne at Stony Point. Rebecca Franks was the most striking figure of a notable galaxy of society lights. She was brilliant, witty and of a winsome presence, the most graceful among the graceful, the most beautiful among the beautiful. Born about 1760, well educated, at home in the classics, familiar with Milton, Goldsmith, Swift, and others, she was of that group of aristocrats, who having derived their wealth and prosperity from the favour of the Crown, sided with the Loyalists and favoured law, order, and property as opposed to mobs and violence. She was a gifted writer and has left in her letters interesting accounts of the society of the days as well as a poem of some fifteen hundred lines written in the summer of 1779, which is a political satire full of unmeasured abuse of the leaders of the Revolutionary War. General Howe was in the habit of tying his horse in front of the house in which the Franks lived and going in to have a chat with the wit of the day.

This sprightly person was naturally one of the belles of the celebrated "Mischianza" given May 18, 1778, by the British officers in honour of General Howe upon his departure. The word is an Italian one and signifies a medley. It was celebrated upon a scale of magnificence rarely equalled in those days and its description reads like a page from Ivanhoe, forcibly calling to mind the days of chivalry.

The guests embarked from Green Street wharf and proceeded in a river pageant to what is now Washington Avenue, where they landed and advanced to Joseph Wharton's place, Walnut Grove, situated at about what is now Fifth Street and Washington Avenue. After this there was a tournament in which England's bravest soldiers appeared in honour of Philadelphia's fairest women, being divided into six Knights of the Blended Rose and six Knights of the Burning Mountain, each wearing the colours of his particular princess. Lord Cathcart led the former, appearing in honour of Miss Auchmuty, the only English maiden present and the betrothed of Captain Montresor, chief engineer. The Knights of the Burning Mountain were led by Captain Watson, who appeared for Miss Franks.

She was dressed in a white silk gown, trimmed with blue and white sash edged with black. It was a polonaise dress, which formed a flowing robe and was open in front to the waist. The sash, six inches wide, was filled with spangles, also the veil which was edged with silver lace. The headdress was towering, in the fashion of the time, and filled with a profusion of pearls. Major André planned most of the entertainment and has left a detailed account of it as well as drawings of the costumes. He painted many of the decorations and Captain Montresor of the engineers planned the fireworks. After the tourney there was a supper with royalist toasts followed by dancing until four o'clock, and all in the midst of a bloody war and within a few miles of the enemy!

After the evacuation of the city by the British army, Lieutenant Jack Stewart of Maryland, calling upon Miss Franks in a scarlet coat, remarked, "I have adopted your colours, my princess, the better to secure a kind reception; deign to smile on a true knight." The beauty did not reply, but addressing some friends in the room exclaimed, "How the ass glories in the lion's skin." A commotion arising in the street at the time, they looked out and saw a figure in female attire with ragged skirts and bare feet, but with the exaggerated headdress of the Tory ladies. The unfortunate officer remarked that, "the lady was equipped altogether in the English fashion." "Not altogether, Colonel," replied Miss Franks, "for though the style of her head is British, her shoes and stockings are in the genuine Continental fashion." When the French Alliance was announced, the patriots wore cockades in its honour. Miss Franks tied one of these to her dog and bribed a servant to turn it into the ballroom where Mrs. Washington was giving a reception to the French minister. It is to be hoped that having lost her manners she lost her dog as well.

In a letter to her sister, Mrs. Hamilton, she writes the most detailed and piquant account that we possess of New York social life during the Revolution.

She thinks that it is in the powers of entertaining that New Yorkers are most deficient:

"Bye the bye, few ladies here know how to entertain company in their own houses, unless they introduce the card table . . . I will do our ladies—that is, the Philadelphians—the justice to say that they have more cleverness in the turn of an eye, than those of New York have in their whole composition. But what ease have I seen a Chew, an Oswald, an Allen, and a thousand others, entertain a large circle of both sexes, and the conversation without the aid of cards not flag or seem the least strained or stupid."

His adherence to the British side caused the confiscation of David Franks' property and, November 22, 1780, Woodford went to Thomas Paschall, son of Stephen Paschall and a friend of Benjamin Franklin. William

Lewis, a famous advocate, also lived in it, and finally, in 1793, it came into the Wharton family, Isaac Wharton being the purchaser. Isaac Wharton was born September 15, 1745, the son of Joseph and Hannan Carpenter Wharton and the grandson of Thomas and Rachel Thomas Wharton. He was married to Margaret Rawle, daughter of Francis and Rebecca Warner Rawle. Isaac's father, Joseph Wharton, was the owner of Walnut Grove in Southwark where the "Mischianza" was held in May 1778. At Isaac Wharton's death in 1778, the partition of the estate brought the seat to his son, Francis Rawle Wharton, who married Juliana Matilda, daughter of Isaac Gouverneur of New York. He was the last private owner of Woodford and it came to Fairmount Park in 1868. It was occupied by Chief Engineers John C. Cresson and Russell Thayer and since May 16, 1887, has been used as a guardhouse. The two small lodge-houses on the place are still standing and in use.

Stenton was one of the earliest and most pretentious of the countryseats of the Philadelphia neighbourhood. The estate originally comprised five hundred acres, but is now a park of some six acres surrounded by rows of the little brick houses for which Philadelphia is widely famous. It is the connecting link between Nicetown and Germantown and is near the Wayne Junction station of the Philadelphia & Reading Railway. The Wingokhocking Creek once ran through the grounds, but is now conducted beneath the surface. Fine oaks, hemlocks, and pines remain about the house but an avenue of scyamores has gone.

The house is built of brick with black headers and is fifty-five by forty-two feet in dimensions with a separate range of servant quarters, kitchens, and greenhouses extending backward one hundred and ten feet farther. The doorway is reached by three curious circular stone steps firmly clamped together with iron banks. It opens into a great hall, paved with brick and wainscotted in white to the ceiling, with an open fireplace on the right. On the left is a dining-room, also wainscotted, with a cup-board for china. The fireplace in this room has blue tiles and an iron fireback ornamented with the initials of the builder, "J. L. 1728." On the right is the south parlour, also panelled, with a fireplace surrounded by pink tiles. A stately double staircase ascends beyond an archway in the rear, on either side of which there are lofty rooms also wainscotted in white. The one on the left is a small breakfast-room reached from the front dining-room through a passageway. Upon the threshold there is a trapdoor in the floor leading to an underground passage to the barns and burying ground, a great convenience in times of stress or storm. In the hallway stands an iron chest to hold the silver, with fourteen tumblers to the lock, and over it are the wooden pegs for hats. In the rear room on the right is a large closet with a sliding top, where a person might be concealed to listen through a small opening to conversation in the hall. The most at-tractive room is the library on the second floor, which extends across the whole front of the house. This once contained the finest collection of books of any private library in Colonial America, presented by the collector, James Logan, to the city of Philadelphia. Here the illustrious book-loving statesman and scholar spent most of his time during his declining years. There are two fireplaces, one with blue tiles and the other with white. There is a little back stairway and two small back bed-rooms for his two daughters. Each room has a fireplace. On the third floor there is no paint on the wainscot or woodwork and there is a little door under the eaves open-ing into a small passageway to the next room. In fact the whole house is filled with quaint nooks and corners which are the subjects of many a strange legend. On the back of a door on the third floor is cut, "Willm. Logan jun. Sail'd for England Octobr. 7th. 1763 Aetat: 1-6-7." The copper boiler, the bake oven, the big fireplace, and the crane are still to be seen in the kitchen, as well as the dovecote on its exterior.

James Logan was born October 20, 1674, at Lurgan, County Armagh, Ireland. He was the son of Patrick Logan of East Lothian, Scotland, and Isabella Hume. He was the descendant of a long line of the flower of Scottish chivalry, scholars and gentlemen, Chief Logan being the Laird or Baron of Restalrig, earlier called Lestralric. Patrick Logan was graduated Master of Arts at Edinburgh University, was a clergyman of the established church of Scotland and chaplain to Lord Belhaven. In 1671 he sought refuge from the turmoil by removing to Ireland and joining the Society of Friends. He took charge of the Latin School at Lurgan and here James Logan learned Latin, Greek and Hebrew before he was thirteen years of age, and became a master of mathematics at sixteen. James later removed to London, where he was, for a while, a schoolmaster, but soon entered the shipping trade at that place and at Bristol. In the spring of 1699, William Penn engaged him as his secretary and together they came to America in the *Canterbury*. On Penn's departure for England he left him in charge of the Province, saying, "I have left thee an uncommon trust, with a singular dependence on thy justice and care."

An account of James Logan's life is an account of Pennsylvania. For half a century he was a most potent factor in the Provincial affairs and was the centre of the volcanic disturbances which affected the Colony. Faithful to the Penn family and loyal to the desires of the Founder, he managed Indian affairs with great skill and it was largely due to him that the friendship and alliance between them and the Province was so long maintained. His correspondence was much with the literati of Europe and often embraced Hebrew or Arabic characters and algebraic formulas. Sometimes his letters convey a lively Greek ode and often they were written in Latin. He published essays on reproduction in plants, aberration of light, translated Cicero's "De Senectute," Cato's "Disticha," and treatises on history, archæology, criticism, theology, ethics, natural philosophy, anatomy, and law. There was no topic of science or literature that he could not discuss with the scholars of his time. He is described as tall and well made, with a graceful yet grave demeanour, a good complexion, quite florid even in his old age. His hair was brown and never grey, but he wore a powdered wig. He was intolerant of the narrow distinction of some Friends and believed in a defensive war of resistance to aggression. Thus he supported Franklin for the protection of Philadelphia in the French Wars. He engaged in business with Edward Shippen, but his trade on his public service never led him from his affection for the muses. He was Chief-Justice, Provincial Secretary, Commissioner of Property, and President of the Council. He acquired a fortune in commerce, in trade with the Indians, and by the purchase and sale of desirable tracts of land in all parts of the Colony which his position of Surveyor-General gave him the opportunity of securing. Thus he was able to live in princely style and to entertain with a free hand. For more than a century Stenton was the resort of notable and distinguished persons of the Colonies and from abroad, and its mistresses were among the most accomplished women of the time. Among the visitors to the house were John Dickinson, Edward Shippen, John Randolph of

Roanoke, Thomas Pickering, the learned and witty Portuguese, Abbé Correa, the French minister Genet, Doctor Benjamin Franklin, Thomas Jefferson, Richard Peters, and President Washington. At Stenton, Thomas Godfrey, glazier, by accident discovered the principle upon which he invented the quadrant. He saw a piece of broken glass which had fallen so as to reflect the sun, and upon consulting a volume of Newton which he found in the library, and with advice from James Logan, he constructed an instrument to the plan in his mind.

On the ninth of the tenth month, 1714, he married Sarah, daughter of Charles and Amy Read, after a romantic courtship. His letters to her are very tender and full of spiritual power. To them were born seven children: Sarah, who married Isaac Norris of Fairhill and whose daughter Mary married John Dickinson; William, who married Hannah Emlen and succeeded to Stenton; Hannah, who married John Smith, and James, who married Sarah Armitt. The rest died without issue.

Perhaps the first and most numerous guests at Stenton were the Indians, who came very often and in great numbers, three or four hundred at a time, and stayed for several weeks. They lined the staircase at night and passed the days in the maple grove. Smaller bands made huts on the grounds and remained a year at a time. The good chief, Wingohocking, standing with Logan on the border of the beautiful stream that wound through the place, proposed a change of names after the Indian custom of brotherhood. Logan explained the difficulty to him and said:

"Do thou, chief, take mine, and give thine to this stream which passes through my fields, and when I am passed away and while the earth shall endure it shall flow and bear thy name."

James Logan died October 31, 1751, and was buried in the Friends' burying ground at Fourth and Arch Streets. He was succeeded at Stenton by his son William, who had married Hannan Emlen. William Logan had been educated by his father and in England. He was the friend of the Proprietory interests and of the Indians, giving them homes and educating their children. He executed the conveyance of the Loganian Library to the Library Company of Philadelphia according to his father's wishes.

The next proprietor at Stenton was William Logan's son George, who was born there in 1753. He was educated in England and took a degree in medicine at Edinburgh University, travelling extensively in France, Italy, Germany, and Holland. He married Deborah, daughter of Charles Norris of Fairhill, a charming lady of very wide acquaintance whose hospitality was shared by most of the distinguished foreigners who visited Philadelphia during her occupancy at Stenton. She was something of a poetess.

General Washington made Stenton his headquarters August 23, 1777, on his way to the Brandywine from Hartsville, Pa. He came with twenty officers of his staff and is described as very silent and grave upon this occasion. Later, as President of the Constitutional Convention sitting in Philadelphia, on Sunday, July 8, 1787, he rode out to Stenton with Major Daniel Jenifer, to see Doctor George Logan for the purpose of looking over some farm experiments. He was interested in a demonstration of the use of land plaster on grass land, which Doctor Logan illustrated by marking out initials in the sod. Where the plaster had been sown on these letters the grass was darker and more luxuriant than elsewhere.

On Saturday, November 22, 1777, Sir William Howe gave orders to destroy the houses of obnoxious persons, and by order of Colonel Twistleton two dragoons came to Stenton to fire it. They told the negro woman whom they encountered there that she could remove the bedding and clothing while they went to the stable for straw. An officer with his command happened to come at the time and enquired for the deserters. The vigilant and faithful negress told him that two were in the barn, so he carried them away and the house was saved. Sir William Howe had occupied it as his headquarters at the time of the battle of Germantown.

Dr. George Logan was an active member of the Agricultural and Philosophical Societies, a senator from Pennsylvania from 1801 to 1807, and was much concerned to preserve peace. Upon this concern he visited France in 1798 and England in 1810. On his death in 1821 Du Ponceau said of him:

"And are thou gone! friend of man! friend of peace! friend of science! Thou whose persuasive accents could still the angry passions of rulers of men, and dispose their minds to listen to the voice of reason and justice."

When Deborrah Logan died in 1839, the estate came to her son Albanus who was born in 1783 and married John Dickinson's daughter Maria. Albanus was an agriculturist and was devoted to field sports. He had a gentle nature and through a long protracted suffering before his death never complained. Two children graced his union with Maria Dickinson: Gustavus, who married Miss Armat of Loudoun, and John Dickinson Logan, who wedded Miss Susan Wister. Gustavus occupied the house and his children Albanus and Maria were born there. Since the occupancy by the Colonial Dames and the ownership by the city they have lived at Loudoun nearby.

The history of the Logan family and of their life at this splendid Colonial mansion, while only one of many similar instances, is, perhaps, the most striking proof of the incorrectness of a common modern idea regarding the Quakers. We see here that they were not stiff-necked ascetics, but were cultured and refined, fond of beauty and pleasant things, and of a lavish hospitality. The portraits which adorn the walls of Stenton are witnesses to all that has been said about them and exhibit the dress, not of a peculiar people, but of those who practised moderation according to the admonition of William Penn:

"Choose thy cloaths by thine own eyes, not anothers. The more simple and plain they are, the better. Neither unshapely nor fantastical, and for use and decency not for pride."

BIBLIOGRAPHY

Deeds, Public Records, Private Papers, Conversation with Aged People and Printed Sources have aided in the preparation of this book. Of the last, the following were the most helpful—

"Early Philadelphia," by H. M. Lippincott

"The Colonial Homes of Philadelphia and Its Neighborhood," by H. D. Eberlein and H. M. Lippincott

"Watson's Annals," by J. F. Watson

"History of Philadelphia," by Scharf and Westcott

Diaries and Accounts by Dr. Alexander Hamilton, Peter Kalm, Jacob Hiltzheimer, Johann David Schoepf, Ann Warder, Dr. Manasseh Cutler, John Adams, J. P. Brissot de Warville, Elizabeth Drinker, William Black, Thomas Twining, and Benjamin Franklin

"The True William Penn," by Sidney George Fisher

Histories by Robert Proud, Gabriel Thomas, Isaac Sharpless, Agnes Repplier

Records compiled by the late Thomas Wynne

Histories of several of the institutions described. The records of the Pennsylvania Historical Society.